THE TIES THAT BIND

THE TIES THAT BIND

by
JULIUS M. MORAVCSIK

C E U PRESS

Central European University Press
Budapest   New York

Published in 2004 by

Central European University Press

An imprint of the
Central European University Share Company
Nádor utca 11, H-1051 Budapest, Hungary
Tel: +36-1-327-3138 or 327-3000
Fax: +36-1-327-3183
E-mail: ceupress@ceu.hu
Website: www.ceupress.com

400 West 59th Street, New York NY 10019, USA
Tel: +1-212-547-6932
Fax: +1-212-548-4607
E-mail: mgreenwald@sorosny.org

ISBN 963 9241 79 2 Cloth

Library of Congress Cataloging-in-Publication Data

Moravcsik, J. M. E.
The ties that bind / by Julius M. Moravcsik.
p. cm.
Includes bibliographical references.
ISBN 9639241792 (hardcover)
1. Ethics. I. Title.

BJ1012.M638 2004
171'.7--dc22

2004004859

Printed in Hungary by
Akadémiai Nyomda, Martonvásár

TABLE OF CONTENTS

INTRODUCTORY REMARKS IN LIGHT OF TODAY'S PROBLEMS

From the vast array of problems the world faces today, this book selects for treatment the relation between individual and community. THIS RELATION HAS BEEN PROBLEMATIC throughout the centuries if not millennia. What do individuals owe communities like state, profession, family? What rights and claims do they have on these? What would be the optimal relations?

Today these questions are more difficult, because while the notions of individual and society were fairly stabile, these fundamental concepts are under fire today. Should communities have independent ontological status over and above that of individuals? Can we agree on a notion of individuals without resolving important metaphysical or even scientific questions? The uncertainty concerning these fundamental notions has a practical impact. For the uncertainty and hesitation regarding foundational issues increases the frustration most people feel already in the turbulent world of today.

Traditional proposals formulated in the past seem less than satisfactory today. For example, making laws and institutions most fundamental, calling for no deeper level of justification, leaves many dissatisfied. Another clearly unacceptable way out is the forming of simplistic slogans, and organizing related violence against those who disagree. For violence spawns more violence, and frustration remains at least on the same level as before the bloodshed. The need to deal with this, whether we regard the perpetrators as rational or irrational, has to become apparent to all since September 11.

The key to the proposals of this book is to see that both "individual" and "community" are partly normative concepts. On the one hand, this means that not anything goes. We cannot just name anything as an individual or a community. But once our notions met certain broad common sensical partial criteria, we face choices in values on two levels. First, there is the normative issue of what we think deserves to be called a community of some sort, and again, an individual of some kind (e.g. capable of taking on responsibility?). Second, both communities and individuals are conceptually partly functional terms. We need to confront the questions of what sorts of individuals are regarded by our theory as better, and how do we extend that kind of characterization also to communities. If we rid ourselves of contemporary stereotypes, then we see that communities can be assessed not only in terms of wealth and power, but also in terms of the relations they foster among the members. We might regard questions about what holds a community together, and what kinds of individual ideals should members be encouraged to hold, as more important than mere material gain and psychological satisfaction. Philosophers tend to characterize the good citizen and good community in rational terms only. But when we take the broader look, we see that emotions are constituents of good individuals, and their absence can be disastrous (indifference in a democracy?). Likewise, greed and loyalty are partly emotional, and play important roles in communal life.

There is an analogy between judging an individual not only in terms of goals, but also in character, i.e. HOW the goals are reached for, and assessing communities not only in terms of how successful they are in meeting goals, but HOW—i.e. in terms of modes of cooperation, regard for others—these are met.

Thus laying out our theory requires laying out what seem to be desirable ways of individual and communal lives. But this does not, indeed cannot (since it has emotions also in the foundations, and we cannot have rules for these) have only, or even primarily, rules rather than guidelines and role models, at its foundation. This approach results in a work that cannot be compared in great detail with what others write in such fashionable frameworks as the purely analytic, or the purely deductively organized material. What is presented here cannot be derived strictly from the meanings or the key words that it includes, and showing a way of life, both individual and communal, cannot be organized in a deductive scheme. Our methodology is to lay out the framework within which the new proposals are made, and as we articulate proposals, we indicate in rough outline how these differ from some of the better known current claims. We leave it to the reader to decide which approach can account in the best way for the salient facts concerning our struggles with values.

Since our approach includes the emotional aspects of our ethical struggles, it enables us to give hints how we might deal with frustration, one of the greatest sources of our problems, in our theory. Roughly speaking, in dealing with individual and communal ideals, we point to liberating aims, projects, that enable people to look beyond grudge and resentment, not as if they thought that the frustration was not justified or that the source can be easily removed, but by seeing how we can look beyond all of this, and build lives, individual and communal, in which the frustrations and their sources do not seem so important.

Thus we do not promise the unrealistic, namely that we can eliminate the paradoxes of today. Today people complain about the lack of stability in their lives but at the same time pursue constant change because they think that it might bring riches and power still unknown. People yearn for ways of sticking together and at the same time they compete as fiercely as ever.

Our theory does not eliminate these paradoxes, but sketches patterns of life in which the importance of these can be minimized.

Within the scheme presented in this book our approaches to the usual topics covered in ethics and social ethics are pluralistic. The scheme construes political ideologies pluralistically. Good individual lives and communal organizations can be established in different ideological settings, and it is likely that in different social contexts different schemes work best as means to the individual ideals and best communal ties that our theory posits. No political or economic system is an end in itself. At best these are means to what a theory proposes as individual and social well-being. The book does not try to give panaceas to the problems of the world. Rather, it tries to build a conceptual framework in which concern with frustration and loneliness, as well as emphasis on communal ties rather than merely on claims and rights, create atmospheres within which more complex conceptual structures can be constructed, in place of giving top priorities to the good vs. bad, right vs. wrong dichotomies.

When we consider the consequences of our theory as applied to the world today, we see that our theory is highly critical of the way most people try to deal with issues. For it says that communal values are more important than speed and efficiency and in its insistence on the humane and considerate, it stands in opposition to efforts to place people in larger and larger groups.

This attempt at returning to the priority of worth while life and good communal relations may NOT SOLVE MANY PROBLEMS OF RAGE, frustration, and greed. But we can do no better than try.

PREFACE

The sources of this book are both theoretical and personal. The theoretical roots are linked to my dissatisfaction, already as a young assistant professor, with the lack of warmth and concrete relevance of so much modern moral philosophy. I felt the need for an ethics that is disciplined and carefully argued, and at the same time addresses what I regarded, and still regard, concrete but all-pervasive human problems such as how to alleviate suffering and overcome one's frustrations. I found an answer to my concern in combining insights from the classical ethics of Plato and Aristotle with some of the insights of the American pragmatists, especially Royce, James, and Dewey. The resulting theoretical framework is applied in the book to problems that relate to experiences that moved me over the past ten years.

It started with my growing awareness that students want to hear more about topics like friendship and love, and not just about duties and rights. The result was a Philosophy of Friendship course that I have been teaching for some time now. More reflection on history convinced me that at the same time I was bringing back into focus themes used to dominate moral philosophy up until the past two hundred years.

Over the past dozen years or so I happened to get involved in a fair amount of travel and lecturing. These occasions became intertwined with some very concrete experiences. My four months of teaching and research in Singapore introduced me to a fascinating culture and ideas—as well as ideals—that do not fit the usual Western democracy–police state, capitalism–socialism dichotomies. My lecturing at seven universities in South Africa brought me face to face with one of the most remarkable changes in culture and politics on our globe. Interaction with South

African philosophers forced me to recognize the importance of moral philosophy dealing with how to change society, and not just sketching ideal ways of building up moral communities from scratch. The post-apartheid South Africa is thirsting for an ethics of change. So is Russia, and other parts of Eastern Europe, as I found out later. My book is meant as a modest beginning to develop ethics that is responsive to this need. During my visits to Moscow I witnessed dramatic events of people's getting rid of a system they no longer thought to be workable. But they were left without any plausible positive suggestion as to what they should do next. The only advice they seemed to get came from foreigners who said: "why don't you do things our way?" Some of the motivation behind this book is the conviction that one should be able to say something deeper and less self-serving in these contexts.

My lecture tour in India taught me how deeply context-dependent even our key notions such as famine, dissatisfaction, distinguishing between nationalism and moral forces, are. It was a matter of sheer coincidence that in those years I was able to talk philosophy with people of such diverse cultures as India, Africa, and Russia. But the necessity to distinguish between surface differences and underlying deep common denominators was forced on me, and had a profound impact on my treatment of many of the topics with which this book is concerned. Finally, it was an eye-opener to be able to reflect on events in the United States, and to sort out the promising from the depressing. For the first time I saw the effort to have democracy in a country of more than 270 million people as a new experiment. I also saw, with consternation, that most people do not see it this way. They think that what worked for smaller units would work also for larger populations, without any drastic changes. This book suggests that this may not be so.

In my peregrinations I came upon many examples of dedication, devotion, determined pursuing of worth while aims, and kindness. It is reassuring to note that the examples represent cultures from all over the world. My book is designed to formulate guidelines for how to MAINTAIN that which is valuable in our practices and traditions, and how to CHANGE parts of our moral framework without these changes bringing harm that outweighs the alleged benefits. If the book stimulates people to think about these challenges and the other key concepts of this book, then it will have achieved its main purpose. If it leads to practical improvements in communal dynamics and communal ties, then it will realize what ultimately every philosophic writing on ethics should endeavor to reach.

My work has been aided by comments from many students, faculty and friends. Among my students at Stanford the main contributors were Tony Pfaff, Lauren Spiegel, and Simon May. From among my students in Singapore Andria Chow and Mary Pan need special acknowledgments. Daniel Bell and David Chan attended my seminar in Singapore, and made many useful comments. In Austria Jozef Zelger and Otto Neumeier have been of help. At Stanford both Deborah Satz and Michael Bratman have given useful criticism while in other parts of the world Philip Pettit, Asa Kasher, and Jonathan Stavi have been sources of stimulating ideas, Frithjof Bermann and Daniel Osherson have inspired much of the early thinking about these subjects, and later Hennie Loetter in South Africa was of great assistance. Finally, I wish to acknowledge the friendly encouragement and much stimulating discussions that Noam Chomsky has provided for many years now.

To all of these people I owe profound gratitude, though I am sure that many will disagree with some of my conclusions. There are many others who contributed to seminar discussions as I kept reading parts of this book in various places. May I just express my thanks and good wishes to them collectively.

INTRODUCTION

Humans have a deep-seated longing for companionship, even under very trying circumstances in which no utility could result from the togetherness achieved. This struck me forcefully at the age of 14 when I witnessed a scene of two soldiers being executed by an army that was under a "take no prisoners" order. The two soldiers were captured in different places and had no previous acquaintance with each other. They were lined up, side by side, for execution. In the last moment they looked at each other and clasped each other's hands.

While acknowledging this yearning for togetherness, we must also acknowledge the human drive for power and competition. One of the key tasks of ethical theories is to reconcile these opposing drives in human nature, and to construct both individual and political ideals within which the two can be brought into balance and harmony, and one of the two can ultimately be given priority. This book has this as its key aim, and it will present the position that the individual and the social must be woven into one theory. We cannot deal adequately with the two components separately. As we shall see, some of the individual and communal goods entail each other, and there are common virtues, shared by individual and communal ethics.

For purposes of better understanding, a contrast in terms of intuitive pictures will be presented. The contrast underlies the difference between most dominant modern approach and the one adopted in this book.

According to the "standard" picture humans are selfish and competitive, at least in the sense that these forces dominate human character if allowed to be expressed without restraints. Thus we need laws to repress and restrain these aspects of human nature. Of course, these laws at their best also protect humans from aggressors. But the protection is gained by restraining others, rather than by changing their overall orientation. According to some variations of this picture, there are purely rational ways of persuading the aggressors to become, at least in conduct, more cooperative. But even within this variant, the human agent remains having a split personality—composed of the aggressive dominant emotions, and reason trying on its own to change conduct. Within this view moral psychology and learning can be reduced to "learning the rules". The cognitive constituents of rule following, and whatever character traits are required for implementing rule following exhaust the moral requirement on humans.

This book, however, represents a radical departure from this conception of a moral theory. For it focuses on the DYNAMIC aspects of ethics. The great modern theories and the classical theories agree roughly on what are good things and right actions in contrast to the bad and the wrong. But instead of arguing over the roles of utility and duty, this book deals primarily with how we can learn about being a good agent, how we can maintain being a good agent, and how a good agent relates to the community to which he or she belongs. For example, Plato does not define either goodness or what moderns call the "right." Instead he concentrates on explaining what psychological forces enable us to maintain goodness and to use it in relation with others. This is not what most moral philosophers talk about today. But the book shows that these are at least as important issues as what mainstream ethics talk about today, and thus deserve a hearing. Thus we do not concentrate what rights and duties people have in a good society, but on what attitudes and cognitive as well as emotional processes hold us together. Our theory then requires attention to processes like overcoming frustration even when it is justified resentment that spawns it. Frustration seems to be the psychological source of much of our anger, bitterness, and hostility. It also threatens the unity of a good agent.

Our theory is concerned with moral learning. This is analogous to the kind of philosophy of language within which one does not merely posit abstract structures as the meanings of words and sentences, but is also concerned with how our natural languages can be represented as learnable by humans. For much of modern traditional ethics mere understanding and following of rules seem to suffice as moral learning. But in our theory we posit a much richer and psychologically adequate learning process. It cannot be mere rule following, since in our theory attitudes are some of the cornerstones of a good agent, and since attitudes also include emotions, and these cannot be acquired by mere rule following, the latter cannot be all there is to moral learning.

Some analytical philosophers might respond by saying that their job is merely the a priori specification of the good and right, and issues of loss and acquisitions are "merely empirical matters." To this we have two replies. The first is that along with philosophers like Quine and moral philosophers like John Rawls (see second book) the theories of this book reject any sharp distinction between the a priori and the empirical, and regard this distinction more a matter of gradations, with the allegedly pure a priori to be found only in pure mathematics. The second defense says that in classical philosophy and modern pragmatism, being occupied with large scale phenomena that are not purely a priori but affect everyone's life, such as the struggle between embracing partly emotional in contrast with purely intellectual virtues, is a part of philosophy. Without such concerns ethical theory would have nothing to say about life. As an informal survey at the Center of Advanced Studies for the Behavioral Sciences has shown, many able people are already drawing this conclusion about modern philosophical ethics. This book attempts to change that picture of value theory.

A clear example is the problem of how to define sound relations between individuals and the communities to which they belong. Most modern philosophers try to prescribe the adequate rights and responsibilities and resulting claims on both sides. Our theory says that underlying such bargaining, there should be the building up of communal consensus on a variety of issues, especially those concerning the attitudes linking people that we deem desirable. As we shall see, our communal ties are fundamentally certain attitudes and the processes that express these, such as trusting, caring and others. This is the fundamental level on which we can bring together the individual and social values.

The current crisis in the USA, as this book is being completed, illustrates well many key points of our approach. A key problem in today's situation is the challenge of adjudicating the conflicting demands of freedom and security. When viewed in a purely a priori manner, there should be no conflict; the two notions are definitionally not incompatible. But empirically, there are situations, in the USA today, in the history of Singapore earlier, when the conflict does arise because of empirical circumstances, and value theory should have some advice.

The choice is clearly not a matter of utility or of duty. We have no duties that would force us to override freedom in the name of security, or the other way around. Nor is this a matter of utility. For one would have to ask: utility from the point of view of which kind of agents? Thus the issue becomes a series of questions about what kinds of human beings we think we should be, and how do the decisions in this area affect communal relations? Do I want to enjoy my individual rights fully even if that will most likely lead to the death of many fellow citizens? Do we want to live in the kind of community in which our relations and communal projects must be maintained knowing that the majority is willing to sacrifice the lives of many citizens in certain types of crises in which some of our civil rights are threatened?

Above all, one would want to know how much loss of freedom is at stake, and how much security will be gained? In such situations trade-offs need to be specified very carefully. Finally, the decision may very well vary, without this variation showing any moral decadence on either side depending on the traditional values of the community in question. Maybe in Singapore there is more concern with the survival of all and much less of a tradition to protect at all cost individual rights? Maybe in the USA it is the other way around? There are objective limits to how much variation can be allowed, but one of the consequences of our theory is pluralism in these areas. I regard this not a law but a positive aspect of our theory.

The alternative presented in this book has the following salient features. First, the choices of overall ends are seen as open to humans. Our final ends may be many things besides pleasure and happiness, though these aspects of life may be among the consequences of having well chosen ends.

Chosen aims need be implemented, and for that we need a variety of attitudes. Attitudes are the key element of the ethics of this book. Attitudes, like respect, consist of a cognitive element and an emotive one that is so closely tied to the cognitive that we cannot identify it separately. Thus we judge someone to be worthy of respect for certain qualities and this engenders the emotion needed to make this judgment operative in what we do and feel. What is worthwhile, then, is specified not simply by rules, or even just by character, but by a variety of adequate ideals (to be defined later) and communal ties.

This view shows the human agent as engaged in trying to live a worthwhile life, with all aspects of his or her psychology. The key notions of approval and disapproval need not be restricted to good and bad, but include the challenge to overcome frustration, and to be open to accept ideals different from one's own, as long as adequacy criteria are met.

This conception requires a much more rich moral psychology and ways of learning about values than what the picture sketched previously contains. This has a variety of practical consequences. Learning by engaging in community work is seen as at least as important, if not more so, than learning rules. Rules, good and bad, and similar notions appear also in this value theory, but on the derivative, rather than on the fundamental levels. The result is a pluralistic ethical theory that nevertheless does not lapse into relativism.

Our approach is thus different from what one might call the right-based approach. Within that conception rights as well as obligations are defined for the individual, and this component is held to be distinct from what would yield utility and satisfaction. The political component has at its bases the delineation of abstract structures outlining what claims the state has on the individual and what rights the individual has in his relation to the state. This book will show, among other things, that the abstract structures are only means to communal ends. The adequate communal

dynamic, to be described in the second part of this book, provides
the foundation for adequate individual and communal functioning. In the first part of the book a conception of individual aspirations will be presented that have both private and communal
aspects, as equally essential ingredients. In some contexts this is
obvious already on the common sense level. These include family
relations and some types of friendship. Some of the deepest forms
of friendship involve sharing what we take to be the best conceptions of what humans should be. These are individual ideals, but
sharing them constitutes also the basis of a very special community, namely that of friendship. A similar context is provided by the
relationship between physician and patient. The complex relationships involved in healing require, in addition to the scientific
and technological ingredients, human elements like trust, loyalty,
and care. These make demands, on the one hand, on the individuals involved, and on the other hand on the ties built.

The theory presented in this book requires the collapsing of several dichotomies favored by such dominant modern ethical theories as utilitarianism and Kantian ethics. It also develops a moral
psychology that clashes with some psychological hypotheses that
are often implicit in modern ethics.

In universities we separate individual ethics from political theory. We give separate courses and seminars in these allegedly sepa-
rable subjects. Thus, for example, a course on political theory
might deal with the conception of democracy and exhibit comparisons with its rivals. A course on individual ethics deals with conceptions of human happiness and its typically being constrained by
duty and obligation. Within the conception of this book, we start
with individual challenges that on the surface seem to be primarily private matters. These include striving towards increase in
knowledge and wisdom, and overcoming even justified resentment.
But resentment is towards others, and the increase of knowledge
and wisdom is today institutionalized. Thus, whether it is popular
or not, this book discusses matters of public policy in terms of how
these affect individual values and aspirations, and regards these
aspirations as presupposing possibilities of belonging to communities that make the realization of one's ideals possible.

Another distinction that is seen as fundamental by the modern dominant ethical theories is that between the prudential and the obligatory. These are supposed to mirror the distinction between our inclinations and our sense of duty. We have seen already above examples such as friendship and healing within which the self-directed and the other-directed are intertwined and how what the best attitudes and activities demand cannot be described simply in terms of obligations. Some of the elements mentioned already involve not only specifications of thought and conduct but also of feelings and aspirations. The latter are only partly within our conscious control, hence cannot be matters of obligation. What in other more popular theories are described as conflicts between duty and inclination became in our theory the weaving together of our ideals, matters of how to relate to others, and how to work towards the more individual aspects of self-improvement.

In ethical theories one can distinguish the highest goods that are simply ends in themselves from the means that led us there. But in our theory the final ends have both instrumental value and value in themselves. To the question "what would happen in a possible state of affairs in which the instrumental is pealed off the final end?" our theory responds that it is not designed to cover all logically possible states of affairs—whatever that means—but is designed only (??) for the world as it is and reasonable projections of it into the probable and possible. Health is a final end. It is also of instrumental value. On the one hand, we define a well functioning human partly in terms of health. On the other hand, we regard health as the key to many processes needed for the realization of some of the best human potentialities. Where these relationships do not mesh, our conceptualizations come to an end.

Obligations and calculations of utility do play roles in the ethical theory of this book. These notions need to play some role in any ethics. But in our theory they do not play fundamental roles, as the following example illustrates this. Friendship and its extended communal versions are based on shared values, cooperation and similar other factors. But once a friendship is made, it does bring with it obligations. The same can be said about many other important relations, like collegial cooperation, or family ties. Similar considerations apply to calculating utility. This cannot be a fundamental notion, since it is relative to agreements on what a good agent and a good community are. But once these questions are resolved, then, with respect to sharply delineated communal projects and predictable circumstances, calculation of utility for various alternative lines of action is an obvious move.

Our theory specifies individual goodness in terms of agency, and ascribes to the good agent good overall aims for life and related character that is not only instrumental to the realization of the overall aim, but is also an end in itself. Since the good overall aim and the appropriately related character together constitute what is called in this book an ideal, the theory of individual well functioning is called Ethics of Ideals (or EI, as abbreviated in the remainder of the book).

Communal goodness is specified in terms of the right kind of ties that bind the community together. Hence the theory is called the Ethics of Communal Ideals (ECI, abbreviated). These theories are supplied with appropriate moral psychologies that differ from currently fashionable ones. Herewith some salient differences.

Our outlook assumes that humans are capable of enjoying a variety of different activities and can take satisfaction in different things. Pleasure or happiness are not the only—or the most desirable—final ends. For example, a child can start out enjoying hurting an animal in play. But as it becomes sensitive to the suffering of other living things, it can cease to enjoy such cruelty, and start enjoying taking care of sick animals or at least bringing them to an animal shelter. This illustrates the plasticity of human nature. It would be absurd to say that torture and healing are only candidates for means to pleasure, and that in the above example the child only changes means. Nobody has specified adequately what this alleged common element of pleasure would be within hurt and healing. We can treat pleasure as a sensation, and compare physical sources such as scratching an itch with the feel of water when taking a shower as means. But enjoyments of hurting or healing are not sensations. These are adverbially dependent on the activities that are being enjoyed. Our conception of ideal building includes choosing adequate overall aims, and hence presupposes the plasticity of human nature.

These reflections show also that our theory requires a psychology within which setting aims is not merely a part of instrumental reasoning, but involves setting final ends that have also non-instrumental value. Such aim setting must have a rational as well as an emotional component. The rational part is the source for the choice of final end and the justification of this choice. But in order to have the striving towards the aim actualized, an emotional element—we could call it aspiration—is also needed. Our ethics does not merely specify criteria for overall aims in life, but also acceptable ways in which these are to be realized. Hence character, another final end, as the second key ingredient. Just as in everyday life, the ways of accomplishing something are equally important as the reaching of the aims, so in this most general case the same considerations hold. For example, for some people the accumulation of wealth is an overall aim, but they specify that wealth brings with it responsibility, and they wish to accomplish their aim with responsibility as a necessary constraint. This does not exclude the possibility that being a responsible person can also be of positive instrumental value in their pursuits for wealth.

This way of specifying the good agent differs sharply from specifying it as merely following the right rules. The first way leaves open the possibility that our basic ethical elements are guidelines, or ideal models to be approximated, rather than general principles. Thus the basic elements of learning will be the different aspects of role modeling in our theory, while in the alternative conception rule following is the basic relevant psychological component of the good agent.

Specifying the good agent and the Ethics of Ideals as we did, brings with it the psychological demand that certain attitudes should be basic for character. Attitudes such as respect, approval, trust and others are characterized in this essay as orientations having both a cognitive and an emotive ingredient. The cognitive element is the judgment that e.g. on the basis of certain qualities a person X should be respected. The emotional element accompanies the cognitive one. In fact, we cannot even specify it apart from the cognitive judgment that generated it, and that it accompanies. This important element of our moral psychology is spelled out in the first part of the book, and it pervades also the second part.

One of the interesting results of our conception is that within it the oft discussed question "why be moral?" does not arise, at least not in that form. As construed, this question typically presupposes that there is a prudential arena for that kind of thinking, presenting at its best how to obtain what we want. The problem then becomes how to close the gap between this kind of thinking and a quite district domain labeled the moral. The latter deals with duty and obligation, in contrast with utility and satisfaction.

Within out theory the most fundamental level is that of choosing overall aims in life. This will cover what we see we should become, and also what we see as the desirable links between us and other humans. We cannot help but set aims, and thus cannot help but engage in normative thinking. In sketching ideals for ourselves and others we deal with matters of how to be good aim setters and also with what kinds of relations to humans seem most worthwhile. Thus considerations of these relationships are also parts of the overall aim setting.

Within the realm of constructing worthwhile aims and formulative ways of implementation we can sort out the ones dealing more with relations to others and the ones dealing mostly with what talents of ours we should develop. But the distinction is not sharp, and it does not mirror the allegedly sharp line between the prudential and the moral. If we have a more wide conception of the self that includes some of our relational attributes, the distinction is blurred. If we have a narrow conception of the self, then it seems fundamental. Hence the key question becomes why develop the wider rather than the narrower concept of the self? Our theory attempts to give at least one solution to this basic problem.

Having sketched some of the more controversial moves of our theory, we shall turn now to a brief summary of the content. Part One, centers on the Ethics of Ideals, as defined. In the first chapter we see the notion of an ideal defined and the choice of this as fundamental explained and defended. A few remarks are added to show that this theory is neither Kantian nor utilitarian. It resembles more the classical ethics of Plato and Aristotle, without falling into the nebulous contemporary rubric of a virtue ethics. The first chapter closes with setting up criteria for better and worse ideals.

In the second chapter we find an analysis of attitudes, in the sense described above. A classification that helps to sort out which attitudes are suitable for inclusion in an adequate ideal, and which ones are not is also presented. This discussion also illuminates the different roles that the intertwining of reason and emotion in attitudes can play. At times the assessment of the virtues of the potential object of an attitude is crucial, in other cases it is the plight the object is in, and in still other cases, neither the merit nor the plight of the object, but rather the circumstances of the situation determine the appropriateness of an attitude to be expressed.

The third chapter concludes the first part. It argues that one cannot do individual and communal–political ethics independently of each other. In spelling out criteria for adequate individual ideals notions like trust and friendship emerge, and these have also important roles in communal and political activities within our theory. The interrelations are partly empirical. Some conditions are causally necessary for the cultivation of certain adequate ideals, and likewise, some presuppositions about the character of a critical mass of the citizenry is needed to describe certain political structures functioning well.

The second part starts with a theory of what an adequately functioning community should be like. The description is quite general, and it specifies necessary conditions that cut across the political and non-political as well as the economic and non-economic categories of communities.

The first chapter in that part, i.e. chapter IV, argues that the key ties for a well functioning community should be agreements on certain attitudes to be shared in the community. Key communal ties are respect, concern for others, trust, and being able to take pride in some of one's work. This conception is defended in that chapter, and evaluations of communities as better or worse are also presented.

The next chapter deals with a notion that underlies and permeates the discussions of both individual and communal ethics, namely the notion of responsibility. Responsibility in concrete implementation has always several aspects. One is the assignment of different kinds of responsibilities to different individuals or groups in a community. The other is the set of conditions under which the various assignments take place. These include certain characteristics of the prospective agent who carries the responsibility. Still another aspect is the range of activities over which any human agent might claim the right to be responsible only to himself. Needless to say, these specifications can be carried out better or worse. Thus criteria of evaluating both the assignment and the carrying out of responsibility are also discussed.

Finally, our theory forges a strong tie between responsibility and freedom. It insists that no freedom is unconditional, but is tied in a variety of ways to actual or potential carrying out of responsibility. In this way the notions of freedom and responsibility are not based on allegedly fundamental rights and obligations, but on the elements of adequate individual and communal ideals. For the individual the ideal consists of aim and character, for the community it consists of aim and the communal ties. Ownership of goods also has its responsibilities, and this is how we arrive in the last chapter at justice, as a distributive principle for goods. In recent times the most popular theory of justice took fairness as its basic notion. In our theory the fundamental notion underlying various adequate conceptions of justice is sharing. It is a well-documented psychological fact about humans that normally everyone wants to share something with someone. This may be restricted to within a family, or friends, or larger communities. The theory of justice in this book starts from this fact and then develops ways in which an individual with adequate ideal, and a community with its adequate ideal, should interact so that the sharing is extended to larger and larger layers of people and to larger and larger collections of goods. This is just a rough idea. It is worked out in some detail in the last chapter. Many important questions about justice, for example, what are goods and what cannot be so interpreted, the acceptable modes of enforcement of justice, and many others, are left out. The aim of the chapter is not to present a complete theory of justice, but to show how such a theory can be constructed within the individual and communal ideals proposed in this book.

The book ends with some comments on how people should behave towards those outside any given community, and how communities should carry in them the potentials of change and growth, without these being in all cases necessarily good for all concerned.

This book will not please those who are firmly planted in the ideologies that maintain the dichotomies we saw our book violate.

Nor will it be compatible with the views of those who think that one specific political theory, democracy, communism etc., must be seen as having non-instrumental value, and should be spread over all human communities. In this book political structures are regarded as means to the final end, which is the development of adequate communal ideals for adequate individual agents. Some readers will complain that this book does not fall within the domain of liberal ideology. But the book should show that one can be outside that domain without becoming an advocate of a police state, tyranny, and other such structures.

The book is intended for an international audience, primarily for those who find the current dichotomies in individual and political ethical theory inadequate and are looking for a framework that is not relativistic, but contains a conceptual foundation that is not specifiable exhaustively in terms of rules and abstract institutional structures, and is at the same time pluralistic in its range of proposed kinds of implementations. It would be impossible to write a book that spells out such a conception completely. The purpose of the book is to arouse interest in this way of viewing individual and community as changes take place in South Africa, China, Europe, and—one hopes—even in the United States. Success for this theory will be if others take up the issues and proposals aired here, and carry these much further to improved conceptions.

Part I

THE ETHICS OF IDEALS

Chapter I

THE OUTLINE OF THE ETHICS OF IDEALS

Philoctetes in the Greek play named after him, faces the dilemma of either overcoming justified resentment, or placing his pride above all else. His choice affects the very core of his values and orientation in life. This kind of a choice contributes to determining what kind of an agent one tries to be, and hence it is not an accidental byproduct of ethical life. He will judge what is or is not useful to him and what kinds of relationships with other humans he should try to cultivate, from the point of view of how he construes himself as a human agent.[1]

Ethics in a broad sense is supposed to help to resolve such agonizing choices as the one Philoctetes faces. Modern ethical theories like Kantian ethics and utilitarianism attempt to solve such problems by separating prudential questions from the purely moral ones. In contrast we find no such fundamental dichotomy in the play. Only after basic decisions have been made concerning the kind of agent Philoctetes should be, are issues sorted out concerning which actions mostly affect the protagonist himself, and which ones affect other humans in important ways. In this book a theory of ethics will be outlined that in this respect resembles the classical outlook more than either Kantian or utilitarian ethics. The first chapter sketches key elements of the proposed ethics, labeled as Ethics of Ideals. Within this theory the most fundamental ethical questions are: (i) what should be an overall aim for human agents, and (ii) how are such aims to be related to character, or general psychological structure? The theory proposes that there should be a conceptual link between aim and character. Within this both are construed as being ultimate ends and having instrumental value.

---

1 Moravcsik, "Development of Friendship and Values in the *Philoctetes.*"

Philoctetes' choice, when arrived at appropriately, requires deliberation, planning, and aim setting. Within the theory of Ideals, this is generalized for all of our ethical thinking. We shall call an overall aim for life and the conceptually related character an Ideal. Some ideals are more, some less adequate. Hence the need for an Ethics of Ideals.

The first section of the chapter deals with what planning is, and how this activity admits of more and less rational as well as self-reflective modes. Our notion of planning is not exclusively instrumental. Hence we need also an account of ends and aims. Non-instrumental aims and aim setting has not been in the main focus of recent moral philosophy. Hence the next section is devoted to an analysis of different kinds of aims and aim setting, and the differentiation of aims from desires, feelings, interest and orientation.

This rich ethical psychology is needed in order to spell out the notion of agent underlying the Ethics of Ideals. Thus the third section is devoted to an analysis of different types of agency, and the presentation of a notion of human agency that is needed to describe a human at his best, setting aims, molding an ideal. The presentation stresses that the notion of an ethically relevant agency must always remain partly normative. To be a human agent is to have certain mental structures, capacities, and undergo certain processes. All of these involve priorities, and the settling of these is a partly normative task.

The fourth section deals with three key psychological and ethical claims that are constituents of an Ethics of Ideals. One of these is the conceptual link between overall aim and related character. Another is the denial of a fundamental chasm between the prudential and the moral, while keeping the distinction as a useful tool for the analysis of problems that confront us once we settled the fundamental issues of what ideal we chose. Finally, the section explains in what non-trivial sense this theory is an agent-oriented, in contrast with action-oriented, ethics, and gives justifications for the stance.

The final section deals with a proposal of criteria of justification and evaluation for proposed ideals, and presents arguments supporting these normative claims.

1. Planning

We shall consider planning in its weakest form, and show how conditions can be added to arrive at the notion of planning needed for an Ethics of Ideals.

On the most primitive level we find creatures that developed expectations about the future and subjective preferences between alternatives. A life based on such planning requires only some instrumental reasoning patterns that need not be conscious, and preferences are based on satisfying desires. In this minimal sense, we can talk of animals as planning creatures.

This conception can be enriched by the addition of consciousness. Thus we plan consciously, envisaging the available alternatives, their likelihood and their value (at least for us). With these abilities, we use imagination to present alternatives as vividly as possible, and exercise a higher, more critical function of reasoning as well. This is the capacity of employing reason to evaluate and assess alternative lines of actions, building up different trees of alternatives at crucial choice points.

Further complexities emerge when we add to the above the abilities to change and modify plans, and to offer justifications for the plan adopted. This is the level of planning and plan implementation that we encounter in typical human undertakings.

Having outlined types of planning with different levels of complexity, we can propose the hypothesis that a certain amount of planning is part of human nature; leaving open the question of the level at which this minimal planning need take place. Suspension of consciousness, instrumental thinking, and choosing seem inconceivable. We have some control over how we utilize these capacities, but not whether we will utilize them at all.

In what has been said we did not assume more than what is called instrumental planning. That is to say a hypothesis such as claiming that all humans are innately so constructed as to want pleasure or happiness, and thus all practical reasoning is merely instrumental in satisfying such a basic desire, is not incompatible with our account.

The following goes, however, beyond the claim of total instrumentality. We can think of human nature and human enjoyment as much more plastic.[2] Within this conception, there is no end at which all humans aim, consciously or unconsciously, and which could not be subjected to challenge. One can enjoy work, classical music, poetry, or volunteering in a hospital. The question can then arise: which activity should I engage in, and how should I mould life?

At this point we arrive at a conception of non-instrumental planning. Planning now involves not only finding means to satisfying my needs, but carrying out intentions and setting aims that will specify what my ultimate ends should be.

Planning can be done better or worse. Envisaging alternatives, judging values and probabilities, as well as reflecting on what should be ends in themselves, can be done more or less wisely or intelligently. Having good imagination, self-knowledge and sensitivity can improve our ability to plan. Furthermore, we need also a variety of practical skills, some cognitive, some sensibilities, some matters of acting in accordance with plans. Thus all of this constitutes part of the foundation on which the concept of an adequate agent must be built. At this point, we shall turn to one of the pillars of the Ethics of Ideals, namely aims and aim setting.

2. Aims and Aim Setting

Aim setting, like planning, admits of layers of complexity. On the simplest conceptual level we find mere goal-oriented behavior and conduct. Examples of this are search for food, shelter, and a mother's protection of her infant in the first days. Though these activities can take place also within complex psychological structures and processes, at the simplest level we find this in both animals and humans, without conscious reflections and choices. If we add to the psychology of the agent consciousness and intentionality, we arrive at a more complex type of aim setting that involves conscious grasp of what the aim is, consideration of alternatives, and justifications of the aim selected.

Still, we should not think of aim setting at this level as a continuous conscious operation. Stages of the development of an aim can take place at various times, without conscious awareness. But

---

2 Aristotle, *Nichomachean Ethics*, book II, 111104b5-25.

there must be some occasions at which the aim selected and its justification is brought to consciousness. For without the possibility of such rational scrutiny, and occasional modification of aims, explicit rational justification is not possible. Both aim setting and justification involves intentionality. We intend certain states of affairs to come about when we undertake to realize some aims, and what our aim is must be stated in intentional (and, semantically speaking intentional) terms.[3]

The following example should make this clear. I may want to become a physician. This, in turn, may be in a context the best-paid profession. From this it does not follow that I want to become a member of the best-paid profession.

Our theory posits the setting of final aims as concerning ends in themselves, and not just mere instrumental aims, or aims forced on us by an innate affective system. In support of this stance let us consider the matter of health as an aim. On the one hand, some might think of health as merely instrumental in giving us pleasure and minimizing pain. On the other hand, there is another view, according to which health is an end in itself, and cannot be defined in purely hedonistic or utilitarian terms.[4] Health is the proper functioning of the whole human being. This sense of "proper" can be elucidated only in terms of a functional account of what a human body does and what structures it must have, and what harmony the various parts achieve. The practice of medicine centers on the restoration and maintaining of health in this sense. Thus health is not just another commodity that we trade in terms of some utility scheme.[5]

Within this scheme of aim setting, we can conceive of an overall aim for a human life. This would be a set of ends towards which life as a whole is oriented. Such an aim can be stated on a very abstract or concrete level.

The following example shows the importance of having our overall aim cover as many aspects of our nature as possible. As Theodor Dreiser describes it, a rural family in the Mid-West of the United States, with well internalized but quite concrete values and

---

3 Bratman, *Intentions, Plans, and Practical Reasons.*
4 Moravcsik, "Ancient and Modern Conceptions of Health and Medicine."
5 Moravcsik, *Health, Healing, and their Values.*

character traits as their ideal, moves to Chicago, and there their moral and intellectual values fall apart. The reason for this is that their overly concrete and specific value system cannot cope with the drastic changes in environment and surrounding humans that the family must face. To cope with changes from a rural to an industrial environment and retain values, the ethics adopted must be sufficiently abstract and flexible.

Overall aims can culminate in one single item such as relieving suffering whenever possible. But these aims can also end up as a disjunctive list, giving the top of the value hierarchy more like the shape of a flat pyramid. This is important to note, since the call for having overall values in life often meets the resistance based on the misconception that such a call can be answered only by a rigid and concrete set of instructions. This is misleading. To be sure, our overall aim must have cohesion, but it can include a number of distinct elements, some relating more to one's profession, some to family relations, and some to economic and communal matters. Furthermore, within each of these areas our final end can be analyzed on two levels. First, the aim can be specified in general terms, e.g. kindness, striving for equality etc. Second, one can ask with respect to any one of these: what are its constituents? For example, one might strive to be kind to others in a variety of contexts, but we must also raise the question in each context: "what counts for kindness under these circumstances?" Different reactions, responses, expressions of feelings are appropriate manifestations of kindness in different circumstances. The traditional ends–means dichotomy is an oversimplified version of the threefold distinction of end, the constituents of end and means. The examples cited above show the need to regard some constituents more salient in one context than in another. But apart from contextual shifts we need to raise the issue of constituency in any case. E.g. someone aims at happiness. The next question should be: what are the constituents of happiness? People can agree on the first point and still disagree strongly on the second. The same applies to many other putative aims. For example, someone says, "we aim at equality." The next and considerably more difficult question is: "what constitutes equality?"

Two dangers in connection with aim setting should be kept in mind. One is that while aims should give direction to our lives continuously, this need not be and should not be represented on the conscious level as an incessant thinking about ultimate aims, for that would rob our lives of valuable spontaneous experiences, so important in the expression of joy, elation, and—as we shall see later—certain kind of sharing.

The other danger is planning too far ahead and in too much detail. As we saw, implementation is a key element in carrying out a life plan, and success in this aspect of the undertaking is difficult to obtain. The difficulties multiply when we construe our aims in too detailed a way. Flexibility is a key aspect of successful implementation, and specifying our aims on the right levels of flexibility and stability is a key element in this task.

So far we have discussed aim setting in individualistic contexts. But we also need to see that adequate aim setting should be an objective enterprise. Our task is to characterize aims that humans can adopt for a good life. This is not a matter of individual subjective choices. If I select one kind of candy over another, normally I do not affect the lives of others, and even apart from that I do not owe rational accounts of what I have done to anyone. But selecting overall aims does not function that way. First, under typical circumstances it does affect the lives of others, in at least two ways. First, the choices will result in actions, and most of these causally affect the lives of others. Secondly, even apart from the consequences of my actions, the decision to adopt this or that value does affect others in terms of their thinking, imagination and emotional makeup. It may open up new vistas or tend to desensitize or dehumanize others. We tend to develop aims partly by exchanging views with others. We are responsible for the impact that such exchanges have on how others think and feel.

Apart from the kinds of responsibilities just sketched aim setting needs to be an objective enterprise also because—as we said before—it carries with it justification. Justification includes giving reasons in defense of choices and decisions. But reasons are by their very nature rationally shared or sharable elements. That is one of the aspects that separate them from mere taste or whim. Hence the conclusion that aim setting articulated must be for humans in general terms, at least to the extent that putative aims must be seen as rationally justifiable for humans under such-and-such circumstances.[6] The justifications must also show the conditions and types of characters that are needed in order for the life centering on the putative aim to be enjoyed.

Such justifications already show a difference between aims and desires. For we can sketch for any given aim and character a range of desires that the life lived with that aim can satisfy. In other words, there is no isomorphism between aims and desires. Let us look at this now in more detail.

The articulation of a proposal for overall aims must also show for which appropriate psychological structure a life organized around the proposed aim can be enjoyable. This requires the human capacity to assess possible sources of enjoyment from an objective and non-hedonistic point of view. Enjoyment involves merely the satisfaction of some desires. Hence we need to distinguish aiming from desiring, and also show how the two can be connected.

In most general terms, to aim at something is to take it to be in some sense good, and to make it the object of activities eventuating either in some acquisition or in the transformation of the agent. We will not treat aiming in the sense in which a missile can aim at a target. We restrict ourselves to conscious and reflective aiming. Even so, there is a variety of aims. Aims can be instrumental or ends in themselves. Even among aims as ends, we can find some that are more mundane and restricted to certain social or economic conditions such as bee keeping or stamp collecting. Others are more general and flexible, such as contributing to human understanding in ways that engender cooperation and improvement of the human lot, rather than mere competition and the acquisition of economic goods. Clearly, not all aims are overall aims for life. One can have as his aim solving crossword puzzles every morning, without this becoming the highest goal in life.

Objectivity has two aspects. It can apply to ends in themselves. That means to apply to what we and others in similar conditions should construe as having values in themselves, and not just instrumental value, and are not associated with human activ-

---

6 Justification must be general; see Korsgaard, *Creating the Kingdom of Ends*, 3.

ities.[7] For example, maybe cosmic harmony is such a good but is not something that humans can achieve. On the other hand, we can aim also at something that may not be of cosmic value, but will pass the test for being an appropriate test for overall aim for human lives.

Our non-instrumentalist outlook on aim setting requires distinguishing aims from desires. The main difference is the relation aims have to reason, in contrast with the analogous role that reason has in relation to desires. I can choose, select aims. Up to a point such commitments are within my control. (Given historical context restrictions, we do not have choices spread across the alleged class of all possible worlds.) In contrast, I cannot choose or select desires. I can, however transform desires by having these directed to modified objects. For example, we can channel desire for food into desire for food that is good for us. I can also work toward becoming the sort of person who no longer has certain desires he had, or has desires he did not have before. Hence the effectiveness of some kinds of drug therapy, and the development of caring people who were earlier entirely egotistic in all of their pursuits. So on the one hand, we are not "slaves of the passions we have," on the other hand, we do not have the kind of autonomy with relation to our desires that we do have concerning our aims. Thus desires are distinct from aims; and experiencing desires from having conscious aims. Furthermore, aims can be justified, while we cannot justify desires, though we can justify efforts to become the kind of person who has certain desires. Desires can be transformed or suppressed. Aims can be formed, abandoned, and modified.

Aims have both intellectual and emotional content. The intellectual content resides in the claim that some X is good (objectively or subjectively) for me, and is worthy of pursuit. (Desires need not have this feature). The component of the relevant feeling depends on the cognitive. As in the case of respect, I cannot describe the feeling that goes with respect apart from explicating the judgment of why and who is worthy of respect. The related

---

7 Distinction between human ends and having intrinsic value, see Korsgaard, *op. cit.*, 9.

feeling helps me to unify various inclinations within me. The same holds for the affective component of aim setting. But this is not true of desire in general. I can identify hunger without ascribing to the agent any conscious selection of object for the desire.

The mixing of judgement and feeling, resulting in the formation of the attitude and related activities that constitute aim setting and realization, can take a variety of forms. It is misleading to lump these all together under some generic notion of "pro-attitude" or "inclination," for this obscures important differences.[8] We shall take up, briefly, three of these: aspiration, orientation, and interest.

Aspiration is the process of trying to approximate some ideal state we typically can never completely fulfill. We aspire to be a perfect physician, or an "ideal" colleague, knowing that total completion is beyond our reach. In contrast, orientation is the centering of the most salient of our relevant psychological structures and capacities around an attainable goal. Specifying orientation can involve giving signposts towards becoming a successful undergraduate, or lawyer, or parent. Thus having an orientation towards certain things in life entails having a kind of unity in our activities and roles as agent. The "kind" depends on how integrated our life is.

Thus, in terms of expectation, aspiration and orientation differ. Often, however, we do not yet know if our aim is fully realizable, thus the striking common elements between orientation and aspiration. These include the presence of intellectual valuing; i.e. construing something as worthy of pursuit, regardless whether at the time of the formation of the aim we have or lack desires directed towards that object.

This last feature can be seen in the clearest form in the case of the notion of interest. We do not have a causal account of how and why people become interested in, e.g. mathematics or chemistry. Our functional account of this well know phenomenon represents the relation between the mind of the agent and the object of interest as an element becoming attracted to something, analogously to the way particles become attracted to magnets. When we become interested, we develop desires, e.g. to spend more time on

---

8 We ignore here recent suggestions of how to reformulate non-cognitivism, since the variations are not relevant to our project.

study or experiments, or other activities related to our interest. But we cannot say that first there is a desire for mathematics and then the interest arises. Nor does it make sense to claim that there is a general desire of curiosity to which then this or that subject functions as instrument. When we develop interest in a specific subject, we also see worthwhile aspects of the subject that cannot be reduced to mere desire satisfaction. (E.g. elegance, something unique about numbers, or human relations, etc.)

These examples show the richness of the moral psychology that our account of non-instrumental aim setting brings with it. The examples cited indicate that this richness cannot be subjected to reductionist technique so as to end up with mere desire for pleasure, or general pro-attitude.

These reflections help us to sketch a general account of those aspects of deliberation that are most relevant to the Ethics of Ideals. The literature on deliberation is enormous, hence we shall select only the essential assumptions that the Ethics of Ideals makes in this context. First, within our scheme, deliberation has two parts. One is aim setting, which includes not only the specification of aims, but also what the constituents of an aim are. E.g. in many political and social interactions we aim at the preservation of equality among co-workers, fellow citizens, etc. in the relevant respects. But we also need to articulate a conception of what counts as equality in a given context. For example, equality among those who should have opportunities for health care is quite different, in its concrete specifications, from the equality of opportunities that should be provided for poor people in remote rural areas who cannot afford transportation to go to a voting place.

The other part of deliberation is instrumental. But this way of interpreting deliberation, i.e. into "parts" does imply that we do not carry out these things in parallel, simultaneously. Furthermore, as John Dewey stressed in much of his work, what seems to be in a context and end in itself can be reinterpreted after more reflection, as means to a higher end. For example, for some people certain economic and political structures, capitalism, communism, democracy, etc. appear as ends in themselves, while to some of us these can be seen as rival proposals concerning means towards adequate political and economic structures for various communities. The second conception involves articulating what adequate economic and political structures can be, without any prejudice in terms of vocabulary or theses regarding the above idealogies.

What we have said so far applies to local and overall aims. For deliberation about overall aims we need some conception of the salient aspects of human nature, and possibilities of their development under a certain set of socio-economic circumstances. In the last section of this chapter this project is developed in detail.

Overall aims must be considered consciously, and distinguished from available alternatives. The resettling deliberation should yield a scheme for orientation (or aspirations) for our lives. Still another part would deal with the implementation of this in concrete terms in concrete circumstances.

In the last few pages we have made a number of implicit assumptions about the relations between aims and thoughts, and desires. These will be spelled out here, and placed within the dichotomy of "externalism" and "internalism."[9] Let us consider the following scheme.

1) X becomes interested in archeology.
2) X acquires some knowledge and understanding of archeology.
3) X's knowledge and understanding and interest of archeology inspires him to major in that subject.
4) As a result of 1), 2) and 3) X comes to enjoy archeology.

As mentioned above, we have no good purely causal account of why X becomes interested in archeology, rather than in physics. The interest, however, creates a mind-set within which the aim of learning and understanding archeology makes sense. His majoring in the subject can deepen his learning. If all goes well, he also comes to a lasting enjoyment of the subject. Presumably some enjoyment also takes place before 4). But two views seem implausible concerning this little story. "Becoming interested," "inspired," "come to enjoy" are metaphorical or quasi-functional descriptions. When we specify aims and aspirations, this is the appropriate set of concepts to use. Not only do we not have a correct causal

9 Explication of the internal-external distinction is given in Williams, *Moral Luck*.

account, but it may be that two people with quite different causal histories could meet the conditions laid down above. So the scheme cannot be reduced to a purely causal account. Secondly, it would be odd to say that some kind of desire or enjoyment must precede 1) in order for the whole process to get off the ground. Interest comes first, enjoyment later. Interest has as its object something understood by the agent. But what would an initial "desire for archeology" be like? Or a "general curiosity" that can be satisfied in that individual only by archeology?

Our interpretation of the scheme assumes that thoughts, beliefs, of some kind can "cause" (evoke? generate?) attitudes that include desires, or sheer desire, or even directly action. Let us look at this more closely. The following is a reasonable account of how we arrive at respecting someone.

1) X judges Y to have respect-warranting qualities.

2) The content of the judgment in 1) engenders in Y the feelings that constitute completion of what it is to have respect for someone.

3) X respects Y, and normally that is manifested also in action.

Note that 1) does not entail or presuppose that X's judgment must have been based partly on some antecedent desire of X. One can simply construe, e.g. the ability to overcome even justified resentment as the sort of quality whose presence makes this a better world, and thus pave the way for respecting in institutionalized form.

Secondly, the example of respect shows that there is no initial reason not to suppose that thoughts or judgments can engender desires, and even that thoughts or judgments cannot directly engender action. Suppose we consider the following scheme.

5) John judges that Bill has respect-warranting qualities A, B, C,

6) This engenders in John respect for Bill.

7) Furthermore, 1) and 2) stimulate a desire to do whatever it takes to respect Bill.

8) John respects Bill

Step 7) seems superfluous and ad hoc. Unless we are already chained to a dogma that we can have a reason for something only in the light of antecedent desires of some sort already in us, we can easily move from the judgment to the realization of respect.

To be sure, other considerations may occasionally override the importance of the judgment. But this hardly justifies the introduction of an ad hoc desire. In this essay the underlying conception of causation is Humean. But the general considerations adduced should be applicable also to theories with non-Humean notions of causation.

So if we admit that thoughts of a certain sort can causally be responsible for the emergence of desires, or even directly for actions, we are embracing some form of non-internalist account of reasons giving and functioning.[10] If we think of thinking as events, the realization of aims as events, and actions as events, there is no a priori reason why any one sequence cannot lead to another. The burden of proof lies on those who would want to insist that only events of certain categories (with ontological distinguishing marks) can be causally related to certain others.

In conclusion, let us review the main factors for the key importance of aims and aim setting for the Ethics of Ideals. As we saw earlier, this ethics is based partly on the importance of an adequate overall aim for a fine human and well lived life. Hence the notion and its intelligibility needs defense. But even if we have done this, one might ask why aim setting should be so important.

William James' pragmatism provides an answer. His view is that certain questions force us to face unavoidable options.[11] E.g. in the face of the academic distinction between theism, atheism and agnosticism, James insists that pragmatically speaking there are only two options. We either live a religious life, or we do not. Furthermore, this is an unavoidable pair of options. Even if we refuse to think about it, in practice we must have opted for one or the other of these two life-styles.

Similar considerations apply to aim setting, and in particular to overall aim setting. Even a refusal to think about it saddles us with a certain overall structure of our life. This by itself does not show why this unavoidable option should be important for our lives. But at this point our reflections about aspiration and orien-

---

10 For explication of a variety of non-contingent reasons see Thorpe, *Non-contingent Reasons*, chapters 4 and 5.

11 James, *Pragmatism and Other Essays* and *Varieties of Religious Experience*.

tation become relevant. A consciously chosen overall aim can have an enormous effect on our life. It gives it direction, and thus makes an overall orientation possible. It can also transform our emotional life; redirecting some desires, suppressing others, and engendering still others. To the objection that this does not prove that such an aim can have answers to most of our key questions, our answer refers to the last part of this chapter, where a detailed account and justification for adequate ideals will be proposed.

3. Agency

We have covered so far two of the pillars of the Ethics of Ideals, namely planning and aim setting. An adequate discussion of aim setting involves an analysis of aims and of the process of aim setting and maintaining. Selecting adequate non-instrumental aims is done—within our analysis—by humans. The planner and aim setter needs various rational faculties as well as a sense of responsibility. As we turn now to implementation, we need the notion of agency. Plans and blueprints for various artifacts and natural phenomena can be implemented by subjects of various sorts. We mean by 'subject' the contextually singled out source of processes. E.g. the car starts, the rain wets the grass. We do not need a notion of agency for these processes. But planning and aim setting and their realization involves envisaging alternatives and selecting among these, as well as initiating actions that constitute implementation. In this section we consider only human agents that can plan, set aims, both instrumental and non-instrumental, and act according to the plans and aims so as to realize these, with commitments concerning the superiority of the alternative chosen and with regards to the consequences of the plans carried out. In this brief discussion many of the aspects of agency will not be covered. We shall concentrate on two points, most relevant to an Ethics of Ideals. First, when we function as agents we need to embrace a structure of priorities among our faculties and capacities that is necessarily normative. Thus the functioning agency must be interpreted as a partly normative notion. There is nothing more fundamental underlying it; especially no non-formative account of human nature. This, of course, does not mean that agential structures cannot be justified and criticized on rational grounds. Agency and implementation of plans can be executed better or worse. In fact, as we shall see, we cannot help but look at the functioning of a human agent as what must be judged in normative terms.

Agency and choices involving responsibility and justification are notions that emerge in ethical contexts. Furthermore, William James would say that these ethical contexts cannot be avoided. What we decide to do has consequences for the welfare of the agent as well as for other humans affected. Thus this way of construing a human being in a necessary role does not arise from purely scientific accounts of human nature. These too, involve— as of now—functional explanations. But digestion is not a process for which we can hold the stomach and various parts responsible, while we can view a human agent that way in the context of accessing his choices and decisions.

We shall now turn to show that while being an agent is a necessary role we play, it is also necessary for us to opt what kind of an agent we should be.

As biological entities we contain hierarchical structures. Thus breathing, digestion contains sub-systems, and can be broken down into further smaller units. But this account does not contain the psychological priorities that need be determined when we opt for a basic agent-profile. In some humans rationality will dominate and the emotions are given less priority as character traits underlying our decision making. In other cases, we find the priority running the other way. In some agent-profiles emotions like benevolence and kindness are dominant, while in others calculations of utility for the agent and those affected are more prominent. Within some respect for the autonomy of others is dominant, while in others the desire to do for others what is deemed to be in their interest has a key role. The latter difference is exhibited typically by types of parents.

At some level an agent-profile is fundamental to a human agent, and hence so is the built in normative priority structure among psychological ingredients. It makes no sense to ask "which profile is more useful to me?", for that question assumes that there is a "me" behind the basic agent-profile. But this would only lead into an infinite regress. Properly viewed, the question just formulated makes no sense, because the "me" in it can have no reference. We first have to have an agent-profile, and then calculate relative to that what is useful for us, and what is not. Mother Theresa had a different agent-profile from that of Napoleon. Thus what would be useful to one, would not be useful to the other, even though some overlap might remain.

The choice, development and justification of an agent-profile can be better or worse. These issues of evaluations will be discussed under the heading of criteria for adequate ideals. We can see from the above that a person with a good ideal is a person with a good aim and related character. But this entails that he is a person with a good agent-profile. His priorities should be guided by his overall aim, and that in turn has implications for adequate agency. The two need be built up so that these can be intertwined.

Not everyone with a good agential profile has a good ideal. But everyone with a good ideal and related character ("related" to be explained in the next section) must have a good agential profile. Else the good aim cannot be implemented.

There is still a "slack" between good aim and good agential profile. For example, one might opt for a more intellectual overall aim, but have a less unified agential profile, so that other aspects of life such as friendship and kindness also play important roles. On the other hand, one can lead a good life also by utter devotion to an aim that is specified without depending much on concrete external factors like the discovery of one specific element or law.

This ethics differs from the variety of theories labeled recently as "virtue ethics." It is difficult to gather all of those theories under a clear concept, since virtues can enter an ethical theory in a variety of places.[12] Virtues can be constituents of the happiness that according to some consequentialist theories we are to maximize. Alternately these can be prominent means to a life morally acceptable to a deontic theory. The Ethics of Ideals leaves open many conceptual places for virtues, i.e. desirable character traits. But what we have said in this section about agential profiles goes beyond the claim that virtues constitute the skeleton of a good life. Theories maintaining this could still posit a basic descriptive layer of characterizing human nature, and somehow relate to that the selected virtues. As we saw in our theory a certain normative structuring of priorities among psychological elements, and their func-

---

12 Arpaly, *In Defense of Deep Virtue Ethics.*

tioning in us as we set aims, plan and implement, is basic, with no further layer of description having claims to fundamentality.

As we consider agency, we need also make provisions within the theory that not only do we keep in mind our role and structure as agents, but also construe the humans with whom we interact as agents. Justification of an agential profile must be in terms of reasons, and these are by their very nature general. Thus our selections for ourselves—if justifiable—must also have implications for how we see other humans. Our choices also commit us to help engender in other humans good agential profiles. If we respect autonomy in ourselves, we should also respect it in others. If we place kindness and compassion on a high plane in us we should also do so in the case of others.

Thus acting so as to exemplify and engender good agency must be an important guiding principle in our lives. It is true, of course, that we will also deal with humans who by our own accounts have inadequate agential profiles. E.g. too much aggressiveness, or insecurity. Thus an adequate agent should have with the profile, structures that enable him to deal both with those who have by his lights adequate agential structures and those who do not. The ethically acceptable conduct cannot be restricted to interaction with those whom we share conceptions of adequate agency.

In this section we dealt extensively with the "good agent." We need to specify the sense in which the agent described is good. As we have already seen, this cannot be a prudential sense of "good," since that would lead to a homunculus type argument. Nor is it a purely moral notion of "good." For many of the aspects of the good agent sketched above are not matters of duty or moral obligation. Having the capacity to form non-utilitarian friendships or to be good at empathy are parts of a good agent, but are not matters of obligation.

Our approach rests on a sense of being good that does not entail either egoism or altruism.[13] A good agent is good in the same sense in which a mathematical proof can be good, or the harmony of our solar system is good. Our conception of the good agent resembles the common sense notion of "a man for all sea-

---

13 Brink, "Rational Egoism, Self, and Others."

sons." For it represents the agency and character that we assume as fundamental for setting good aims, carrying these out and interacting with others. We understand well what is meant by a good father, a good teacher or a good friend. One might think of the goodness of a good agent as the generalization over the various ways in which we can be good at the tasks and challenges that human life brings with it.

It is important to note, however, that the Ethics of Ideals does not assume some sort of metaphysical truth specifying what the basic function, and hence goodness, of humans should be. Divine or naturalistic sources of this goodness are not assumed. There may be, of course, overlaps between such theological views and the theory articulated in this essay.

Various ethically relevant attitudes are either self-centered or altruistic. But all focus on what is good for either the self or others. This good needs analysis. Either it is merely subjective preference, in which case it is not clear that we need to honor it. Or it turns out to be the kind of good that also characterizes the good agent of our theory. Within our theory there is a list of goods in this "basic" sense, and egoistic as well as altruistic attitudes are based on these.

4. Relating Aim and Character in the Person with a Good Ideal

A good overall aim for life can be realized by people of different natures. One can achieve intellectual goals either in very competitive or more cooperative ways. The key intuition of this section, and hence one of the intuitive pillars of the theory, is that good aims should be realized by right kinds of people in order to have a complete ethics.

One might wonder why we need to bring in the notion of character at this stage. Why is it not enough to say that a person with good ideals has a good aim and a good agential profile? Our answer points to vital human capacities, such as certain feelings and modes of thought that complete the human potential but need not play important roles in action and what goes into these being well planned and justified. These include being imaginative, capable of fantasies or being in states of peace and tranquility. The latter can be achieved in different ways by different people, but many of the features of a good character rule out an "anything goes" stance in these matters.

These examples show that a fully specified good character goes beyond, though it includes, a good agential profile. The constituents of good character must be ends in themselves, else these would be good only instrumentally, as means to aim realization. One might ask: so why not just two elements, good aim and good character that are independent and represent intrinsic goodness? This would go against the intuition listed at the start of this section, namely that the ideal should involve good people realizing good aims. The good character within this theory is constrained by the condition that it should fit the range of good aims we can select. For example, two quite independent elements are: political contribution as an overall aim, and sensitivity to suffering as a key element in the separately specified good character. Such a life can lead to grave conflicts, with little left in the theory to resolve these. An example of the two intrinsically good elements being intertwined as our theory demands would be Plato's conception of a good overall aim such as increase of wisdom, linked with the agent having also a good, for Plato harmonious, character within which reason "rules."

The dependence can also run the other way. For example, one can discover that one is very good as an efficient director of various types of operations. This could become a reason for choosing the kind of overall aim the realization of which is facilitated by having that kind of a character. The fact that in the theory both elements have intrinsic value does not exclude their also having instrumental value.

Another way in which we can compare good overall aim and good character as ingredients in an ideal is to see that both help to unify the human agent but in different ways.[14] A good overall aim unifies the human agent by giving him or her what we called above orientation. Orientation helps to clarify means–end pyramids. Even if we end up with a pyramid that has a "flat top" (several ultimate ends), orientation helps us to establish their compatibility.

---

14 K. Korsgaard in an unpublished paper presented conceptions of stronger and weaker unities of agency.

Good character also unifies, but in a different and compatible way. Good character need not give us orientation, but it unifies the decision-making process. It spells out what the agential profile should be, and which characteristics should be judged as important for promulgation when we plan action affecting others or ourselves. A person with good character can be quite different in different contexts. More compassionate and sensitive when helping a friend in need, and more bent on enforcing rules when working within a financial institution. But good character must bring with it a good sense of judgment that prescribes for the agent when to realize which of his or her cognitive and affective potentials. A surgeon or a professional athlete may need a certain kind of supreme confidence as they perform what is required. But they should also know how to change their attitudes towards others once they leave the hospital or ballpark.

Thus being dedicated and occasionally also single-minded is an important aspect of a good life. But it needs to be complemented by having a character that contains a variety of affective and cognitive elements, thus giving us a variety of capacities that should be realized in the right contexts in our lives.

These remarks show how aim and character are related in an "ideal" and why we need the notion of character in addition to that of agential profile. In this entire discussion, however, we dealt with the whole human or the human agent. It is time to defend our ethics as an agent-oriented ethics.

The very distinction of agent- and action-oriented ethics might seem counter-intuitive. Don't we need both? Ethics must include analysis and evaluation of both agents and actions. In reply, we can point to the key basis of the distinction, namely priority. The roles of both are acknowledged, but in our theory the delineation of the good agent is conceptually prior to the specification of good deeds, hence more fundamental. The priority can be spelled out in terms of dependency, which in this case means definitional dependency.

We cannot reduce the notion of a good agent to the performer of a certain independently defined range of actions. For the good agent is defined in terms of good aims, agential profile, and character. This, in turn, is explained in terms of capacities like that of dealing with frustration, insensitivity and others. These capacities defy reduction to actual or possible performances. The ethical life cannot be given a job-description. In fact, job-descriptions typically fail even in the concrete work environment, since new contexts, challenges and emergencies can always emerge.

Still even if this is accepted, one might try to give an independent characterization of good actions. To be sure, there are general descriptions that we can give of some types of good actions. For example we can say that good actions in general should reduce suffering. But this raises the question: whose suffering? This theory does not accept any "no-ownership" theory of suffering. In the typical context the suffering in question involves that of agents. So we need some theory of agency to explain why we should reduce suffering for certain kinds of creatures. We may also accept the thesis that creatures that do not have all of the agent-constituting characteristics of humans should not be left to suffer when possible. Suppose we eventually reach the minimal level—any creature that can experience pain. Are we not tempted to add: "and can react to the pain of others?" Or if we do not, are we not at least reducing the amount and kind of ethical concern for the suffering of entities that can register pain but cannot understand and react to the suffering of others?

In sum, the definition of a good agent is prior, and the delineation of good actions is derived in several ways, or is at least dependent on, our conception of the good of those with whom we interact, which in turn depends on some conception of agency, or elements of agency.

This not only influences the architectonic of this theory, but should also affect our conceptions of ethical education. The action-oriented ethics stresses the learning of rules for action, taboos, and rule-following. Our kind of ethics has as the main focus of ethical education role modeling, with rules and rule following occupying second place. We shall return to this in the second chapter.

These discussions about agency and character did not draw a distinction between the moral and the prudential. If we see this theory in the light of classical considerations, then the lack of that distinction is not surprising, for it does not exist in the classical writings either. To be sure, on some level the contrast does arise. In many ordinary circumstances one might ask whether a proposed action is in one's interest and whether performing it violates one of the duties we have. But what is an issue here in regard to our theory is not such contextual differentiation, the value of which is accepted by all concerned, but an allegedly fundamental dichotomy between prudence and duty. There is a "picture" that motivates the positing of such a contrast as fundamental. Within this picture human interest and inclinations are seen as needing some external constraint in order to maintain fairness and order among humans. Thus morality is seen as having a different source from that of prudence, and ethics is construed as the workings out of the appropriate ways in which the moral places constraints on the prudential and on inclinations. One might call this the "legal model" since we often construe the criminal legal system in this manner. In the alternative conception, within which we do not find this chasm between the moral and the prudential, the moral is seen as primarily enabling. It enables us to find worthwhile ways of interacting with others, and does not need the dichotomy at issue.

We can question the legitimacy of this alleged sharp distinction in two ways. First, examples suggest that the distinction is more a matter of degrees than of a sharp division. Secondly, we can question the need for having this dichotomy play such a key role in ethical theory.

The following phenomena seem to fall between the purely obligatory and the merely prudential. Take the example of not merely utilitarian bonds of friendship, such as friendship in which loyalty is based on shared overall values.[15] Participation in this kind of friendship is seen as an important enriching factor in a well lived life, and the capacity to enter into such friendships is ethically valuable, since it constitutes one key way in which humans can cooperate and share. Yet one could hardly say that we have a moral obligation to develop such friendships. Nor can we say that such friendships are always useful, without specifying the kind of agent whose utilities are assumed to hold. Within our theory the capacity to enter into such friendships is seen as a constituent, rather than a mere means within a good agent.

Another example showing the same situation is the development of trust in contexts in which rational evidence neither justi-

---

15 Aristotle, *Nichomachean Ethics*, Books VIII and IX.

fies nor disconfirms the feasibility of such a development. Developing trust under such circumstances is often a "forced option" in the sense discussed before. We either "take the leap" or end up with a community riddled with distrust and enmity. The ability to develop in some circumstances this kind of trust and to have it in relations with members of a given community has ethical value in the same way in which the kind of friendship discussed has. Yet such a development is neither a matter of obligation, nor is it useful in some absolute sense, without specifying the types of agents involved in the interactions.

Other examples, such as caring, compassion and overcoming justified resentment come to mind showing once more the doubtfulness of seeing duty and inclination as a fundamental moral dichotomy.

But distinctions cannot be judged solely by how sharp these can be drawn. The theoretically more interesting question is: is there really a justification for giving this distinction, sharp or otherwise, a fundamental role in one's ethical theory?

As defense one can cite the ability of a theory with this dichotomy to explain certain kinds of conflicts. These involve what we on the basis of common sense would label as clash between what we would like to do, or think to be useful, and what we ought to do if we are to remain moral beings. Such cases can involve self-sacrifice, forgoing certain pleasures for fulfilling our obligations to others, or giving up certain activities in order that we can take better care of loved ones. In response, one can show that these conflicts can also be resolved without the questionable dichotomy. For many humans self-sacrifice in the ordinary sense is also a form of self-fulfillment; i.e. the realization of a capacity they deem as crucial in human character. Furthermore, what is within the other model presented as a clash of duty and inclination can be reinterpreted as a clash between two conflicting inclinations. For example, we can contrast courage with seeking a quite comfortable existence not as duty against inclination, but as one form of delineating the good agent with good character, in conflict with another.

On the basis of interpretations of this kind the need for a basic duty versus inclination distinction can be seen as not needed in an adequate moral psychology in which we can represent human nature as plastic and capable of being trained to include a variety of types of states as possible source of enjoyment.

★

To sum up, in this section we first argued for character not being equivalent to agential profile, for its being the object of ultimate end, and at the same time being intertwined with having a good aim. We also showed the need for both aim and character by showing the different ways in which the two unifies the human psyche. The good aim in terms of overall orientation concerning what we want to achieve, and the other in terms of maintaining the kind of psychological background for decision making and for implementation of a well lived life that a person with appropriate ideals—in our sense—should have. We have then showed that this theory being agent-oriented and not having a duty versus inclination dichotomy at its foundation can be defended.

We shall now turn to the criteria of evaluation of good aim, agency, and character.

5. Criteria of Evaluation

The criteria are organized according to basic elements of human nature, and the bonds holding an ideal together. Thus there are sections concerned with reason, emotion, relations to others and aims. This classification cuts across the distinction between aim and character. Furthermore, it does not separate criteria for agency and those for character. Some of the criteria for any one part of human nature would apply to more than one of the ingredients mentioned. The totality, however, delineates adequate ideals, and thus serves as a guideline for developing these.

The criteria are conceptually distinct and do not entail each other. Hence there may be ideals that meet only some of the criteria. Furthermore, criteria can be met more or less completely. These considerations show that having adequate ideal is not a yes/no issue. Some ideas may be more and some less adequate, and the dimensions of assessment represent different vectors.

The following is a summary of the criteria of adequacy for ideals.

(A) Rationality.

    A1) The agent must be able not only to reason inductively and deductively, but also be able to articulate the social–cultural position in which he finds himself. He needs to be able to characterize his ultimate aims and values, envisage alternatives to these, and rank-order the alternatives. Thus he needs developed capacities of planning, choosing, self-knowledge, imagination, and the theoretical and practical wisdom to justify the decisions he makes and the ideals for which be opts.

    A2) The agent should have the skills needed for the implementation of his ethically relevant plans, and have the rational character and consistency to maintain his ideal through vicissitudes brought about by external factors and changes in internal psychological structure.

    A3) The rational functioning of the agent should be combinable with affective factors needed for the evolution of cooperative attitudes like trust, respect and concern for others.

    A4) Ultimate aims should be justifiable with reference to A1)–A3) and with reference to reasonable conceptions of the human potential.

(B) Affective Factors

    B1) In addition to the usual functioning of appetites, desires, and feelings, the sound agent has also a reasonable array of the following three kinds of emotions: self-centered, altruistic and emotions centering on matters of intrinsic goods or at least what can be regarded as final ends for humans. Examples of the first type include feelings of satisfaction, pride and self-esteem. For the second type sympathy, sensitivity towards the suffering of others and well wishing count as illustration. The third type is illustrated by certain types of appreciation, aspirations and spontaneous joy.

    B2) The adequate agent with the appropriate ideal should be in psychological states in which the life implementing the ideal can be enjoyed.

    B3) The agent with the appropriate ideal should be capable of generating and having spontaneous emotions, and feelings that have their source in the agent's character and not outside manipulation or persuasion. Such an agent would feel, for example, spontaneous care for those encountered who are suffering, and could feel spontaneous joy of pride in accomplishments that he or she deems to represent non-instrumental value.

B4) The adequate agent should have a psychological structure that enables him to find meaning in his life and can make sense of it. This enables the agent to go on with life even under dire circumstances, to find ways to contribute to goals of social units larger than the individual, maintain interest in some aspect of life, and place his life into larger contexts and thus units of reality. He or she should have thoughts and feelings that enable him or her to face death without anxiety.

(C) Relations to Others

C1) The agent should have a psychological structure enabling him or her to appreciate and take pride in work deemed by him or her and others to have value for individuals and communities. He or she should be able to have as one orientation in her life the realization of communal values.

C2) The agent must take responsibility for his or her actions that affect the welfare of self and others.

C3) Adequate relations to others require a certain domain of emotions. These include kindness, concern for others in bad state and for those involved in developing worthwhile relations, and the emotions required for placing in the appropriate contexts cooperative attitudes above the competitive ones. Also included are the emotional factors needed for the formation and maintenance of friendships centered not on mere mutual utility but on shared fundamental values involved in ideal building.

(D) Aims

D1) Adequate agents should not only have instrumental but also non-instrumental ends and aims. These can culminate in one or several but consistent final ends. These ends and aims organize life into a coherent whole.

D2) The realization of overall aims should be consistent with maintaining the conditions for adequate agency and character articulated in A)–C). The latter must be a part of the set of overall aims. Thus both these aims and others organizing life into a coherent unit should be ends in themselves.

D3) The Final aims should represent values that the agent can see as having objective value, and not represent merely as subjective preference.

As we survey this summary, we can see how many of the conditions rise out of the notion of successful ideal building. For this fundamental activity we require the kind of rationality described in A), and the affective component specified in B). This requirement leaves us a wide range of ideals to choose from. So why should everyone attempt to become a good ideal builder? This translates into: why should we develop a rich structure of rationality, emotions involved in various activities of cooperation, and psychology needed for happy interrelations with others, reaching way beyond mere mutual gratification?

Ideal building is—in the terminology of William James—a forced option. We will develop in our lives ideals in the sense defined here, in one way or another. Furthermore, these will have a great impact on our lives. It seems then foolish not to become aware of ideals we formed non-consciously and try to gain control over this activity. We should then consider human potentialities, our social nature and ways of bringing all of this into harmony. This is basically what these conditions spell out.

As we turn to A1), we should distinguish "thin" from "rich" conceptions of rationality. "Thin" or minimal requirements on rationality include concept formation and inductive as well as deductive reasoning capacity. On the face of it, this is not sufficient to characterize the rational part of an adequate agent attempting to build and maintain an ideal. Hence the additional elements listed in this condition. One might reply that according to some philosophers all of the additional conditions can be reduced to the "minimalist" version. Such reductionism, however, is yet to be shown possible. A crucial element in the concept of rationality in A1) is making sense of things, hence explanatory power. But whether something is explanatory or not cannot be reduced to purely formal, logical structures.

We should not assume that the notion of rational order has only one universal structure. Charles Taylor argued convincingly that fundamental conceptions of rationality emerge in different cultures and contexts.[16] In some cultures having a mathematical–geometric model of reality counts as ultimate explanation. In others, success in giving causal explanations for natural and man-made phenomena counts as the final stage. The conception of rationality needed for adequate ideal choosing agency sketched in A1) can stay neutral with respect to that controversy.

A1) presents rationality at its best with a variety of elements included. This shows that in our system rationality is semi-normative notion. The plurality of distinct factors help us to see at once that by having more of these or less, and having any one of them to a greater or lesser extent, we can achieve better or worse rationality. Furthermore, rationality of the A1) kind enables us to transcend the boundaries of the conventional thinking of our environment. It does NOT posit human ability to survey "all logically possible worlds," but it says that once we become aware of some deeply held view in our society, we can envisage alternatives to it. This makes change, and hence occasionally progress, possible. So this is the more limited Platonic, rather than the unlimited Kantian or analytic freedom that A1) posits for ideal builders. It gives us partial, not complete autonomy for reason.

Our conception entails that one of the most important human elements is the ability to survey and reflect on what we aim at, how we implement, how we can combine reason and emotion. This self-knowledge is not a guarantee that we will always be able to change ourselves in any way we want. Perhaps some cognitive structures are given to humans innately, and though many of these are useful to us, perhaps others are not, and may be beyond changeability. Still, the ideal builder always relies on self-knowledge, no matter how limited this may turn out to be. We have no alternative.

This stress on the need for self-knowledge and examination

---

16 Taylor, "Rationality."

should not be read as implying a ban on spontaneity, not only in feeling but also in thought. We might reflect on one part of the mental structure and at the same time allow free flow for another part. Our views of ourselves are at any time only partial.[17]

We leave this justification for A1) with a speculative note. As we see, it is good to reflect some time on this, and at other times on something else. But how do we know what is good when? This leads us to a second-order of reflective activity. But spelling this out, and protecting it from infinite regress is beyond the scope of our current enterprise.

As A1) specifies seeking and maintaining concepts and principles A2) sketches the requisites for successful implementation. Relationships between theory and implementation are complex, and the ethical assessment of implementation varies with different conceptions of morality. Thus, for example, on some versions of the morally right, the key emphasis is on intention, or faith in supernatural values. Behavioristic models yield the opposite result. This essay rejected behaviorism from the start. At the same time, this is an ethic that revolves around agency. Hence implementation and successful ways of realizing aims are key elements in the ethic of ideal building.

In classical philosophy we find two quite different conceptions of how theory and implementation in ethics are related. Within the Platonic model, implementation is not given the role of a separate constituent. Relying perhaps too much on the paradigm of mathematics, where indeed theoretical insight cannot be separated from ability to construct proofs and calculations, Plato seems to take for granted that if we have the right insights, we will also be able to carry out their practical implications. In contrast, Aristotle gives theory and practice separate treatments, and has a number of suggestions concerning some overall strategies of how to implement moral ideals. This essay adopts the Aristotelian stance with respect to this issue. The key consideration leading to this decision is the heavily context-dependent nature of implementations of values. With this context dependency comes the plurality of skills and abilities need-

---

17 Moravcsik, *Meaning, Creativity, and the Partial Inscrutability of the Human Mind.*

ed to implement, e.g. how to be a good physician, and how to function well in a political–economic community. Nevertheless, some general guidelines can be articulated. This serves two purposes. On the one hand such a sketch is a justification of the insistence of seeing ethical value in implementation skills. On the other hand, it shows the pluralism in context need not lead to relativism in theory.

In order to achieve successful implementation, the agent must have an analysis of the goal in terms of the end, its constituents and the means for realization. The latter will vary in different contexts. The difference between constituent and means is crucial for implementation. For example, in some contexts we attempt to achieve equality in some respect between members of a community. The discussants may know what equality is in general, but they also need to agree on what the constituents of equality are e.g. in the context of economic opportunities, etc. After these matters are decided, we turn to means or instruments of realization. Here further contextual elements may enter. E.g. distribution of food may require one set of means in one cultural context, and another set in another.

As another illuminating example, we can consider the promulgation of genuine friendship between members of a community. In some cultures, the means chosen may require a lot of leisure time. But if we think of friendship among members of an agricultural community in Africa, who work 10 hours a day in the fields, we need to think of other means.[18]

Implementation requires cleverness in knowing what the reasonable available means are in a given context. It also requires a good sense of judgment. For example, what may be intended as being concerned and helpful may turn out to be in fact a case of overbearing conduct, doing more harm than good.

Implementations for the more deep ends in our lives take place over longer periods of time. This has the result that we must be prepared to alter the means to some extent as cultural conditions change. It also brings with it the demand on mind and character to be able to remain consistent in more general abstract terms. This needs both consistency in our thinking, even in

---

18 I am indebted to Joan Bresnan for helpful comments.

changed circumstances, and also determination of character to remain consistent in action.[19]

We cannot say that good implementation is not within our power, because it depends on external circumstances that are beyond our control. SOME circumstances are within our control, and can be changed. Thus perfect implementation is often unattainable, but it can remain a standard to be approximated. To assess the adequate agent we need both theory and implementation, in the same way in which we expect this from mathematicians, physicians, and practicians of other vocations.

Underlying the right practices we find attitudes of cooperation, respect and others. The notion of an attitude, so central in this kind of ethics, will be analyzed in depth in the next chapter. For our purposes here it will suffice to see its main structure as a combination of judgments and feelings evoked by these. For example, we judge X to be worthy of respect in virtue of his having respect-warranting qualities Q1...Qn. A3) states that our rational activities and underlying structure must be such that these combinations be possible. Elements in the Q-set will have to include concepts to which we produce certain emotional or valuational responses spontaneously. E.g. health is seen by everyone as at least prima facie something good to be aspired to, and the same can be said about notions like courage or wisdom. This may not be a mysterious magnetic property of some concepts, though one can easily imagine that something like this is involved and is deeply embedded in human nature. Alternatively, we can conjecture that some of these concepts have a built-in normative aspect, and we are forced to respond to this positively or negatively, prior to overall rational assessment of their role in any given context in terms of utility or duty.

So the language of the adequate agent must contain words and judgments that can evoke feelings that contribute to the emergence of action. What would it be like to have languages that lack this feature? For example, it would be a language in which all words denote behavior only as far as description of human activity is concerned. Furthermore, the behavior would be described solely in terms of movements, changes in location, etc. Alterna-

---

19 Bok, *Freedom and Responsibility.*

tively, the language would contain only descriptive terms that admit of complete mathematical analysis; a kind of "Pythagorean ordinary language." These outlandish examples are listed here only to show that A3) is not an empirically empty claim. It is probable that on a very basic level every natural language meets A3), and that humans have the necessary cognitive equipment for understanding these parts of languages. But A3) can be met more or less, and our conceptual world can be more or less adequate for analyzing this aspect of human thought.

6. Emotion

We have dealt with conditions on rationality, but in A3) we transgressed the line between conditions on reasons and on emotions, since the formation of attitudes, in our sense, also required that certain feelings could be evoked by the use of certain types of expressions. (Contrast in this respect: "I respect Jim" with "yepee" or "hurrah;" latter are purely expressive of emotion, former is not.)

Our B-conditions are meant to take into account the highly likely empirical fact that the development of certain types of emotions depends on the human being's early exposure to certain types of affections. This suggestion emerges from recent studies of juvenile criminals who murdered tourists in Miami, and seemed incapable of understanding the idea that they were causing suffering to humans. As one social worker put it, when looking into the eyes of the criminals: "the lights were on but nobody was home." The hypothesis was formed upon further examination that unless a human receives some form of warm positive affective input in the first 4 years of life, they will not be able to understand the notion of causing suffering to others.

B1) deals with the kinds of emotions that an adequate agent should have, in addition to the usual desires dealing with survival and reproduction. The adequate agent should also have emotions and desires falling into three classes, the self-centered, the altruistic and the feelings centering on projected goodness that is construed as objective and providing the foundation for a description of human nature relative to which one can talk of objective utility. The justification for this condition is that an adequate agent will need some of each class in order to form and maintain an adequate ideal.

The agent needs self-centered feelings, since some of these will be involved in various projects of self-improvement, and also in the psychological struggle to maintain the chosen ideal. As we shall see, a full presentation of conditions of adequacy for ideals includes sound relationships with others, and these will include some altruistic feelings, like concern for the welfare of others regardless of the utility of this for oneself, as ingredients. Finally, our pursuit of ultimate aims and ends will have to include emotional factors that have as their objects elements seen as either of intrinsic value, or at least as non-instrumental human ends. For example, wisdom may have some instrumental value, but on some level it will have to be defended as a key constituent in an adequate human character. Pushing for justifications terms of utility, duty or satisfaction must have an end at some point.

This requirement, however, leaves open a wide range within which ideals involve a more gregarious existence, others more room for solitude. There is no magical formula that would dictate some exact proportion for the right combination of the tree categories of feelings and attitudes. (For the legalistically minded, this may be bad news, for those of us who think that ethics leaves room for creativity in constructing our ideals, this is a welcome message indeed.)

B2) should not be confused with the hedonistic claim that would simply demand the adequate ideal to be maximizing pleasure, for such a claim must be challenged by the question: "pleasure for whom?" An ideal may be enjoyable for humans with one psychological structure while not be enjoyable for people with a different psychology. There are activities that give people who are like Mother Theresa a deep sense of satisfaction, while these activities do not please gamblers, and soldiers of fortune.

The best way to delineate the kinds of people for whom the ideal must be enjoyable, is to specify it in terms of the psychological adequacy conditions in general, that this scheme prescribes. This is not circular, since the scheme allows much variety of ideals and psychological portraits within our theory. Furthermore, we must guard against overly quantitative conceptions of enjoyment

in general. We must distinguish pleasant sensation, e.g. one resulting from taking a shower after a tennis match, from the general
notion of enjoyment that includes enjoying a concert, a book, or a
successful semester of teaching. It makes no sense to ask in each
case which of these are more enjoyable, and even less sense can be
assigned to questions like: given two ideals for people with different (but within the theory acceptable) psychological structure,
which combination of agent and ideal yields more satisfaction or
enjoyment? Who derives more enjoyment from their daily work, a
dedicated mathematician or a dedicated gardener? Such questions
presuppose scales of comparisons across types of enjoyment and
psychological types that do not exist. B2) prescribes a basic kind
of enjoyment and delineates a basic kind of acceptable physiolog-
ical structure, and lays down in terms of these an enjoyability condition. There is no precise way of delineating either a level of
enjoyment or the class of psychological types whose enjoyments
are to be considered.

Even with all of these caveats, we still face the question: why
have an enjoyability condition at all? In order to answer this question we need to clarify the claim that maintaining a certain ideal
is to be enjoyable to some. Clearly, we cannot mean "enjoyable at
all times, in all contexts," else the adequate ideal holder will
resemble the perpetual smiling character of toothpaste ads. There
are also "sayings" such as: "Some suffering is good for you; it
develops character." B2) treats the enjoyability of an ideal as a
conception within which the enjoyable life is treated as a holistic
unit, and we speak of enjoyment as the overall mark over larger
stretches of time. Even then one must add that this holds for idealized conditions; environmental factors can make the holding of
an ideal very painful and difficult. Obvious examples are: being
antifascist in a fascist country, advocating women's rights in a
rigidly sexist society.

With these admittedly vague qualifications, we can see why
the enjoyability condition is justified. We face a forced choice:
either the ideal will be enjoyable or neutral, or brings mostly suffering. But an adequate ideal is like the blueprint for a smoothly
running organism. We assume that what is running well should
place the agent in a position of well-being, and enjoying the right

things should thus be one of the marks of things going well. (This is similar to Rawls' point about goods.[20]) The suffering endured during a good life should be either for the sake of eventual or over-all higher values, or the consequences of unfavorable external circumstances. Enjoyment is partly responsible for a state of satisfaction, and is also a good motivating factor.

B3) is the analogue of what moral philosophers call rational autonomy. The autonomous reason can form concepts, judgments, arguments, without these being coerced by external factors or internal purely physical elements, or whatever causes obsessions and other forms of insanity.

Emotional autonomy is meant to protect at least a part of our emotional structure. It claims that in an adequate agent building or maintaining an adequate ideal, not all emotions should be merely causal effects of external circumstances, be these brain washing or factors such as starvation, making the development and expressions of normal emotions either impossible or at least very difficult. One key reason to support this claim is that we need a certain kind of spontaneity and autonomy in forming attitudes that are fundamental to adequate ideals, such as cooperation, respect, trust, etc. For example, registering the love and caring attitude of a mother differs radically in quality, depending whether the feeling is interpreted as a mere reflex to some environmental condition, or as the result of the kind of union of reason and emotion that we sketched earlier as the basic structure of attitude. If I form respect towards someone, this should be a matter of a free rational judgment as to what relevant properties the other person has, and the feeling attached to the judgment should also be a freely formed occurrence, not the result of e.g. mere conditioning.

In some professions emotional autonomy plays a key role. Medicine is aiming at healing. In many contexts this requires a caring attitude on the part of the physician. But this is seen by the patient as reassuring only if it is felt to be "genuine," which is the common sense term for what we mean here by the autonomous feeling.

B3) calls for the realization of conditions for emotional autonomy. Many of these conditions are empirical. As we saw above, the

---

20 Rawls, *A Theory of Justice.*

ability to understand the suffering of others is most likely a part of the right empirical external conditions, and having the freedom for a physician, not bothered by rules of for-profit HMO organizations, to develop the caring attitudes that the physician judges and feels to be appropriate to given relationship with a patient is also a condition needed for the emotional autonomy linked to that profession.

We see, then, that emotional autonomy is a vital condition for a healthy psychological structure enabling an agent to develop adequate ideals and to maintain these. This autonomy can also affect communication, especially in cases in which emotional autonomy affects the quality or the communication, such as being kind, sympathetic, expression of loyalty.

We turn to the last of the B-conditions. This one is situated squarely between A and B domains. It is listed here because the B-aspect is so crucial, and more difficult to describe. B4) states that the adequate agent and ideal builder must have a mental structure that enables him to find meaning in his life. Finding meaning in one's life may involve finding meaning for life (answering to the agent's satisfaction the "meaning of life" question) but it may not. Finding meaning in life enables one to go on with life even under extremely harsh conditions. For example, the widow of O. Mandelstam found as meaning in her life her hope, even when at one stage she spent most of her life going from office to office of the KGB, trying to free her husband. James Stockdale has described vividly in lecture how certain philosophical reflections gave meaning to his life and thus enabled him to go on with life even in at times hopeless circumstances in a Vietnam prisoners' camp. Finding meaning in one's life also helps to make sense of one's life in an overall assessment. Perhaps one's achievements, contributions to what are deemed to be matters of intrinsic value or having been able to enrich the lives of others through personal contact, helps to see one's life as having had "a point." Finding meaning in one's life is often linked to having found something—be it intellectual, artistic or personal—that attracts one's dominant interest for long periods of time.

Finally, finding meaning in one's life helps to face death without much anxiety. A German magazine asked once a number of well known public figures how they wish to face death. The former leader of Bavaria, Franz Josef Strauss, said that he wishes to die having made his peace "with God and men." One's first reaction may well be that these are very high expectations. But on further reflection it becomes clear that what Strauss proclaimed can be interpreted as admitting matters of degrees. If one has a viable conception of the larger units of reality within which one has been placed in life, and one can say that we did our best in coming to understand that, and based on that understanding found ways of contributing to what at our best speculation are the good worth while things, then one can face death more peacefully. Prof. Jonathan Stavi once said that the most one can hope for is that in the final summation one will be able to say, "one did one's best." (Characteristically, he added immediately that this brings up two questions: "what is your best?" and "how do you know that you did your best?")

Not everyone needs to find meaning in life. Some enjoy most of whatever comes their way and feel no need for general reflections of the sort just sketched. But the ability to be able to find meaning in one of the ways listed is part of good ideal building, for humans can never know when such reflections will seem to them practically forced on their mind, or when merely doing interesting things loses its value to them, and boredom sets in. The A- and B-conditions function well as foundation for searches for meaning. One needs to add only that one needs also the ability to shape the capacities listed so as to be focused on these searches. The question of "meaning" in this context arises out of looking for larger explanatory structures than those emerging in everyday practice. The emotional sensitivities need to be supplemented by senses of awe and appreciation of tranquility arising out of having reached satisfactory ultimate explanatory schemes.

C1) stresses the ability to place high value on communal work and the appreciation of its value as an essential ingredient in ideal building. Work for many in industrial and agricultural societies has come to be a mere means to earn enough money, or to acquire things that we need for our own indulgence. Yet all of us engage at one time or another in communal activities, i.e. activities that more than one person must partake of, and cannot be reduced to a conjunction of two separate actors doing two separate things. Dr. Michael Fehling pointed out that even on the most basic level we find examples like a handshake and what it symbolizes. The handshake has to be performed as a joint cooperative with the pair as the subject, not the mere conjunction of the two participants. C1) states that the recognition of high value for such activities, and the appreciation of the potential for our enjoyment of these is a part of the good ideal builder. Partaking in such essentially joint activities is needed for most of our important communal activities, and—as we shall see in part II of this work—lay also the foundation for sound and lasting communal ties.

In part II the notion of work will be subjected to detailed analysis. But we need a preliminary conception of it for our purposes here. C1) shows that work need not be seen as merely something we want remunerated, but also as what at its best enables us to express basic good human potentialities. It construes humans as not just rational, but also achievement oriented creatures, where achievement is not reduced to hedonistic experiences but as a natural function of humans. Seen this way, taking pride in work as an end and as in many cases requiring the essentially cooperative can serve as the foundation of social structures that have as their basis sharing. In handshake-like activities we necessarily share feelings of affections, or respect, or promise keeping, or a combination of these. If we come to enjoy and appreciate this, then perhaps we can build on sharing and essential cooperation a basis for distributive justice that is not restricted to fairness as its foundation, nor to utilitarian considerations.

C1) then, has the appreciation of work and essential cooperation at the very basis of our interpersonal systems. It leaves room for rules, laws and agreements, but does not regard these as the most fundamental level of human coexistence.

C2) is linked to C1). For making responsibility a distinct and essential ingredient of ideal building, it draws on the experiences of necessarily communal activities that are not conceivable without some sense of responsibility.

The work envisaged within C2) covers a wide range that includes not only legally defined jobs, but activities that help the maintenance of the legal system by making it intelligible to wider segments of the population, or organizing cooperative efforts to fight lack of hygiene in one's community.[21]

---

21 Tyler, *Why Do People Obey the Law.*

Responsibility structures concern for others. Mere concern might not be productive at all. We can be very concerned, and yet our irresponsibility prevents us from expressing the concern in fruitful ways.

So far we have dealt with responsibility in contexts in which it is essential for us doing good things. But responsibility by itself can also help evil designs. A diabolic agent can carry out plans much better and coordinate these with the plans of his diabolic friends, if all participants can take for granted that each will take on responsibility for the acts performed and their consequences. So responsibility does not have a necessarily benevolent orientation. Applied to human interactions it always affects the welfare of others, but we cannot arbitrarily build into the conception that the affecting of the welfare of others will not be harmful, just because the agent is a responsible person.

We can take as part of ideal building responsibility as a necessary condition. What we said elsewhere in conjunction with work and cooperative actions of other sorts ensures that responsibility will be developed in humans primarily within the framework of such cooperation, sharing, and the development of positive affective qualities.

Finally, a key condition on meeting successfully C2 is that the taking of responsibility is recognized by the agent and is recognized, as well as expected, by other members of our community. For this recognition plays a fundamental role in building up other attitudes that are constituents in adequate relations to others. The recognition that the others take on responsibility is already a ground for respect, and helps bring about trust in the community.

Responsibility in the sense employed here presupposes what we called earlier autonomy of reason. For without such at least partial autonomy there are no genuine choices, and thus responsibility makes no sense. We see here once more how the Conditions must be formulated such a way as to be consistent with—though not derivable from—the A- and B-conditions.

C3) should be placed in a wider context. We have a great variety of emotions: greed, anger, hatred, resentment at what frustrates us, and many others. There are also morally neutral emotions, such as liking, disliking, being scared, feeling bored, and many others. C3) singles out what we might call intuitively the positive affective emotions, and states that their presence is essential to that aspect of ideal building that concerns our relations with others. Thus it matters that we should be able to trust others and have them trust us. It matters that we should have the kind of psychological structure that enables us to develop non-utilitarian friendships.

What is required for friendship? The key elements are: the ability to share, cooperate, to have loyalty, to be able to respond to shared values, to have compassion towards others, and retain special feelings towards a few individuals. The latter is a special requirement that we drop when we attempt to extend the realm of friendship to a whole community. This does not mean that everyone will be a friend, but that in our relationship to others in our communities there will be ingredients of friendship.

Why should this be a condition of adequacy of ideal building? Why not envisage the possibility of a cold but cooperative and peaceful community in which people help each other out of a sense of duty, but express no kindness, love and care? Maybe this would not be a pleasant community to live in, but why is it not an ethically adequate community?

Our answer goes back to the handshake and to the empirically attested need for positive warm affection towards the very bound in order to awaken sensitivity towards the suffering of others. Helping each other to build and maintain rational and emotional autonomy are among our most fundamental challenges. So is spontaneous sharing and cooperation. If we do not develop the emotional capacities listed in C3), we deprive others of what—on empirical grounds—we can see are important needs to fill. In fact, perhaps humans would not be able to lead a happy social, cooperative existence without the emotional background C2) posits. Again, there could be very moral people who are incapable of forming non-utilitarian friendships, but they would miss what is attested across history and cultures one of the most moving experiences in a human life. We turn to others with care and respect when we detect in them not just rationality, but the kind of attitudes under discussion here. Thus a whole dimension of human life is cut off the "cold moral" community. And the evidence that a sense of duty is better justifiable rationally than benevolent attitudes, or that it is more likely to survive even environmental changes, is simply not there.

7. Ends and Aims

Ideals were defined earlier as a combination of adequate ends and related character. We saw in our review of criteria of adequacy, that the relevant aspects of character include those of agency. Ideal building requires not only adequate ends, but also an adequate agent who has the cognitive equipment to select the right ends, and has the right combination of cognitive and affective structures to implement these. The ends we are considering are primarily non-instrumental (or not purely instrumental) ends. Since we assume that humans have the capacity to select ultimate non-instrumental ends, and these can be assessed as better or worse, we need criteria primarily for these. Criteria for adequate means are also discussed in other ethical traditions, and the Ethics of Ideals has nothing unique to offer on that topic.

Since the right character is already included among the adequate aims, we know that there is a strong conceptual connection between end and character. But the other important link is the claim that an appropriate end may be realized in a number of ways, and our theory insists that the aim be realized in accordance with the appropriate characters delineated by our previous conditions. For example, one might select the increase of wisdom as an adequate final aim. But this can be realized in a number of ways. It might be the case that one way of realizing does not give the learners any autonomy or any sense of community with other learners. Our conditions will rule such paths out. We can see a kind of incoherence in a position that tries to instill a system in a society with means that are inconsistent with what we try to implement. A good example is forcing a society into a democratic system. How can such a learning process, if we can call it that, have a lasting positive effect on the learners, and if it does not have this effect, how deep can the implementation be? It remains a surface procedure, with results depending on further force.

These reflections show the need for aim evaluation, and its effects on the resulting ideals. Let us look at the conditions in more detail.

D1) rules out a completely pluralistic view of life as what an adequate ideal should specify. Complete pluralism comes usually from an implicit pessimistic epistemology, and extreme individualism. It says: "everything changes, how can I have overall aims, life is a continuous series of adjustments, etc." It says also: "why should I box myself in; why not allow myself the freedom to change even overall aims any time I feel like it?"

If taken seriously, this stance rules out rational planning, and thus construes human life as a basically chaotic set of processes. When people say that everything changes, they seem to have mostly superficial aspects of existence in mind, such as technology, political changes and other such items. Following Aristotelian lines our theory interprets character and ethical overall aims as moving on a deeper level than the above. For example, the means to retain friendships and express the feelings involved can change from civilization to civilization, and historical stage to another stage. But, as both historical and cross-cultural surveys show, the basic ingredients of friendship do not change. For example, Aristotle's delineation of non-utilitarian friendship need not be accepted by all, but to the extent that it is adequate, that adequacy can be defended today in so-called Western societies just as much as in Aristotle's Greece.

Again, the need to sustain some overall values, and thus give life some unity and persistent structure, can be seen when drawing a parallel between a well-lived life, and a long lasting business company. Concerning the latter, Prof. Porras has shown that if a company has a value statement and attempts to stick to it, it has a much better chance of survival than those that do not.[22]

Aims can some time slip away, without our noticing this. Hence the need for self-reflection. We need to ask periodically whether we really know what our aims are, whether we live up to these, and what the available remedies are for repair.

D1) does not intend to rule out aim development or even a change in overall orientation. We need to preserve some flexibility in our thinking. But on the topic of how much and what kinds of flexibility are encouraged, neither our theory, nor any alternative has anything to say other than banalities, and vague references to an alleged "golden mean."

---

22 Collins and Porras, *Built to Last.*

D2) asserts the need for both good character, as defined in A, B and C, and also good aims. The latter should have both communal and individual implications. Why do we need overall aims in our ideals in addition to those constituted by the ingredients of adequate character? Intuitively speaking, the initial answer is that one could have good character and the unity of a good agent, and still not know where one should go. Good character is, alas, consistent with being misguided. It is also consistent with having, e.g., two ends taken to be ultimate that are incompatible. One might want to include among one's final ends good citizenship and decent behavior towards others, only to discover that at a certain stage of life the two become—within a context—incompatible. Hence even in a pluralistic pyramid of values, priorities in terms of possible choices need be maintained. This is, to be sure, idealized picture. One cannot have a conception of all possible empirical circumstances in which two or more of one's ultimate aims conflict. But this should not keep us from trying to envisage conflicts and set priorities as far as we can. It shows that the human implementation of ethical theory is, even at best, only partial. Of such stuff are tragedies made.

D2) does not generate a decision procedure, but sets guidelines. For example, the level at which the general overall ends need be stated must be abstract and general enough to allow for flexibility. But again, there is nothing non-trivial to be said about how abstract the ends should be, other than the reminder that the overly abstract ends (e.g. the cliché: "Let us all love one another") say nothing that affects ideal implementation.

The notion of meaningful work, on which we touched above, helps to steer us towards adequate overall aims. Not everyone with adequate character knows what work will in fact aid the community, and help to engender pride and cooperative attitudes. This is, then, an area in which aim selection and efforts to achieve at least partial correction have real bite.

Finally, the sound overall aim should allow for the agent a partial autonomy from the conventional values of the environment. E.g. the slogan: "Even if everyone else will seek only material enjoyment and instant gratification, I will not organize my life in such directions." Such a claim can be justified in terms of D1).

For instant gratification and random hedonism fail to imbue a human life with sufficient coherence. This has grave psychological consequences, and can destroy adequate agency. To see the significance of D3) we need to consider two uses of "end" and "intrinsic value." In one use these expressions are construed as complete. So something can be a final end, without qualifications. Of course, an end has to be an end for someone, but the specification can be as broad as "for all humans" or "for all rational beings". There is another, relational, use. Within that use we can talk about a human or humans regarding something as their ultimate end. The latter notion can easily degenerate into mere subjective preference. D3) states that we should be able to interpret our ultimate ends as having the unrestricted and thus objective status. This involves, typically, placing ourselves, or our community, into larger schemes of reality. For example, claiming not only that a certain amount and kind of order is a constituent of human representations of reality, but that reality itself, apart from how we see it, acquires some value on the ground of its exhibiting order. Alternately, some might say that the universe is a better entity if it contains creatures that have the capacity to transcend both selfishness and altruism and form friendships based in shared values that have goodness beyond utility and mere deontic value.

Thus the overall aims that this condition rules out as inadequate include: enjoy life in any way you can, or have power over others.

One can raise the following criticisms against the latter pair and many like them. How does everyone trying to enjoy life in any way they can, lead to a happy and purposeful community? Secondly, how does this help us in relating to larger parts of reality? Even if admittedly we know, and are likely to know, only a small percentage of reality, should we not have concern for how our enjoyments help or hinder treating the rest of reality as entities for which we should also have concern? Finally, the general empirical fact, that humans in various parts of the globe, even if not known to one another, are interdependent economically, environmentally and in other ways, suggests that we need some intersubjective agreement on some ultimate ends, and that in terms of justification the interpretation of these in terms of objective goodness seems most plausible.

These conditions sketch admittedly without much detail the anatomy of ideal building. The details we would add are extremely context-dependent, and thus difficult to summarize. The conceptual details of two key psychological notions, namely that of aim setting and attitudes will be treated in greater length in the next chapter.

To complete this chapter, we add the following general comments on ideal building and the adequate agent.

As we step back and look at these criteria of adequacy, two questions arise. First, what are the criteria for? According to the main design of the chapter, these should be criteria of adequacy for ideals. But the subdivision of the criteria into four species does not reflect directly criteria for ideals. And yet, aspects of assessment for ideals can be read off from our list. The order of listing A, B, C and D does not reflect any conceptual priority. In fact, there are good grounds for holding that aims have at times psychological priority. For overall aims define orientation and have crucial roles in shaping character. Ideals are ways of orientation and standards for character needed to fall within patterns of orientation in appropriate ways. Furthermore, ideals are ways of living, not just abstract rules. Ideals have to be implemented and maintained. Hence the heavy stress among our criteria on agency. Agents choose, implement and maintain. Hence one way of approaching the issue of adequate criteria is: what kind of agent would choose the right criteria? At the same time, we saw that good agency is not enough. Hence category D. The aims help with orientation, and agency as well as character gives the orientation concrete substance.

Our ideals are supposed to cover all of the salient aspects of human nature. Hence the extension in our list from agency to character. A good agent may still lack some highly valued characteristic, e.g. trust.

Our second main question that the survey brings forth is: why not just grade agencies, why divide into demands on reason and emotion? In reply we point to the approach of this essay to character. We are not interested in a mere list or virtues. We are interested in the underlying psychology of the person with good character. For this we need the trichotomy of reason, emotion, and—

orthogonally—the attitudes needed for sound relations with others. Our specification of character did not yield a "sacred" list. It did show cognitive and affective elements needed to build up character-types that represent, in a variety of ways, the fulfillment of the good sides of human potential. If one tried to derive a list of virtues from our conception, it would have to be a disjunctive list. Our characterization is compatible with the more gregarious as well as the more solitary life style. It can be satisfied by the more intellectually and by the more practically oriented individual. Ideal building principles specify the basic framework of adequacy, not concrete rules and patterns of conduct.

This chapter has dealt with ideals and their approximations. One might complain that not enough has been said about negative evaluations. Should this framework not be supplemented by some more traditional verdict, such as not to cause harm and pain to others?

In reply, we can point to the various features of the ideal theory that amounts to an equivalent to such a verdict. Our criteria of the social aspect of ideal development already include concern and respect for others. Without these the ideal remains inadequate since it would lead us to psychological states similar to what is so well sketched in S. Eisenstein's moving film *Ivan the Terrible*.

The ideal specifications that we sketched entail that one's concern should not only be with how we can build an ideal for ourselves, but also with how our ideal buildings affect others. Given the descriptions it is clear that these do affect others. We cannot construct and implement our ideals on lonely islands. Human conditions being what they are...

Our range of disapproved attitudes and practices include more than what is usually in Western societies meant by "moral." For example, we can hurt people by indifference or by our lack of effort to overcome frustrations of various types. Such flaws too prevent us from having in our lives adequate ideals.

Thus within our theory there is much to criticize everyday human conduct. But this criticism deals with actions and attitudes in matters of degrees of inadequacy, rather than a sharp "right–wrong" dichotomy. Correspondingly, the remedies for inadequacy as agents will be more varied than what we find in a typical criminal law system. There are signs that the population at large is beginning to understand this. The growing practice of "sentencing" people to years of community work instead of mere incarceration is a step in the right direction. The impact of this does not seem to have yet affected most philosophical ethics. This book is a modest attempt to stress such communal responses to social inadequacy.

Chapter II

IDEALS AND ATTITUDES

The previous chapter provided an outline of the Ethics of Ideals (from here on EI) and its criteria of adequacy. As we saw, this type of ethics centers on selecting adequate overall aims for our lives, and characters or psychological structures that has both non-instrumental and instrumental value. For it presents psychological structures that are instrumental to reaching the selected aims and maintain these. At the same time they have value as final human ends as well. These place constraints on HOW the adequate overall aims are to be reached.

We construe neither aim nor character as completely definable in terms of rules. Rather, both are seen as aspects of agency. An adequate agent is characterized in terms of the attitudes and orientation he has. These cannot be analyzed exhaustively in terms of rules and principles. A good agent takes responsibility for a certain part of life. No matter how detailed a job description we construct, there will always be new and hitherto unpredictable circumstances emerging, and the agent is challenged to respond to these, giving new implementations to the characteristics and attitudes he or she already possesses.

In some ethics reason has only instrumental roles. It seeks the means towards ends predetermined by alleged basic desires for general items like pleasure or happiness. EI rejects this conception, and construes the adequate agent as selecting final ends and constituents of the ends as well as means. Furthermore, in EI there is no sharp distinction between the ethical and the prudential. The criteria for adequate interpersonal activities are whatever constitutes the harmonious development of adequate ideals in our sense. Thus in this ethics we also find a strong unification of reason and emotion. As we shall see, the strongest unity between reason and emotion, both conceptually and empirically, can be located in our attitudes. Hence this chapter will provide a general analysis of ethical attitudes and will show these to be the cornerstones of selecting and realizing ideals.

I. What are Attitudes?

In our theory attitudes are not mere dispositions to act. Attitudes like respect, care or trust include cognitive judgments, related feelings and ensuing actions. But attitudes are not mere conjunctions of separately working cognitive processes, emotions and activities. For as we shall see, the emotional component of an attitude cannot be identified apart from the cognitive conceptualizations that engender it. Here are some examples of attitudes:

admiration	apprehension	trust	being abusive
respect	anticipating	loyalty	hatred
kindness	greediness	loving	resentment
compassion	joyousness	care	pushy
sympathy	unselfish	concerned	irresponsible
awe	being power-hungry	indifference	aggressive
cooperative	cautious	competitive	scheming

The O.E.D. yields descriptions of attitudes as "holistic ways of regarding something" or "settled manner or acting as representation of a feeling." These accounts seem complementary. One emphasizes the cognitive aspect of attitudes, the other the affective aspect. So this is not a matter of a word having two meanings, but rather a concept having two aspects and in a given context one of the other may be more stressed. In "how caring a person he is" we are likely to stress the affective part, in "he does not confuse caring with dominating someone" we stress the appropriate cognitive side. In this chapter we shall select some ethically relevant aspects of attitudes, rather than attempt yet another definition. The aspects selected are constituents of the dictionary description we listed.

We shall start by considering the principles of individuation of attitudes and their components, for this will bring out the strong unity of attitudes. Let us consider respect as our example.

The logical form of "respect" is: x respects y on the basis of y's having qualities Q1...Qn. The object, i.e. what falls under "y," can be an individual or a group of individuals. One can respect a person and one can also respect a research team or a community. As construed in this theory, the "x"-slot is always filed by a human or humans. Furthermore, respect calls for justification, and this is furnished by reference to what are regarded as respect-warranting qualities. Thus we need in an ethical community agreement on: the status of respect as a positive ethical attitude, what respect consists of, and which qualities should count as the respect-warranting ones. The last point is crucial. We cannot build an ethical community if half of the people respect only money and power and the other half cooperative attitudes and the search for what is good for people. As we shall see shortly, there are attitudes in which the justification does not depend on attitude-warranting qualities. But we shall see this as a variation on the analysis offered here.

The agent who respects needs to have the capacities to understand and be able to describe varieties of human character in order to locate the relevant attitudes. He or she also needs to have the cognitive and affective qualities needed to evaluate the different attitudes encountered. This requires more than just observing sensibly given data and inductive–deductive reasoning.[1] Thus understanding the attitudes of others and self as well as evaluating these takes place in a rich texture of human interactions. It is an ongoing dynamic process, unlike a mathematical proof that can be completed at a given time.

We must have reasons for respect. We cannot just walk up to someone, and in answer to the question: "what are you doing?" reply: "oh nothing, just respecting you." As we shall see later there are different kinds of reasons why respect in a certain context, as well as other attitudes, are justified. In the examples listed above we find many cases in which the attitude in question needs be extended on the basis of merit. In short, being the object of attitudes like respect, admiration, concern, etc. has to be earned. This is articulated in our scheme in terms of the attitude-warranting qualities. The assigning of these is a complex matter. In different

---

1 Moravcsik "Understanding and the Emotions."

contexts we might respect people in view of different qualities. Some we respect for their kindness, some for their wisdom, some for a combination of both. According to some authors, there may be some all-purpose respect-warranting qualities, such as lists of traditional virtues.[2] Then again, presumably there are qualities that evoke respect in contexts like that of Mother Theresa, and others for the achievement of people like Goedel and Kant. Fortunately, we manifest respect in restricted contexts most of the time, otherwise we would face the daunting task of constructing a large map of all of the respect-warranting qualities that emerge in some context, and try to form a coherent conception including all of the quality assignments. Given that the number of relevant contexts is infinite, such a task could not be carried out in actuality.

The judgments and evaluations making up one part of respect should evoke and be blended with feelings as well. "Blended" is not meant to be a metaphor. It indicates those aspects of the feelings that make their independent identifications impossible. For we can identify the judgments and evaluations that constitute what with some oversimplification we can call the cognitive part of respect, but we cannot do this with regards to the feelings. We can identify introspectively feelings of pain, joy, surprise, and others. We cannot do this with the affective component of respect. We can say, "I am happy but I don't know why." But we cannot say: "I feel respect, but I don't know towards whom and I don't know why." We identify the feeling with reference to the judgment that engendered it and that it accompanies. Thus one can say "I have a strong feeling of respect towards Max, based on his courage, strength and attentiveness." But the question: "could you have that particular feeling towards someone else, on the basis of other qualities?" makes no sense. It is like a serious—not Lewis Caroll-like—attempt to present the smile of the Cheshire cat, without the cat. Thus different conceptions and quality assignments help individuating attitudes like respect. The component of feeling is a necessary condition for respect, but by itself does not contribute to the individuation.

These reflections show that since agency is the key marker of a good human being, and agency consists of a unified framework

2 For example Plato, *Republic*, Book IV.

of attitudes, the ideal agent is not a purely rational creature. Rather, it is a combination of reason and feeling, intertwined in the manner just described. When describing a good agent, we end up with an enumeration of cooperative attitudes. These will include concern, care, kindness, sympathy, trust, loyalty and others. There are also attitudes centering more on the maintaining of inner harmony. For example, self-control and the variety of attitudes dealing with how to deal successfully with frustration. Needless to say, in some contexts some of these attitudes are more important than in others. We can see, then, that the actual fabric of the morals of daily life is very complex. Though it leaves room for abstract, higher order assessment in terms of better and worse—or good and bad in a few simple cases—its basic functioning is the shaping, modifying, implementing of attitudes, and the never ending task of defining over and over again what we should regard in a given context as the attitude warranting qualities.

In explaining attitudes, now in more detail, we shall turn to comparisons between attitudes and other psychological phenomena, showing the distinctness of the notion of attitude.

One might try to identify attitude—or at least some of the attitudes with wishing. This idea would rest on the similarity between the logical structure like respect, and wishing. For "wish," it is: "x wishes for y on account of y's having qualities Q1...Qn". But as we have seen, having this structure is only a necessary, not a sufficient condition for being an attitude. Attitudes—under normal circumstances—have action as one of their components. If someone claims to respect X, but never does anything about it, he owes us an explanation why this is so, and if no explanation seems possible, we doubt the veracity of the claim of his being respectful. Wishing, on the other hand, is not so restricted. Wishing need not be action oriented, because the objects of wishing are not restricted either to the actual or to the actual and likely possibilities. We can wish for what is in naturalistic terms impossible. A child a hundred years ago could have wished for a space ship. Some still wish the Easter Bunny were real.

The phenomenon of liking is simply being attracted to something or someone. Thus by itself it is not an attitude. In some contexts we can, but generally need not, give a defense of our likings. And in many cases we cannot specify the qualities in view of which we like something. Perhaps there are no qualities. On a conscious level, liking can be like magnetism. Liking can have dominantly emotional spontaneous roots. It need not have the cognitive architecture that attitudes require. Liking also differs from wishing since it must have real entities as its object.

We have already seen why mere feelings cannot be attitudes in the sense defined in this essay, for on our accounts attitudes must also have a complex cognitive component, involving description and evaluation. Hence benevolence, construed mostly as a feeling and viewed in modern moral philosophy as an important ethical notion, cannot be an attitude.[3] Benevolence is not like compassion. Compassion is not earned by merit but is evoked from people on account of the object suffering in some ways. Benevolence, however, is an overall feeling extended to anything living. Benevolence can be presented as an important ethical feeling, accompanying many ethical attitudes, but it does not require justification in the way that the attitudes do. "Why be benevolent?" requires some justification as an answer, but "in virtue of which qualities have people earned the right to have benevolence extended to them?" is a malformed question.

Attitudes are not intentions and vice versa, though the two are linked. Various attitudes surveyed also have intentional components,[4] and intentions often rely on the agent having a variety of relevant attitudes. E.g. the intention to bring flowers for someone is typically embedded in assumptions such as aesthetic attitudes, concern for the ill, etc. An agent having intentions presupposes the agent also having feelings, but there are no feelings that are conceptually, in terms of individuation, dependent on intentions.

Finally, one might want to identify attitudes with rational desires. Rational desires contrast with non-rational desires like thirst or hunger. The sources of these desires are needs that the human body has. The object of thirst as such is any object that will satisfy this need. Thus the only reasoning needed in reaching fulfillment is instrumental. A rational desire involves taking a non-rational one and transforming it by giving it an object selected by reasoning involving both instrumental and non-instrumental cal-

---

3 Benevolence plays a key notion in David Hume's ethical writings.
4 Bratman, *Intentions, Plans, and Practical Reasons.*

culations. Thus desire for healthy drink is a rational desire, since mere desire for drink has been transformed into desire for healthy drink, and health can be construed as a human end, not just a means to something. One can have a strong desire for victory in competition, and one can also have a desire for victory achieved by fair means. The latter is what we call here a rational desire. We see, then, that certain desires can be modified by reason, also involving non-instrumental considerations. But we have seen that attitudes too can be modified by reason; e.g. respect or admiration on the basis of good grounds. So perhaps what we called attitudes are rational desires.

There are, however, important differences between the two. First, rational desires are peculiar complex entities. Their genesis involves taking something general and indeterminate like thirst, and then modifying it. So thirst exists in both unmodified and modified form. This is not true of attitudes. Respect on account of qualities Q1...Qn is not a complex made up of something called unmodified respect and then a rational modification, while rational desires do have this character. One can see intuitively the reason for the difference. Respect arises out of intellectual consideration concerning values that are attached at times to human nature, and feelings that these should optimally engender. The main source of respect, sympathy, concern and others has a very strong rational component. But in the case of the rational desires this is not so. The basis is a need, yearning, drive, or simply the affective quality of desire. Rationality enters as a—temporally and conceptually—secondary element.

Furthermore, in the case of rational desire, the rational modifies some desire that can exist without it, and is thus not dependent on it. This is not so with attitudes. We cannot say that respect for cooperative and concerned individuals depends on something that could exist independently called "respect in general".

This little conceptual map helps to indicate the wide variety of psychological elements that lie outside of strict rationality. Furthermore, the different kinds play different roles in ethics. It is good for the adequate agent to be both builders of rational desires by modification, and to develop a set of coherent attitudes that underlie the functioning of good agents. This difference is obscured by careless reductionistic programs that try to reduce the non-rational in all of its aspects to desire, or even worse, to some obscure catch-all expression like "pro-attitude." There is a difference between the process of modifying a desire for companionship to a desire for good companionship, and building up friendships based on shared values as both a pleasant way of interacting with others and as a relationship that has ethical value. Having right kinds of attitudes and related values is more fundamental for EI than the modification of desires by rational means, though the latter too plays an important instrumental role in the building and rebuilding of ethical life.

2. Types of Attitudes and Their Role in Ethics

The previous sections clarified what we take for the purposes of our theory attitudes. Clarifications should be followed by classification. There is a large variety of ways in which attitudes can be classified. The classification to be presented provides the foundation for how attitudes are viewed within EI.

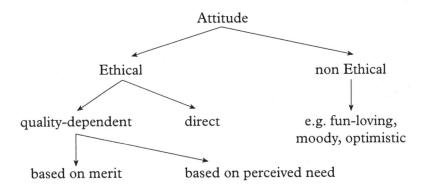

The first division articulates the obvious truth that not all attitudes are ethically relevant. A good person can be either an optimist or a pessimist. Some good people are apprehensive in face of strangers, others are not. The distinction is not meant to suggest that the non-ethical attitudes are not important for us. Some of them can affect our mental health, and thus also our ability to function as agents. But a person in deep depression does not have ethical but other flaws.

A key distinction lies between the quality-dependent and

direct attitudes. Direct attitudes like love, trust, joy (at least by one interpretation) are "unconditional" within contexts. That is to say, they are not earned or evoked by undeserved misery. Our directing these attitudes towards others does not depend on their having merited this by the possession of the relevant attitude-warranting qualities. Offspring often yearn for this kind of direct love. "I want them to love me no matter what." We placed "unconditional" in quotes above, because not being quality-dependent does not mean complete unconditionality. For expressing a direct attitude towards someone may take place under appropriate circumstances or inappropriate ones. There are many cases of misplaced direct trust, direct love or joy. In many cases we regard direct attitudes as carrying with them spontaneity. But this does not mean that the good agent should not have a second-order control over when and how to let the spontaneous be expressed.

In order to look at the direct attitudes in more detail, we shall first complete the survey of the quality-dependent ethical attitudes. In our treatment so far we have dealt with the ones that needed to be earned, or be bestowed on merit. But there is also— as our scheme shows—another group, where the attitude-warranting qualities are not meritorious character traits of the object, but rather attributes representing different kinds of suffering or need, and thus evoke from us attitudes of sympathy, compassion, readiness to help, and others like these. The logical structure is the same as in the case of the meritorious quality-dependent attributes, but psychological content is different. The merit-based ones call for positive evaluation of what might loosely be called the virtues of the prospective object of attitude. In the cases of types of compassion and meeting need the key cognitive element is the ability to understand and detect types of suffering, and assess the nature of damage and be able to judge issues of desert. Consider "x is compassionate towards y in view of y's having qualities Q1...Qn, which designate different types of need and suffering". We need to decide what the appropriate substitutes are for Q1...Qn. Not everyone who suffers is an appropriate object of compassion, pity and other such attitudes. Some people suffer because of what they did to themselves, and the nature of that deed may be such that the actor should have known better, was careless or had other such attributes. These attributes render the object in many typical cases not appropriate for compassion. "Maybe this will teach him," we say at times (too often?).

Much of our ethical life is spent trying to have as operative in our life the appropriate qualities for becoming objects of respect, admiration, or sympathy, and concern. In some cases both kinds of quality-dependent attitudes are to be directed to the same person. Being the object of respect need not imply being good at responding to suffering. Being a good judge of something does not entail being good as the agent in that context, and this is also true the other way around. It helps to develop in both directions if we are surrounded by the right kind of community. This means that our community should have among its members a large overlap both in terms of how they judge merit and need, and also in terms of what they aim to exemplify. Most of the attitudes we discussed require for implementation and expression interpersonal contact and activity. Agreement on what is to be respected, be concerned about and so on, and on what basis, can aid greatly in the development of the good agent. Conversely, disagreements on these matters can hinder agent development considerably. This may go against the intuitions of some according to which every human being should have an equal chance at being ethically adequate, but this "democratic" sentiment seems to fly in the face of facts. From the classical philosophy to today's social worker there is a somber tradition that thinks of ethical achievement as depending to some extent on the individual, but also depends for high level of realization on the environment.

In this analysis we have not said much about the causes of attitudes. The reason for this is that there is very little one could say about that except in great detail, with constant contextual variation. One key philosophic thesis about reasons and causes, however, does underlie this work. The thesis states that in many cases the same thing can function both as a cause and as a reason. Though tacitly assumed in antiquity, this thesis was presented in recent times in vigorous fashion by Donald Davidson.[5]

In our analysis the quality-dependent attitudes provide a stable foundation for individual and communal ethics. For the logical structure as we have sketched, provides for consistency. If

---

5 Davidson, "Actions, Reasons and Causes."

I respect x for qualities Q1, Q2, then—*ceteris paribus*—I should also respect z if he or she has Q1 and Q2. As we have already seen, in this respect quality-dependent attitudes are different from the less stable direct ones.

To be more precise, one can see one kind of stability in the quality-dependent ones: they are stable as long as the qualities in question are maintained by the object and recognized by the subject. These are also consistent, and hence stable in that way. If I approve of an exam on the basis of qualities Q1...Qn, then I should approve of all other exams with the same quality-structure. We gain consistency but lose loyalty to individuals who change their character.

In the case of the direct attitudes we gain loyalty but lose consistency. Loyalty to the individual can survive character changes, since the attitude does not depend on the set of warranting qualities. At the same time, we lose consistency across possible agents. For because of their directness and independence of normative quality structure, we cannot infer that if the attitude is directed towards someone with qualities Q1...Qn, it will also be directed to anyone else with the same quality structure. Since respect admits of degrees, it can happen that at one time *A* is the person I most respect, later his or her place is taken by *B*. Since we want in a community some level of basic respect, some level of good or potentially good conduct and inner life must be assumed in everyone.

There are also views according to which the more deserving humans should also receive more care and sympathy from others than the less worthy ones. This essay remains neutral on this difficult thorny issue.

Agreement in a group on what are key positive ethical attitudes and the criteria of bestowing these is needed as a foundation for many worthwhile activities. For many of these underlie important communal activities in the sense that without a critical mass of people having these attitudes the activities cannot go on smoothly. This is illustrated by activities such as building a new hospital or devising new curriculum for a high school. There must be some agreement on what the purpose and function of the hospital should be; e.g. only serving patients with expected illnesses, or also a research institute, specializing on this or that rare disease.

Should it mostly serve the local community, or be of international repute or should it especially serve a certain social-economic class in the community, such as Highland Hospital in Oakland, where the predominant patient group comes from among the economically disadvantaged. The discussions on the relation between research and healing are partly about respect. Whom to respect more, and on the basis of which qualities?

In the case of discussions on high school curriculum, there is a need to agree on responsibility assignments. For example, how much freedom do the teachers have in assigning material, what are minimal requirements that the community expects. In such a complex undertaking mutual trust must be built up, else the discussions will degenerate into different parties protecting narrow self-interest.

General discussions of good and bad will not answer such questions such as: with whom should we cooperate in this or that context and on the basis of which qualities? In a given context what kind of concern should be expressed for the welfare of those involved in the activity, and what kind of alleged concern will be perceived by those affected as interference in their lives and attempts to dominate?

These reflections show the daunting complexities of ethical life; distinguishing the different kinds of attitudes, establishing priorities, considering contextual implementations and try to balance the demands of the various attitudes judged as desirable.[6] The attitudes also differ in ranges of application. For example, we need not admire everyone whom we respect, and conversely, not everyone who has some admirable characteristic need be an object of respect. I might respect someone because he or she shows at least minimal levels of cooperation, but that need not be sufficient to generate admiration, or even trust. Approval has yet another range. Roughly speaking, we approve of agents or actions for either instrumental or non-instrumental values that they possess, but we respect people for some of their values and characteristics that we judge to be ends. Lastly, we might approve of firemen in virtue of one set of qualities, and of physicians for another set.

Some of the traditional ethical problems that are phrased in

---

6 Moravcsik, "Two Types of Ethical Attitudes."

terms of goods, or the good life, can be fruitfully rephrased in terms of the moral psychology offered here. For example, one traditional question centers on whether a good life depends on prestige and power or on ethically fine character. At least one aspect of this rather vague question is whether we should show respect towards people on account of their character or their achieved power and prestige.

To answer this question, we need to consider what we judge to be adequate ideals, and how these relate to good character, power and prestige. A hedonistic calculus is of no help in these cases, since the answer to the question of which kind of life brings more pleasure depends on the point of view from which we judge the matter. Mother Theresa will give one answer, a newly rich entrepreneur might give another one. EI at least gives us a way of assessing ideals, as the previous chapter showed. Prestige and power may be acceptable goods if they are gained for appropriate reasons and are exercised in appropriate manners.

Within the ethics articulated here, responsibility is a quality dependent attitude. Hence it cannot be unconditional. Responsibilities are assigned by communities, and there are better and worse ways of making such assignments. If we think that some responsibilities (or rights) should be bestowed on every human, we must show what characteristics are either possessed by humans universally, or at least are part of what could be described as the human potential. What these characteristics might be, and how these could be realized universally is a question on which lively debate could ensue. EI is neutral with regard to that issue.

This review of variety among quality-dependent attitudes should now be compared to the variety among the direct attitudes. Some of the terms we use can be applied both in quality-dependent and direct ways. These include trust, loyalty, and caring. In some contexts we trust on the basis of qualities indicating reliability. In others we are forced to trust or not, even though we have little or no evidence about the character of the agent. This can be illustrated by situations in which a certain social–economic–ethical order has broken down, and there are no communally agreed upon standards of conduct and attitude. Under these conditions the direct attitudes can perform a vital task. For these will be the glue that can link people together in constructive ways (as opposed to e.g. fear), and serve both as an interim ethics, and as laying the foundation for the kind of community within which a new system of values can evolve.[7] Without these direct attitudes total chaos can surface, with selfish people grabbing anything they can. Stores and abandoned houses are looted, and violence is all-pervasive. Some might try to cling to the earlier quality-dependent values, but these are not likely to be effective, since no consensus is backing them any more. In such situations, even if some sort of order is restored, as long as no communal consensus exists with regards to what to respect and what to strive for, wholesale corruption is likely to emerge. That ethical nihilism breeds corruption can be illustrated with many examples from recent history, from Russia to the early days of South Africa.

Another context in which positive direct attitudes play an important role are emergencies like earthquakes, or infectious diseases.[8] A whole community is in danger of being wiped out, and even if much of it survives, in the aftermath communal cooperation of hitherto unimagined nature is required in order to cope with what there is left, and start the rebuilding. The right direct attitudes will spread from person to person, since there will be causal links among those cooperating. This analysis of communal cooperation in the face of emergency helps to explain both the good and the dark side of public reaction to earthquakes like the Loma Prieta Earthquake that hit San Francisco a few years ago. People who did not know each other cooperated in valiant ways, but when things were normal again, the old selfish attitudes returned. According to our theory the reason for this is that the cooperation was based on direct attitudes among people causally linked. Once normal circumstances begin to appear, people move back into their earlier lifestyle within which they did not have direct contact with most of the people involved in the emergency cooperative efforts. No causal links (or direct contact) no direct attitudes. This seems a far more plausible analysis than the one given usually, in terms of a strengthened awareness of the traditional quality-dependent attitudes during the crisis and a "spiri-

---

7 For example, the feeling of suddenly becoming poor in B. Pasternak's
   Dr. Zhivago.
8 A. Camus, *The Plague.*

tual weakening" afterwards. Quality-dependent attitudes do not lead to the intense personal and "no questions asked" help and cooperation that we see in cases of emergency. They call for careful assessment of the proposed object. Direct attitudes call for a careful assessment of the circumstances, not the object about which we do not know much in these contexts. Of course in the case of an earthquake a "careful assessment" of the circumstances need not take much time; we know right away that that is a direct attitude-warranting context.

The danger with attitudes is that these are more easily misplaced than quality-dependent attitudes. Thus unconditional love may grow spontaneously but fade when the unworthiness of the object becomes apparent. Some direct attitudes like trust survive as long as the causal link between the agent and the object persists. Love of certain types, however, is expected to survive even if the causal link is broken for long periods of time.

At times the behavior of the object can become so depraved that it destroys the direct love, and we do not find the agent blameworthy.[9] The loss of love in such cases is not a matter of decision. Just as we cannot decide to love someone, we cannot decide to stop. The depraved conduct has just too much negative causal impact for the positive earlier love to survive. And yet, while a voluntaristic psychology does not help with the gain or loss of positive direct attitudes, there is much that we can do to maintain or lose a direct attitude. One cannot force oneself to stop hating, but one can think of thought, activities, and gestures that make the gradual disappearance of hate more likely.

We have talked so far about direct contact and causal links between agent and object. Those are not the same. Direct contact is a kind of causal link, but not the only possible one. With today's means of communication, contact via telephone or e-mail can also count as direct contact. There is no general answer to the question: can direct love, trust, or care survive if the sole basis is one of the new modes of communication. Yet this exploration also shows promise. With increased communicational means—some of which introduce more and more humane elements—one might be able to create collections of people tied to each other via direct

9 For example, the figure of Strelnikov in B. Pasternak's *Dr. Zhivago.*

attitudes. We do not know, however, how strong such ties will be. Perhaps one should think of these communicational potentials more as assisting rather than replaced traditional direct contact. At times working together for a cause, or institution, helps to generate positive direct attitudes. Evidence for this are the various loyalties that we see springing up between "comrades" or co-workers.[10] One account of this phenomenon could be given on the hypothesis that we deal in these cases with quality-dependent attitudes. Agent A has loyalty to B because they are working for the same cause which is good and warrants one having loyalty towards comrades. But on this view the loyalty would cease if the company dissolves, or the cause is seen by those who have fought for it to be no longer worthy of pursuit. There are many cases, however, in which loyalty springs up between co-workers, including military structures, and it survives long after the fight for the common cause is over (for example, veteran's associations). Furthermore, the source for the attitudes may be genuinely direct. It may have arisen and is continuing without any joint commitments to ideals. One was for the war, the other against. In the trenches they become friends and develop loyalties. They remain friends long after the fighting is over. Similar considerations give adequate interpretations for former school friends.

In some cases sentences seem to describe attitudes ambiguously. For example, the sentence "I love all those who mix kindness with following their duty" can be read in two ways. One interpretation makes this a quality-dependent love. The affection depends on the object having a certain quality, and need not be in causal interaction with the agent. The other interpretation construes the love as direct, and the object as each particular individual with whom the agent had some contact and who mix kindness with duty.

The first interpretation introduces a strange kind of love. What kind of a feeling is this that one is to extend even to people with whom one has had no contact but concerning whom one has favorable information? One can imagine admiration or respect on such grounds, but love is hardly amenable to this kind of description.

---

10 Royce, *The Philosophy of Loyalty*.

The second reading should imply that the attitude will persist even towards those of the collection who no longer mix kindness with duty. So perhaps the most reasonable reading is that this kind of love, if it exists, should be called "conditional love". It is direct, and depends on causal links, at least for some of its early stages, but will attach itself to the objects only as long as they have a certain quality. If parents would have such an attitude towards their child, the child could rightly say: "so you don't really love me."

These brief remarks show the complexity of coordinating in an agent all of the ethically relevant elements. These will include beliefs, attitudes of both kinds, implementation routines. Coordinating the first with the attitudes like hatred and dislike can clash with some of our quality-dependent attitudes. It is easy to respect people we like, but more difficult to respect and get along with those we do not like. Yet in a well lived life, in which we are parts of different groups at different times, it is important to be able to cooperate with unpleasant people, perhaps even obnoxious ones.

Unity of agency need not mean that all of our quality-dependent and direct attitudes are in harmony with each other, but that we will have priorities deciding conflicts. In some cases individual loyalty can take precedence over doing something useful for the community, and in others our instinctive personal likes or dislikes will have to be sacrificed for the sake of higher goods.

Having developed the analysis so far, we need to face the question: what good are direct attitudes? This is distinct from the question we did explore, namely how do direct attitudes complement an ethics based on quality-dependent attitudes. First, we should ask ourselves whether a human person is conceivable with only quality-dependent emotions. How would emotions develop? Presumably given the current state of knowledge, we think of infants starting predominantly with direct emotions. As instrumental reasoning helps develop ends–means patterns the quality-dependent attitudes also develop, and eventually become quite complex, as the cognitive structure maturates. This conception does not entail a mechanistic–hedonistic scheme. There is not good reason to suppose that the early direct emotions must be utility or pleasure oriented. Direct attitudes develop partly as a result of spontaneous positive emotions such as joy, delight and others.

These spontaneous feelings are directed towards humans or

other entities in the environment. But we must not suppose that these entities with which through some form of communication causal link is established, act as the stimuli necessary for the awakening of the attitudes under examination.

Perhaps the best way to present this account of the need for direct attitudes in a human personality is to coin a new phrase EMOTIONAL AUTONOMY, and in articulating this, present the case for the need we just posited. Emotional autonomy is to be thought of as analogous to the philosophically well-known notion rational autonomy. Rational autonomy covers two conditions. First, that the human possessing is allowed to have reason, work out plans, new concepts, and other cognitive elements needed for an adequate full employment of human rationality. Secondly, a stronger condition can be added, namely that the functioning of the human mind is also at least partly independent of stimulus–response processes, and that its functioning is not completely determined by perceptual processes and other psychological element-outside of cognition. On this conception reasoning is an "automation" i.e. self-governing entity, in the traditional sense.[11]

Along parallel lines, some of our emotions are not fully determined either by utility and sensations of pleasure, nor are they automatic reactions to environmental stimuli. Thus emotional spontaneity is a part of what we mean by emotional autonomy. Freedom from external interference that could be described as brainwashing is another condition. This second condition states that our emotional lives should not be manipulated by outsiders. The first condition states that with the second met, there should be a psychological structure in the adequate agent that allows the spontaneous emergence of emotions that go with joy, elation and the like.

The place of direct attitudes can be described in terms of the following dichotomies. Some of our attitudes in everyday life relate to humans with whom we do not have any direct contact. In many other contexts we need attitudes to form the basis of our interactions with those who are in direct contact with us. For dealing with the first group the quality-dependent attitudes are sufficient. But this will not do for many of the contexts in which

---

11 Chomsky, *Cartesian Linguistics.*

we are in direct contact with people, action is forced on us, and there is no time to try to ascertain whether the person with whom we are dealing possess these or those attitude-warranting qualities. In these cases the first set of attitudes have to be unconditional in the sense described already. We should try to make sure that the circumstances are indeed as just described, but we cannot assess the qualities of the person.

A typical context in which this problem arises is the physician–patient relation. Over a longer period of time, mutual assessments can develop. But in the initial stages—for example in the emergency room—no such grounds are available. Furthermore, it might even take time to determine whether the patient has some of those qualities that evoke compassion or sympathy. In the first stage, it is a matter of human meeting human, without previous acquaintance or knowledge of each other. The direct attitudes governing the encounter need not last long. Some direct attitudes like love are expected to last a long time. Others, like initial caring and being concerned, can change into quality-dependent attitudes. But to have positive direct attitudes in the initial stages of ignorance is very reassuring for the patient.

It is easy to see that what we described applies to many other situations. Relations towards small children, initial teacher–student relations, relations in initial stages of interviews for jobs are some of the more obvious examples.

Given, then, the general conditions of human living, direct attitudes occupy a vital role in our psychological structure. For developing adequate relations and making initial decisions we need the direct contact and related attitudes. Thus any for profit HMO that does not give the physician who is in attendance of the patient the final word on treatment, cure, and manner of caring violates the conditions to which both patient and physician are entitled.

Finally, we can see that given the variety of ways in which any implementation or expression of attitudes can take place, we need flexibility when there is a need for some overall coordination among fellow workers on what are acceptable and fruitful ways of expressing how we feel. This too requires—if it is to be successful—the presence of positive direct attitudes.

3. Criteria of Assessment for Attitudes

Our classifications of attitudes cut across the division between desirable and undesirable attitudes. For example, the theory should show on what grounds we should regard envy, hatred, aggressiveness and the like as undesirable. Undesirability in our framework means that anything with that common sense characterization would not fit into an adequate ideal, in the sense defined in the first chapter. To be sure, there are attitudes that in some contexts are desirable and in others not. Anger, or wrath, is an obvious case, since in some cases justified anger leads to constructive activity, while in others it is destructive. We also need to keep in mind that there are two levels of assessment. On one level we assess the choices for attitude-warranting qualities given a certain attitude. For example, respecting people for their wisdom of kindness is to select the proper qualities, while respecting them merely for their power, or prestige is to use the wrong qualities as the base. We shall not deal with this problem. In rough outlines, the selections will depend on the ideals we regard adequate in context. We will deal, however, with the evaluation of attitudes that are clearly in the undesirable category. Examples will be given showing how the various criteria of adequacy we gave earlier for assessing ideals can be used now to show that this or that attitude is to be excluded.

Criterion A2 rules out attitudes that lead to or constitute in an agent lack of purposefulness or determination to hold unto attitudes formed. Examples of these are carelessness and disloyalty. A careless person does not pay enough attention to factors that lead away from the aims and designs that the agent chose. We say in the vernacular "pay attention to what you are doing," but what we really mean is: pay attention to features of your activities that show lack of concentration on what is prescribed as to be accomplished. If one person is operating, nobody cares what his shoes look like. If one is to appear at a reception given by a head of state, inattention to shoes may be highly relevant.

Disloyalty is a sign of not being able to focus on the fundamental psychological structure of the person to whom we are to be loyal, and on the hierarchy in values that we share with the object of our loyalty. Loyalty requires perseverance and the inner discipline of being able to maintain—among others—the attitudes that underlie our loyalties. The stress on attitude is important. It brings up once more the point that stances of loyalty and lack of stances such as manifested in types of carelessness are not merely matters of rational conviction. They must also include the emotional elements that depend on and are also essentially intertwined with judgment.

Traditional views on excellences often assume some kind of unity among these characteristics. Our theory makes no such assumptions. For example, one can imagine one of the Borgias or Medici to be very careful and to have strong loyalties, and at the same time to be lacking many of the characteristics that an adequate moral agent should have.

Further constraints are placed on acceptable attitudes by criteria A3 and A4. A3 lays down a condition that is fundamental for the development of the kinds of attitudes we considered as candidates for inclusion in the character of the good agent. For it says that our rational makeup should be such as to make it possible that reason and emotion can achieve fusion as in attitudes like respect or trust. This is not a trivial condition. One can imagine a reasoning device that goes along with desires in our sense (like thirst and hunger in general) and never fuses with these or with feelings so as to modify the appetite and give it objects like healthy water and good food. At the same time, we must consider the possibility that we do not know how to work on achieving in our psyche the kind of harmony of reasoning and feeling that respect, approval and other attitudes require. Here talk about examples and illustrations do not help much. One might posit some kind of innate potential in humans to have and develop such attitudes, and then the challenge would be to try to understand what factors can block such developments, and to create conditions that are causally efficacious for the developments.

We do posit some structure and some potentialities that we regard as fundamental to human functioning. At the same time we should admit that our conception of that basic layer in the human makeup has changed from time to time, and is likely to change in the future. This is not a fatal objection to E.I. It simply requires the addendum when we talk of the human potential that we rely on this concept "understood as best we can." Science has not collapsed just because at some stages of history we think that we need to initiate drastic changes in our conceptual frameworks. Within our theory, neither should ethics take in this context a pessimistic stand. There are ethical breakthroughs and periods of steep ethical decline. We must simply work with what at any stage of history we have available. Our theory denies that at any stage of history we have available in our mind and imagination of all logically possible ethical alternatives. As Plato has shown, we can transcend the views of our environment, but such steps still leave us with less than perfect knowledge.

Condition C3 imposes further constraints on acceptable attitudes within proposed ideals. This condition might seem questionbegging, for it assumes that cooperative attitudes should play key roles in our relationships with others. But this is illusory. In defense of C3 we can cite the fact that everyone wants cooperative attitudes in some contexts, e.g. family or friendship. Thus the condition merely expands the range for types of attitudes by the fact that we are forced to consider how we fit into larger and larger layers of communities, and that in most cases we may choose which ones, but we have no choice over the need to be related in one way or another to such larger units. Thus condition C3 rules out as bad all attitudes that conflict with the development of kindness, concern for others and the like. It also rules out attitudes that, when dominant, prevent us from forming friendships based on shared goals and values. Through these constraints we can look to building up those attitudes that reduce conflict with others and within us. These constructions lead us to the kind of inner and outer harmony that Plato sketches in Book IV of the *Republic*.[12] Though such harmony also has instrumental value, it is seen in ideal building as one of the final human ends. Reason has a lion share of the work of ideal building, and it cannot function in this way without the harmonies we just described. In summary, we can say that ideal building at its best also requires attitudinal structures at their best in the ideal builder.

So far we have dealt with the distinction between desirable and undesirable attitudes, and illustrated how we can justify the division by reference to the criteria of adequacy for ideals articu-

---

12. Plato, *Republic*, Book IV, 437–442.

lated in chapter 1. We also need to face however, the problem of deciding in context what the domain should be and to what degree we should express this or that attitude. We can call this the problem of moderation and of the golden mean. Popular and time-honored as these labels may be, they are misleading. It is misleading to ask "how much fear should I experience and express in this or that context?" It makes more sense to ask: "What kind of fear is appropriate in this context, and how should one express it?" For example, in case of threatening weather one rushes to help the neighbor farmer to bring in the hay. The question is not "how much fear should we as farmers have of the impending storm?" bur rather how the fear we experience can be justified, i.e. as fear of something objectively harmful, and how we should channel the fear into constructive action. "Good" fear comes with preparation of appropriate defense. Moderation could be best rephrased in these ethical contexts as appropriateness. Quantitative comparisons of fear and other such emotions captured by mass terms admit of comparative judgment, but these are very rough, and difficult to apply across different types of phenomena. We can say that we are more afraid of a hurricane than of getting a bit soaked in a rain. But it is difficult to make sense of question such as, for example, those comparing our fear of going bankrupt with our fear of suffering from a debilitating disease. This is analogous to the absurdity of assessing in quantitative terms our pleasure of listening to a Beethoven quartet with the pleasure of solving a difficult problem in logic. So we can transform the "moderation" call into a call for contextual appropriateness, and solve this by not considering attitudes one by one, but in groups.[13] Thus the appropriateness of a type of fear in context is partly determined by what other attitudes, such as caution, concern for others, regard for others, and similar complexes have bearing on how we face certain situations. "Express your elation moderately" is good advice when disturbing others in a concert hall, but an irrelevant comment when the expressing is about to take place on a mountain top in the Sierras, with none else in sight. The determination of which clusters of attitudes should be considered in which context is yet

---

13 On the topic of unified agency I am indebted to an unpublished manuscript by K. Korsgaard.

another task for "practical wisdom" or simply having a good sense of judgment.

4. Role Modeling: Learning Theory for E.I.

Unlike in the classical period, in modern times it is not customary to attach a theory of learning to an ethical theory. One of the reasons for this is that two of the most influential ethical theories require no special kinds of learning to accompany them. Kantian ethical epistemology can be construed as the ability to understand knowledge and belief, and to participate in rule-following. Even though the big rules are different, the same can said of utilitarianism. So in both cases we have rules in the form of commands, and then a deductive system of maxims, which can be understood as any other deductive system.

Neither Plato's ethics nor that of Aristotle can be represented in this form. Their respective ethics—to sum it up briefly—center not on some fundamental rule of action, but on presenting as ideals the good human agent. Their conceptions of agency cannot be exhausted by sets of rules. The characterizations are, rather, in terms of sets of attitudes, orientation, setting overall aims for life, and psychological structures that provide unity and coherence for the human agential structure.[14]

E.I. has an underlying moral psychology that resembles that of the classical writers, and thus differs sharply from Kantian and utilitarian ethics. It too centers on specifying ideal agency to be approximated. Agency is specified in terms of attitudes, in such a way as to exclude defining these in terms of mere dispositional properties. Since the attitudes posited have an emotional element, we cannot formulate rules for them. "Don't be angry," can have an exhortative power, or a guiding impact, but cannot be construed as a rule.

There are rules in E.I. but these are derivative from the agent specifications and are context-dependent. E.g. they can have the structure of "in such-and-such a context the good agent will set himself such-and-such rules that help streamlining his

---

14 For the contrasting emotivist notion of attitude see Stevenson, *Ethics and Language.*

contributions to his ideal and that of the community to which he belongs."

Thus we are forced to consider learning strategies other than those of gathering information and rule following. To be sure those two will also have some role in the development of an adequate ideal successfully implemented, but these are not the key modes of acquiring understanding and ability to embody aspects of ideal agency. The learning mechanism for that is what we call role modeling. This is hardly a new idea. Role modeling crops up in Aristotle's ethics when he urges people to conduct themselves as the "man of practical wisdom would." In plain English this means that they should develop a good sense of judgment. Furthermore, it is crucial to standard clinical training in medical school hospitals. The proper training does not result merely in proper bedside manners, but in abilities to develop and express concern, sympathy and similar attitudes.

Nevertheless, we are treading on rarely furrowed ground, because philosophers have not concerned themselves with role modeling as an important mode of learning. It falls outside of modern philosophical epistemological interests. This is most regrettable, if we are to develop epistemology that covers all of the typical human cognitive processes.

We need role modeling in explaining how a human can develop the right attitudes, the good sense of judgment in singling out the appropriate attitude-warranting qualities, and skills of implementation.

Thus a young intern selects—ideally—the right role model for illustrations of correct attitude, practice of interacting with patients, and overall orientation. Role modeling also plays roles in people learning how to become teachers, parents and organizational leaders.

Role modeling is easy to illustrate, but difficult to define. It carries a good deal of conceptual burden in religion-based ethics such as Christianity, and in ethics such as various strands of ancient Chinese ethics. Within E.I. role modeling should facilitate becoming like the appropriate agent in terms of conduct, emotions, ability to combine emotions with cognitive elements so as to form what we called earlier as attitudes, in forming correct judgments about self and others, and basing correct evaluation of these on the judgments formed. We cannot leave role modeling without conceptual clarifications, because there are at least three ways in which role modeling can misfire. One of these is the pattern within which role modeling degenerates into mere following of another person. This results in indiscriminate imitation. The key to role modeling is to know which characteristics are to be embodied in the student, and which ones of the purported role model are merely accidental to the project and hence to be ignored. Blind following has no positive contribution to make to E.I. and can have in the case of misguided fanatics disastrous consequences. The second possible misfire is the general phenomenon of imitation. This can emerge even if the student has singled out the relevant aspects of the role model's nature that are to be incorporated in the life of the student. Imitation neglects the contextual elements of implementation. Socrates is courageous in the final scene of his trial. One can construe this as to be emulated. But implementation cannot be mere imitation, since the court rooms and various offices are quite different from the context in which Socrates stood up for his convictions. Finally, our choice of the appropriate role model can become badly flawed under the influence of certain direct attitudes. The best role model in a context for the learner may be a certain person who, however, evokes in the learner negative direct attitudes. For example, some people cannot turn with the appropriate appreciation towards certain others who have a bad odor, or an annoying personal habit. We lose, however, a great deal if we cannot abstract away from these trivial matters in our choice of role models. The ignoring of the incidentals is also a matter of character.

The selection of a role model brings up the "Paradox of Role Modeling". The selection of the appropriate role model presumably requires knowing quite a lot about what it is that we are to embody in our own lives. But if we have all of that knowledge, why need the role model at all? Alternately, we can start with the assumption that the selector knows very little about what is to be learned from the role model. But then how can we minimize the danger of selecting the wrong role model? For example, someone wants to become a drug counselor but he does not know anything about what practitioners call "tough love." (This involves, among other things, explaining in extremely realistic terms why the addict is likely to die in great pain within a short time if he does not change habits.) So the learner selects as role model a counselor who seems to be very nice and gentle and kind to the addicts at all times. This may turn out to be a big mistake.

In order to consider at least one way of resolving the paradox, let us remind ourselves that role modeling involves attitudes, and that attitudes have a cognitive element. Thus concentration on that element can give one a theoretical account of what the attitude is. For example, one comes to understand what judgment one is to have in order to form the cognitive aspect of respect. For example, one could phrase it in terms of regarding the other as having non-instrumental value and being an agent. So as the first step one would seek humans who practice what is described as respect. But the fact that they claim so is not enough. How do we know that the emotive component is there as well? At this point we invoke the "by their fruits we shall know them" principle, and see in which cases and involving which individuals do we find evidence in their interactions that respect is in fact the attitude the prospective role model has and that the appropriate emotion is expressed.

This way of resolving the paradox leaves us with the residual problem of how we come to know whether the expression and implementation of a given attitude has been successful? It is not a matter of mere behavioral observation. We need to have certain sensitivities to discover whether a certain person feels and thinks that a certain other person cares for him. So we have not gotten out of the problem of needing sensitivities to discover whether sensitivities are expressed. But at least we worked ourselves out of the blatant form of circularity with which we started.

Resolving the paradox is only a first step towards conceptual clarification. We are left with important epistemological questions concerning how we know that a certain person respects us, how we know whether we have been successful in learning how to develop and express certain attitudes. There is empirical evidence that humans can discover these things. For example, small children can tell the difference between a mother's genuine affection directed toward them and having merely soft warm things to be touched in their environment. We also know that typically humans can distinguish between genuine caring and mere caring behavior, e.g. the kind exhibited by the staff of certain department stores.

Of course, the situation might turn out to be analogous to other basic elements of human nature like language learning, or learning mathematics. In both of those cases we specify success in learning more by results and much less in terms of our knowing—or rather speculating—what is going on inside the mind. The mystery of some aspects of language learning has not prevented us from developing techniques of how to teach second or third language competence. It is to be hoped that the same applies to the learning of the development of attitudes. Success in the case of some family relations and hospital training should give us a least a start.

There are many epistemological issues left open by this chapter. But at least we showed why these psychological structures, ill understood as these may be, are needed as the underpinnings of E.I., and that the structures are not incoherent and we have achieved limited success with these in certain areas.

Chapter III

INDIVIDUAL AND SOCIAL–
POLITICAL ETHICS INTERTWINED

Some of the attitudes analyzed in the previous chapter, such as respect, concern or trust, indicate conceptual ties between individuals and communal virtues. Communal concern for those less fortunate is a necessary mark of an adequate community, and it must also depend at least partly on concern being regarded by individuals as a part of their ideal. The same holds for respect. Members of the community respecting each other for sound reasons is a part of communal well-being, and it is also a part of an adequate individual ideal.

Some concerns, such as with a child crying in a public place, cannot be reduced to being either solely a matter of interest to the community or a source of exclusive individual reaction on the part of a relative.

Before commencing with the details, herewith a brief sketch of the admittedly metaphorical "intertwining." Using this word does not mean that one could not do, e.g. tax collection without discussing individual ethics, or that we could not consider courage for being placed among the virtues without bringing in political theory. But even in these cases, things work out better when one keeps an eye on communal questions while working out individual ethics, and vice versa. Taxes can be administered in more or less humane ways, and some types of courage should be more stressed than others in a given social context. Once more, one should not sacrifice the priority of dynamical communal values and individual ideals over speed and efficiency.

In some cases intertwining amounts to acknowledging the mutual reliance between individual and social values, such as in the case of responsibility. The responsibilities between citizens and state must be reciprocal in an adequate society. Citizens can be expected to meet their responsibilities toward the state better if the state makes it clear what it will do for the citizens, and fulfills these promises. The same can be said with regards to how the state performs when citizens meet their responsibilities.

In some cases the intertwining consists of the same psychological element being shared on a concrete not generic level between the individual and the communal. In our relations with communal organizations we trust both the organization and the individuals representing these. I trust the government and the Prime Minister. If I do not know how to trust an individual like a minister, I will not know how to trust an organization either. Communal trust brings with it individual trust. But though this is less obvious, the same also holds in reverse. A person who can trust people should also be able to trust a collection of people in which the whole is more than a mere sum of parts. We may not want to trust everybody, but it is difficult to find rational grounds for being distrustful towards communities in general, just because many people are involved, and they are joined in a holistic social structure. Of course we may feel distrustful towards specific communities on the ground that these have reputations for having members who hide behind the structure and do not give their share in building and maintaining a trustworthy community. But analogous things can also happen on the individual level. We might not trust a person because we think he is exposed to more temptation than he can bear.

There are many examples of the many-faced nature of such concepts. Respect, concern for others, and loyalty are some of these.

Empirical ties between the individual and communal ethics are those that are contingent and show causal interaction. Conceptual links are those where we can show a key concept to be a common element between the two, or show an individual and a communal principle in some logical entailment relation.

In the first section we shall review empirical dependencies involving an example in which the individual ethics requires social ethical context, and one in which the reverse dependency can be shown. Our third example involves very general empirical conditions on the possibility of having an ethical response to human suffering.

Subsequently five conceptual dependencies will be presented. First, we will see that some varieties of friendship need be included in any viable individual ethical theory, and also in any account of communal dynamic underlying socio-political frameworks. Secondly, we will see how individual and social decisions must be involved in fixing the moral domain, i.e. the determination of the kinds of creatures whose suffering and general welfare is deemed to be relevant to both individual and communal decisions. Thirdly, we will find examples of both individuals and communities making judgments about priorities in which individual and social ethics must be intertwined. Our fourth example is educational policy. Here again societal and individual needs and rights need to be combined in order to come up with viable proposals. Finally we will deal with the problems involved in balancing economic and technological advantages and advances with the maintaining of humane values in a society.

The metaphor of intertwining was purposefully chosen on account of its flexible meaning. The two levels of the individual and the communal are distinct. Some issues such as declaring or not declaring war are matters for eventual communal decision. Whether one places one's professional commitments ahead of everything else or not is a matter of individual decision. But there is a variety of ways in which decisions of these levels require modes of interaction and cooperation. These in turn rest on qualities and among these the communal and the individual are interrelated. One could handle these matters in isolation but as we shall see in chapter 4, a well functioning community and adequate personal ideals need be interrelated in a variety of ways. Thus the pragmatic gist of intertwining is that optimally we should develop the two kinds of virtues and life styles in relation to each other. Good communal ties must take into consideration how their implementation helps the development of adequate individual ideals, and the criteria of goodness for the latter includes concern for good relationship with other people and the community at large.

It is clear that in the cases of friendship and trust the individual and the communal are not the same. But both of these attitudes and relations are complex, and there are ingredients in both that have the same psychological source. We cannot expect in the case of civic friendship to find all of the immediate contact and intimacy as in a good personal friendship. But we do find efforts to share and develop values, achieve projects requiring cooperation and the like. In individual friendship we do not find the same kind of cooperation that we find in many communal projects. But we do find the sharing of our highest values in the individual cases, just as we do in well functioning communities.

It must be admitted that the intertwining will not eliminate completely clashes between what we regard as individual interests and communal or political interests. But working with enlarged conceptions of the self in which many of our key social relations are also seen as parts or aspects of our selves, and the effort to build value-based and not merely legal institution based or economically forced communities, will cut down greatly on the occurrences of such clashes. There will be some inevitable conflicts that admit only less or more unhappy "solutions." But this also happens with clashes involving only individual or only political interests.

In these discussions individual ethics is construed as the ethical characterizations of adequacy for individual human character, agency, aim, motivation and action. Chapter I presented conditions of adequacy for this domain. Social ethics involves a conception of how the social and the political should be interrelated from an ethical point of view, the ethical values that a successful society must have, including appropriate legal structures, distribute principles, relations to individuals, and the nature of the communal life that is to underlie legal provisions.

Today many societies are ambivalent on this issue. On the one hand, we teach separate courses on individual and social–political ethics, and divide research accordingly. On the other hand, we tend to accept the slogan: "good societies require good participants, and good individuals require good societies." Some interdependence is also acknowledged in recent philosophical literature. For example, John Rawls argues that there must be congruence between conceptions of distributive justice and conceptions of the nature of the goods to be distributed. This congruence, together with adequate conceptions of human goods, provides stability for societies.[1] The conceptual links to be presented here are even stronger than this thesis.

---

1 Rawls, *A Theory of Justice*, 395.

Most analytic philosophers today would disagree with my claims and approach. But there are at lest two traditions that would endorse my stance. One of these is the ethics of Plato and Aristotle. The differences between their respective ethics is conjoined with the common claim that individual and social ethics must be developed together, as humans are essentially social beings, and any adequate society must make provisions for individuals to be able to develop into good individuals. For example, Plato's conception of a good human includes certain roles that we must play in society.[2] Aristotle, in turn, insists on the right kind of civic friendship underlying adequate social and political organizations.

Among modern theories, pragmatism involves the claim that individual and social ethics need be intertwined. This is clear not only in some of Dewey's writings,[3] but also in the moral theory of Josiah Royce, that sees devotion to certain types of causes as a key element in a well lived human life.[4]

1. Empirical Interdependencies

In the discussions that follow it is assumed that humans are essentially social beings, and that this is reflected both in rational and emotional components.

This claim is articulated explicitly in Aristotle's *Politics* I.2. Humans are by nature born into communities, and they also tend in adult lives to form communities for the sake of attaining or realizing certain goods. A number of factors show that individuals are not self-sufficient, at least from the point of view of realizing the full human potential. Aristotle stresses defense and safety, as well as attitudes that involve interpersonal relations and not purely self- but rather other-oriented emotions and accompanying judgments. The profession of medicine illustrates these well.

One could add the empirical evidence that a certain amount of interpersonal contact is needed for a human at a rather early stage of life if he is to master fully a natural language. Aristotle also believed that thought was essential to humans, and that this includ-

---

2 Plato, *Republic*, Book IV, 433–443.
3 Dewey, *The School and Society.*
4 Royce, *The Philosophy of Loyalty.*

ed determinations of what is good and useful. But such considerations will have to include views on what are better or worse relations to other humans.

In addition to the need for social contact, Aristotle also held the view that the evolution of political units is a part of basic human nature. For humans have the capacity to adopt legal systems, and within these to formulate principles of justice. These, he held, are what leads a human unit, a society, to self-sufficiency, and in this sense he thought of the "polis" as having priority over the individual (1253a25). So in a way Aristotle is committed to a mild form of holism, but also to a kind on moderate individualism, since he also holds that the job of the statesman includes helping the citizens to become good individuals.[5]

With these conditions in mind, we turn to the first dependency illustrated by the virtue of kindness. Kindness is an attitude, and thus it involves thoughts, feelings, and action. Kindness is expressed in actions. To be sure, one could be described as kind if conditions prevent the person from ever exercising the virtue, but this is a derivative notion of kindness. Kindness typically develops through interaction with others, and it is maintained in this way. Kindness tends to atrophy without human interactions. Persistence is fuelled by active expression. This expression takes place in a variety of contexts. We are kind to a variety of types of being. To be kind in the usual general sense thus requires interaction with many different kinds of humans and other sentient creatures.

It is easy to see that the above can be generalized to cover many other virtues, such as trust, concern for others, respect, and so on. To be sure, the amount and kinds of kindness, trust, respect, etc. vary with context. There is the kind physician, parent, friend, landlord; in all these cases different modes of implementation are needed. But in all of these cases continuous maintenance requires social interactions of one kind or another. Hence the empirical dependencies of individual character constituents on social interactions.

We shall now look at a case of the reverse dependency, namely ways in which social and political goods depend on individual ethics. First, a general empirical dependency. In the case of political laws and rights acknowledgements, stability is required for

5 Miller, *Nature, Justice, and Rights in Aristotle's Politics*, 197–199.

maintenance. There is empirical evidence that in the optimal cases stability is assured by the citizens having understanding and respect for the laws and trust in the legitimacy of the enforcing institutions.[6] But such characteristics require the ethical commitment to a certain ethical ideal, i.e. combination of overall aims and character that is in harmony with such aims. To be sure, this dependency affects not the genesis of our political structure; i.e. not what analytic philosophers call the "definition," but the persistence and maintenance of the political life dictated by the laws. The methodology of this essay, in harmony with the methodology of much traditional moral philosophy, requires that we outline implementation procedures for any proposed legal or economic structure. Definitions of ideal states of affaires without "bridge-laws" connecting these to the dynamics of the actual flow of history seem empty of serious content, be these in ethics or the sciences.

Let us turn now to a further dependency, showing links between a specific political structure and individual ethics. One might call this the "optimality condition." In order for democracy, involving accountability, representational government and the other usual features of this political form to work well, the citizens should have respect for the structure as well as for each other, trust in the government, have concern for communal aims in addition for the self-interests of various members, and ability to think for themselves. These are traits that need to be incorporated into the individual ethical ideals that are desirable in a democratic political unit. One might say that the mere structure as defined has value, apart form "mere empirical questions" of implementation and persistence. But this sounds hollow. One has to look at the delineation of a political system like democracy in conceptual ways we use when examining concepts for artifacts like a knife. To understand what a knife is, there is a need to understand not only its constituents and structure, but also its functions. Thus to understand what a knife is entails knowing what is a better or worse knife, and to see that the line between a very bad knife and a stump that is not a knife at all is very thin. Thus to understand what a democracy is includes understanding how it is supposed to function, and hence what are better or worse modes of function-

6 Tyler, *Why Do People Obey the Law.*

ing. But these differences involve both political and individual goods. Also, goods that cannot be sharply classified as belonging exclusively into this or that category. One of these is the virtue of being cooperative, and the conception of this as one of the most fundamental ingredients of the social dynamics that most underlie any successfully functioning democracy. A very bad democracy becomes—as Aristotle indicated—mob rule. We can find similar dependency relations among the individual social and institutional values in units like hospitals or schools.

Consideration of such dependencies also affect ways of choosing between political structures. Ranking alternatives is not sufficient. One needs to ask how close one's first choice can be to optimality in terms of implementation. One might prefer the second choice if this can be implemented more optimally in relation to its ideal functioning in our context than one's first choice.

A general dependency need be added to the examples considered. Some psychologists are considering—in the wake of the murdering of tourists in Miami by very young criminals—the hypothesis that unless a human is exposed to some warm positive affections—regardless of source—within the first four years of his or her life, this human will not be able to respond with concern to the suffering of others.[7] If this is correct, it places an important empirical constraint on ethical outlook and conduct, given the obvious assumption that concern for the suffering of other humans is a prerequisite for sound ethics.

In summary, if we are concerned not only with definitions of political, social and individual goods (values), but also with possibilities of implementation and persistence, then we need to be concerned with dependencies such as the ones illustrated above, and hence work on the three levels of values with their interwovenness in mind.[8]

---

7 For discussions of these matters I am indebted to Professor Herbert Leiderman.

8 For an extended account of such approaches see Putnam, "The Moral Life of a Pragmatist."

9 Miller, *op. cit.*, 209. Miller sees that social friendship could not be the highest Aristotelian friendship, but only a utilitarian one. An alternative, advocated in this chapter, takes out a number of ingredients from Aristotelian virtue friendship, and projects these unto larger social units.

2. Conceptual Dependencies

In this section we will be concerned with cases in which a concept plays foundational roles both for individual and social–political ethics, and the roles need be worked out together. Hence we will have conceptually common elements between individual and social–political ethics. The first such case is friendship. We will consider friendship based on shared utility and, in addition, shared values. The following considerations show why such a friendship, or at least some of its ingredients, should be a part of any adequate individual ethics.

As a preliminary, we should note that in the case of individual ethics, the moral worth of the agent is characterized partly in terms of the capacity to have friendships of the sort described. Implementation may be hindered by external circumstances. In the case of the social, however, actual realization need be a part of communal life, and not mere possibility. Without actual cooperation, etc. political institutions will not survive.

Friendship can be analyzed into ingredients like sharing overall values, respect for each other, cooperation, concern and other such aspects. Some of these would require close contact. But we can also consider friendship without including all of the ingredients. One might call the full friendship "close friendship" and still leave room for a kind of friendship in which the actual close contact—at least on the physical level—is absent.

Friendship on this general level is seen by all major moral theories as a constituent. For Kant it was very good training for the kind of universal good will needed for the purest part of the moral, for the utilitarian friendship can only be a constitutive element of the happiness to be maximized, or a prominent means to it. In ethics stressing character as the fundamental element, the ingredients of friendship contain the virtues we most often associate with the well-lived moral life.

Civic friendship, or at least a cluster of many of its ingredients, is needed as an essential underlying element for the communal dynamic that makes the social group a well functioning unit, and the appropriate foundation for the maintenance and continuous improvement of the associated political structures.[9]

In summary, the argument takes the following form:

(1) Humans are social beings, in the sense articulated earlier.

(2) The highest forms of friendship, or at least most of its ingredients are needed for the realization of this aspect of human nature.

(3) Humans who realize this aspect of human nature are needed for a sound communal life in which people support not only each other, but also work together for communal aims that cannot be reduced to sums of individual aims.

(4) So the individual virtue of friendship is also a key constituent in the communal virtues.

(5) A sound community that is based on civic virtue is needed as an underpinning for an implemented political structure that functions well and has the potential for maintenance and persistence.

The last point needs stressing. It has been pointed out in recent literature that Aristotelian civic friendship helps build robust social units, but would not be accepted by proponents of a minimalist state i.e. one in which governmental activity is limited to defense and protection of individual rights and property.[10] In response this essay argues that a political structure, defined in the abstract, will not function well, and will not have the vitality to adjust to legal and political changes unless its activities are interwoven with robust communal civic friendship. This interaction is also needed for the settling of the next dependency, the delimitation of the moral domain, to which we now turn.

Determining the moral domain is to delineate the class of beings whose welfare and possible suffering is morally relevant to both individual and communal decisions. Members of the moral domain have ethical claims on us, such as respect, concern for their welfare, sensitivity to their suffering, trust, care, and others. For our purposes we need not delineate the domain in any specific way, and can admit that the domain might admit layers of priority. Our main point is that this determination must involve both the individual and the community.

The following report from the so-called Watts riots illustrates our concept. At a cross-section in Los Angeles a white person lay

10 Miller, *op. cit.*, chapter 10.

badly wounded. A Japanese gentleman, considerably risking his life, helped the wounded man off the street and called for medical assistance. A reporter passed by and asked him why he, as a Japanese man was helping this white person. He replied: "because he is a human being." Given the atmosphere in which many said that they were primarily black or white and only secondarily human, this was a non-trivial reply. The attitude exemplified here contrasts sharply with the "help your friends and harm your enemies" attitude that we find recorded in early Greek literature.

The story of the Good Samaritan who helps someone who does not belong to his cast, also illustrates the expansion of the moral domain to humanity. These are so far individual choices. Such choices may or may not lead to institutionalization of the new expansions.

In Sophocles' drama *Philoctetes*, we have a case of an individual decision that does suggest the need for institutionalizing a new delineation. Neoptolemus, one of the main figures, decides at a crucial junction of the play to defy the Greek army and restore goods to a suffering person on the grounds that his previous deed of theft was a case of harming a fellow human being. So here individual decision clashes with political institutional demands. This also shows the need to reach communal agreement, or at least large areas of overlap, on the extent of the moral domain.

The structure of the delineation must follow the following pattern. The members of the moral domain are the claim- or right-bearers. Hence we need to specify what the right-bearing warranting qualities should be. One can view these qualities as either matters of desert or as basis for inclusion apart from desert. For example, we can regard responsibility, or wisdom as warranting qualities, but we can also regard being a sentient creature as a warranting quality, though this has nothing to do with desert. The key point is that some list of the warranting qualities need be made, and that the list can be submitted to rational critique. This does not mean that the list might not have some of its origins in human capacities for compassion, and sympathy with those who suffer.

The conception of the moral domain must emerge on three levels: the individual, societal and political. The political element enters because rights need be implemented, institutionalized and maintained in order to be effective. Mere individual good will cannot decide what in this or that unforeseen political context constitutes doing justice to the moral domain. For example, even if everyone has the right to vote, further political steps will have to be made in order to enable those who have this right now, to be able to put it into practice. Thus prospective voters who are weak need be brought to the polls, education need be expanded to reach all prospective voters, etc. But even if the right institutions are erected for realizing enabling conditions, the successful execution of what these institutions should do depends on a cooperative communal dynamic. The community must support the extension of the moral domain, and initiate action in a variety of unforeseeable conditions. This can be seen from examples like the abolition of slavery in the USA and the end of apartheid in South Africa.[11] But eventually, since the respect for the rights of the members of the moral domain includes individual acts involving attitudes, i.e. combination of reason and emotion, individuals will also have to accept the task of maintaining the moral domain. The attitudes involved in the task must become parts of their individual ethics. Given this situation, though one could start a change in the moral domain solely on the political level, individuals need be involved as soon as possible so that these can see the legitimacy of the new delineation and its rightness.

Thus the individual has a certain attitude towards others (e.g. no prejudice, cooperation), this becomes part of the foundation for certain communal aims and activities (education for all, etc.), and these in turn require political protection and adjudication of conflicts in which we need to agree, given scarcity of resources, how the effort to maintain the moral domain will be supported across the board.

None of this denies that in some cases the redrawing of the moral domain is an individual achievement. For example in Lessing's drama, *Nathan the Wise*, the hero resists getting even with Christians who murdered his family, and extends love and kindness towards a Christian orphan. In cases like these, the effort and achievement remains on the individual level, and eventually some laws protecting individuals from persecution may be formed. But

---

11 H. P. Loetter, *Justice for an Unjust Society*; and T. Lott; ed. *Subjugation and Bondage*.

when it comes to elements like the right to vote, to own property etc., the purely individual effort will not do. Thus in cases in which the rights and claims involve political and economical matters we need the political level. But this by itself will not lead to actual implementation unless the population joins in the effort to bring the process to a successful conclusion, and help it to persist. There are other cases, on the other hand, in which political laws and regulations are useless. Presumably a sound community has some agreement on whom a human should love under certain circumstances such as family, or volunteered support, and other such relations. But just as love and kindness will not install a voting system, so political rights will not create a happy family or circle of friends.

At this point one might wonder why we cannot simply agree to extend the moral domain to all humans. But certainly, the so-called human rights doctrine by itself could not do this. Mere specification of a fundamental set of rights does not, indeed cannot, by itself delineate also its domain of application. Thus we need to look for arguments supporting the claim that all humans should be included. This must mean that all humans, just by being human, automatically have membership in the moral domain. But what are the warranting qualities? Merely being a member of a certain species? Or being a member of the same species of which those raising the question are members? Or the alleged characteristic of autonomy? We cannot enter into detailed discussion of these matters at this point. All that is relevant to the argument at hand is that political, communal and individual commitments need be made concerning the warranting qualities, and that communal as well as legal agreements need be made as to which right can be secured through which means.

We also need to note that acknowledging rights is in some contexts a matter of degrees. We do not accord criminals the same rights as others, and membership in a community or political units is not a guarantee of equal rights with everyone, regardless of how responsibly or irresponsibly these rights are being exercised.

Returning to our scheme, the membership-warranting qualities must be related to a conception of the kinds of agents to be included, and the kinds of social activities the member are expected to perform. Thus the notion of a good or acceptable agent is a common element between the individual and the social–political ethics. In individual ethics the good agent must be the subject in relation to whom we specify utility, and also the object of many of our moral attitudes, not in the sense that only the good persons can be such objects, but that the selection of the appropriate object includes the assumption that at least potentially such a human could meet the relevant conditions. The good agent is also a key element in our communal ethics, since this conception will guide our establishing the right warranting qualities for the moral domain. Again, the domain includes good as well as not so good people, but the minimal warranting qualities are set with an eye on what it takes to be a good agent.

The delineation of the moral domain, then, includes both an ethical characterization of the entities to be admitted, and of the community from the point of view of which the delineation is carried out. Hence the intertwining of the individual and the social. This is illustrated on a smaller scale within friendship based on shared values, the highest form of friendship according to Aristotle.[12] Within such a friendship being cooperative is both an individual and social value. For it is seen as an individual virtue of intrinsic value, and at the same time it is also an essential ingredient in that kind of a community. We can see this also in Royce's ethics.[13] Loyalty is both a part of the individual and the social ethics.

If we ask: "how is Aristotelian friendship good for me?" we need to specify the nature of the agent, the "me," from whose point of view the question is raised. The specification has to be at least partly in moral terms. There is no value-neutral conception of an agent from whose point of view asking this question makes sense. If one is striving for certain virtues, then this kind of friendship will be the highest fulfillment.[14] If one is a narrowly hedonistic person, then this kind of friendship will be of minimal value. Thus this kind of friendship is good from a certain individual point of view, and to be that kind of an individual is good from the point of view of a certain normative conception of a society or political unit. This is not a vicious circle. It shows only how ethics

12 Aristotle, *Nichomachean Ethics*, Books VIII and IX.
13 Royce, *The Philosophy of Loyalty.*
14 Moravcsik, "The Perils of Friendship and Conceptions of the Self."

must be built by a "bootstrap" strategy in which the social–political and the individual are intertwined.

At the heart of our ethical lives we do not find so much debates about what is good or bad, but rather the setting of priorities between the conflicting values that we need to confront constantly in our lives. The simplistic "good/bad" or "right/wrong" dichotomies may provide a necessary conceptual ingredient on a foundational level, but in daily life priority setting is the most frequent challenge. The conflicting elements may be ethical values, or matters of utility. The conflict often involves a clash between the demands of the individual and the community. There is no "super-science" that can deal with such conflicts. We need to establish transcategorial priorities, and also to recognize the importance of values that are conceptual parts of both individual and communal well-being.

First we shall consider a relatively simple case and see that even in such matters it is difficult to sift out some allegedly purely individual value to be contrasted with societal demands.

A few years ago I was working on a paper on Aristotle in a rural Swiss setting, in a house surrounded by farms. Suddenly a storm seemed to be brewing up. One of the farmers had much of his hay still out in the fields. Those of us in neighboring houses stopped doing whatever we had been up to, rushed out and helped bring in the hay. This had to be done, because the farmer would not have been able to do all of this by himself in time, before the storm. The farmer was no friend of mine, and I was not a regular member of this rural community. Furthermore, I was not going to stay long in that area. Still, I joined the crew of helpers. My choice was not designed to serve the utilitarian consideration of ingratiating myself with these people; given the circumstances that would have been neither possible nor productive.

In my very brief deliberation the following considerations played key roles. First, here was a fellow human being in dire need. Secondly, his endeavors had a commendable purpose. Both the helping of others under these circumstances and the work of Aristotle had for me intrinsic value. At the same time, both the values of the two endeavors, the farmer's and mine had for me intrinsic value, but incommensurable. The fact that under these circumstances the farmer's loss would have been greater than mine did affect the choice, though in other contexts this might not have been relevant. He could have been using his wealth irresponsibly, my work might have been of great value in understanding our past and present. Similar scenarios could have changed the priority.

So utilitarian considerations played little if any role in the decision. At the same time I felt under no obligation to rush to help. Neither the choice to help nor the alternative not to help would have involved not to treat the farmer as an end. Two considerations that one cannot classify utilitarian–deontic, or strictly individual–social did play major roles. One of these was my conception of how I would like to respond to the plight of fellow human beings, i.e. what kind of an agent did I strive to be. Within my conception my functioning as an agent should include the readiness to form ad hoc communities with people in need involving worthy causes. Secondly, I place great value in being part of communities that are tied together by mutual respect and commitment to worthy causes.

These considerations led me to act as I did. Within the framework of the decision some of the priority setting conditions cannot be classified within the usual rubrics of utilitarian–deontic and individual–social.

One might think that the choice and the issues involved in this case were not of paramount importance. But the same issues as well as further complicating factors also emerge in struggles that are of greater significance. A beautiful account of such a situation is described by Sissela Bok in her account of the life of her mother Alva Myrdal.[15]

Alva Myrdal was a politically influential person, an intellectual, a mother, a wife, and an individual who is described as trying throughout all of the upheavals of her life "to retain one's self." The values that were likely to clash occasionally included the individual, the social, and the political. But on a deeper level, the example of this wonderful life raises the question of how well we can separate these three domains. Some of the factors causing conflicts are felt obligations, to family, to humanity, to the self. But not all clashes are on that level. Some of it seems to be the effort to be "good at" the tasks that life throws at her (good mother,

---

15 Bok, *Alva Myrdal.*

good wife, etc.). This is surely distinct from questions of obligation. It is more like striving to embody certain ideals. Finally there
are the morally relevant emotions, love, compression, concern for
others, that also demand expression. The concern for retaining
one's self thus presents an enormous challenge. From the point of
view of the outsider, the reader of the biography, it is very difficult
to describe the self that she wanted to be. How much of it involved
a desire to be occasionally withdrawn from people, how much of
it was constituted by regarding some of her deepest feelings for
others as also parts of herself? Faced with such an inspiring but
enormously complex life, one is tempted to wonder: where did the
self stop and where did external relations start? Need one, should
one, try to draw a sharp line here at all? Choices between conflicting values could be best seen, perhaps, not piecemeal, but as an
attempt at balance over longer periods of time. It is fortunate for
human life that we can discern at least the main concerns that
emerged continuously in this remarkable life without being forced
to try to squeeze it all into the philosophical dichotomies sketched
in this section.

Today many women lead much less dramatic lives within
which, nevertheless, the same issue, conflicting values, emotions,
clamor for attention. This essay suggests that one might have to be
more pluralistic in our acceptance of different conceptions or
"thin" and "thick" portraits of the human agent, and to accept the
claim, formulated long ago in Greek drama, that the insoluble
moral dilemma is an essential part of the human condition, across
historical contexts.

These reflections on examples that show the enormous difficulty if not impossibility of keeping the individual, social and political ethical elements separate is strongly influenced by the thesis
articulated earlier concerning the essentially social nature of
humans. Hence it is appropriate to make a few remarks about a
very different tradition that gave rise to many individualistic conceptions of ethics and politics. J. J. Rousseau wrote the lines that
became a famous quotation: "Man was born free, but today he is
everywhere in chains." [16] This statement suggests construing individual freedom in term of release from social pressures, institu-

---

16 Rousseau, *Du Contrat Social*.

tions, inherited obligations and other relations that we have not entered voluntarily. Our participation in political units are like chains, and gaining our freedom should be the struggle to get rid of all those links that we have not formed voluntarily, thus ending up as much as possible only with free contract-like bonds. A treatment of Rousseau's view and the ethical theory known as contractarianism is beyond the scope of this essay. Here we can only contrast these views with that of this essay, and show key points that need to be considered in any adequate debate between these.

If we take the quote as describing literally what is in fact the human conditions, then it seems patently false. No human being was ever born free. Human beings are born into families, states, tribes, and other social and political communities, and derive the means for much of their development (in terms of linguistic, logical, and ethical competence) from the interactions that inevitably take place. Thus even the strongest innatist position will maintain that at certain stages of life certain social interactions are needed, in order for human nature to develop to an adequate degree.

Rousseau and his friends knew all of this. Thus a more sympathetic reading will interpret the claims as idealizations. They prescribe abstracting away from all of the ties, relations, and influential interactions in which humans are involved since birth, and regard from the point of view of constructing a sound social–political theory humans as what is left over after the abstractions have been completed.[17]

We shall consider the abstractions first on the level of the social or communal aspects of human nature. The abstractions would not work. If we take away social interactions and communal belonging, then—as we have seen—language, thought, sensitivity of suffering of others and other emotional ties would have to be deleted from the "equation," and there would not be enough left to reconstruct the human agent confronting ethical choices.

We should consider the remarks of Rousseau, and those of the contractarians on the political plane, since this is clearly what they have mostly in mind. But such consideration in isolation runs against much of what we said about the interrelations of the communal and the political. Many of the so-called "chains" referred

---

17 Taylor, "Atomism."

to above can be seen as enabling conditions. These enabling conditions are key elements in the role of the communal dynamics as underlying the successful maintenance and persistence of political structure. Thus there is already that much interaction.

Should we consider some aspects of political ties and structures as enabling conditions rather than chains? Does the assumed idealization require that we should be able to consider all of our political relationships and then make the decision of what is or is not an enabling condition voluntarily? Humans are thrown into a web of political relationships as soon as they are born. It is not feasible to think of a human life as having the possibilities of considering all political ties "from scratch". It is more plausible to hope that a human being under desired conditions can reflect to some extent on alternatives that within his or her context open up and seem more adequate than the ones in existence at a given time. This is a picture that suggests "relative autonomy", i.e. reflection being able to transcend given political bonds and being able to come up with some alternatives that are conceivable in any given context. This is weaker than the suggestion that at any given time the human mind can reflect on "all the social-political conceptions," and is hence in conflict with this essay. The conflict is of an empirical nature; the idealizer has to abstract away from all of the evidence that has been brought up by intellectual historians. We need to consider whether the idealizations seem the same from different contextual points of view. Political structures try to combine in different ways three factors: freedom, security and economic well-being. Communities differ on the ways in which they want these three factors combined. Different geographical and economical conditions make different combinations more or less reasonable. This casts doubt on the viability of the idealizations we have been considering.

Someone might say that in all of this we have been considering a political structure within which the state or other political unit has within its power much besides defense and the protection of property. How does our account and main thesis fare when compared to the "minimalist" conception of the state and its relations to its citizens? Within this conception the functions of the state are limited to defense, protecting rights to property, enforcing human rights and taxation, as well as the maintenance of a criminal law structure. The citizens' relationship to the state consists of obeying the laws, paying taxes, and having some ways of holding the state accountable. It seems that within such a conception individual ethics and political theory are kept separate.

In reply one can point to elements playing key roles in political life that are also tied to communal and individual ethics. For example, as was mentioned above, Alva Myrdal worked tirelessly for peace. Issues of peace and war are political decisions. But underlying these are questions of how we value peace, how important it is, how we rank it in comparison with demands of individual and political autonomy, and economic conditions. It is senseless to insist that the state has the right to declare or not declare war, and to ignore the question of whether the population will support the decision made. Attitudes of nationalism, tolerance and intolerance, etc. will have much weight in determining whether a purely legal decision can culminate in a successful military campaign. Determination of duties—in social units like a family, or in a political unit—must have underlying them a supportive communal dynamic if the duties are to function successfully in a socio–political community.

We shall turn now to education, our fourth example of the need to have individual and social–political ethics intertwined. In discussing the role of education William Frankena writes: "If both individuals and societies must be concerned about the acquisition and transmission of certain dispositions rather than others, or of what we have termed excellences, then the next question is: How are excellences acquired? Can they be transmitted from the older to the younger, and if so, how?"[18]

This statement is designed to open up a vast area of issues around which a philosophy of education must center. Our purpose here is only to point out how any adequate theory of education must combine individual and social–political ethics. Frankena's sentence already points to the key issue: if education is to develop certain dispositions in individuals, then this must be done both with an eye on what individual human agents should be, and with consideration of what kinds of individuals the community and related political unit or units need. But answers to these questions

18 Frankena, *Three Historical Philosophies of Education*, 4–5.

must be interwoven. The conception of what kinds of individuals the state should have depends on views of the state from different points of view. In different contexts a state confronts certain economic and political problems that need solutions of one kind or another. The citizens are forced to face such crisis, and need to come to agreements, even if such will be drawn from individuals with a variety of outlooks on life. Political and economic problems place a constraint on how much disagreement is possible within a community in a given context.

In some countries ethics courses are offered on the high school level. In others efforts in this direction would be drowned out by shouts of "whose ethics will be taught?" Though some of us hold the view that there are basic matters of what a community is, what loyalty is, how sharing can take place in a community etc., and that a discussion of such matters is both vital and can be kept neutral between various types of morality, this stance unfortunately has not attracted many believers.

An educational curriculum is balanced typically between subjects that everyone is supposed to know and subjects that prepare humans for special types of jobs. This raises immediately the question of whether the special training could not be and should not be left to prospective employers. It is quite misleading to describe discussions of these issues as "discussion of social problems". Such description covers up the fact that there is no way of settling such matters without some stand, implicit or explicit, on what are desirable character traits in the humans that are supposed to come out of the schooling process. This is Frankena's basic insight, shared by Aristotle, Dewey and many others.

Finally, the issue of programs for the gifted child raises once more the same problem of reconciling individual rights with communal needs and resources. One way towards reconciliation is to ask what we expect of the humans who come out of the educational program. Should they have an appreciation of the vast area of knowledge that not everyone can master? Thus should the gifted also have appreciation of sharing, and the less gifted of the purpose of helping the gifted to eventually explore new regions of what can be known and explained? These ruminations will seem strange to those used to the legalistic battles fought over this issue. The comments here will certainly not provide some magical cure-all to end all such debates. But they point out that from the point of view of this essay, the quality of the communal bond among students is also a relevant issue, and that help for the gifted should not be conceived by the students as mere privilege, but as an aid to the expansion of knowledge. Likewise, the gifted should appreciate the need to share resources, not just from the point of view of the state, but from the point of view of a conception of agents who at their best exemplify both valuing advancement in knowledge but also the quality of communal life in which sharing is a highly valued virtue.

To illustrate our point further, a few remarks about an earlier educational document, namely James Bryant Conant's "General Education in a Free Society." There were around that time other educational plans dealing with education other than mere preparation for jobs or further specialized training, e.g. Great Books programs. But Conant's was clearly conceived as a project for education in which individual values and social values were harmonized to the point of sharing common conceptual ingredients. Implicit in the conception was the idea that certain virtues, such as those one can gather from humanistic material, were needed both to develop humans into good human beings and to develop them into good (useful) citizens, provided, of course, that we had the right kind of state or society in mind. The General Education program was both a guideline towards helping develop certain individual human potential and a guideline towards acceptable forms of state; i.e. those in which the same virtues also formed communal aims and ties.

One might regard the aim of the Conant conception to produce in students virtues that are both civic virtues, and given the social dimension of humans, also individual virtues. Alternatively, a Kantian might argue that a citizen has obligations to the state, beyond paying taxes and obeying the law, and that these include the obligation to develop those individual virtues that also serve as civic virtues. This view is not compatible with the claims of this essay. A virtue or desirable character trait is a combination of belief, feeling and action. Feelings cannot be commanded. Hence a virtue cannot be commanded. We might have obligations to try to develop certain attitudes, but no command to actually have those makes sense within the moral psychology of this essay.

Volumes more could be written on the moral aspects of any adequate theory of education, and these sketchy remarks do not amount to a formal proof concerning the conceptual interdependence of individual and social–political ethics in all conceivable moral systems. But the considerations adduced support the hypothesis that not only is this interdependence a necessary feature of all traditional moral theories, but also of alternatives and various refinements.

We turn now to the last sphere of interdependence, namely the relationship between the demands of technological progress with its ensuing economic advantages and the maintenance of humane values and thriving civic bonds underlying successful political functioning. Again, the following remarks only touch on a few aspects of this complex problem. Our approach here is restricted to adducing considerations supporting the claim that only the interrelation between individual and social ethics can provide the appropriate ground for dealing with this cluster of problems.

We shall deal with three points of contact between the individual and the social in the meeting of the challenge of technology and new economics. First, the problem of economic success and the effect on communal life and individual ideals. Secondly, the effect on modes of communication, and thirdly, the effect on modes of cooperation.

Recent technology has changed the way we work, the modes of personal interactions open to us and the way a community can keep civic virtues alive. Some changes have been enabling. Communication is possible with persons physically distant, information can be gathered by a wide range of people who were earlier excluded. Other factors have negative effects on these aspects of life. People are under stress, work is monotonous for many, work with machines often makes people feel that they are also machinelike.

In some societies, like Singapore, these matters are the topics of grass-roots discussions between government officials and groups of citizens. In a small city-state this is easier done than in large countries. In Singapore the prime minister goes from apartment-block to apartment-block, exchanges views with the inhabitants on these issues and listens to their concerns. In my experience, the following topics often come up in these exchanges. Many people feel that though technology and economic success has

enhanced their life in terms of physical comfort and level of economic wealth, it has made their interactions more impersonal, and
leaves less time for communal activities. Cutting down on unem-
ployment and educating larger segments of the population for
work requiring more than manual skills raises the level of overall
education, but often leaves people tired as they come home from
work, and leaves them without interest and energy to focus on
close relationships with family and neighbors.

Many people spend long hours working at computers. Much
of this work leaves them little chance for creativity, and exposes
them to medical problems, such as problems with eyesight damaged by staring at the computer screen, mental problems arising
from that kind of cognitive processing, and serious back problems.

In some parts of the world we see efforts to alleviate some of
these problems. In Switzerland some companies allow people to
work only at 75% rate, thus letting the employees spend some time
on their own efforts, such as artistic, athletic or social work. Still
others work on new forms of work schedule and instilling more
variety, options and responsibility in what were routine and
monotonous forms of work.[19]

In these efforts and deliberations we must consider the conceptions of what kinds of humans we want to be, and what human
achievements, types of work, an economically successful and technologically not backward country, or other political unit, demands.
Empty slogans like "you cannot stop progress", "economy comes
first" etc. only obscure the problems. Many of the issues again
bring up priorities. E.g. how much effort to put into making computers user-friendly in contrast with mere speed and efficiency of
production and how much effort to put into the manifestation of
kindness and other humane qualities into the work of the physician in contrast with mere efficiency focussing on speedy elimination of local problems whose solutions may or may not bring overall health and psychological well-being to the patient.[20]

These examples, culled from different parts of the world give
only a bare taste of the complex problems we face in this area. But

---

19 Frithjoff Bergmann in Ann Arbor and Detroit is doing interesting
   work of this kind.
20 Aiken, Mechanic, and Moravcsik, "Organizational Aspects of Caring."

the key point of this essay in relation to such needed discussions is that we can take neither romantic views of individual bliss, nor crude economic efficiency and drive for profit for granted. As Conant's "dream" about education, in this context too, we need to look for economic and technological arrangements within which the quality of life including individual ethical and psychological needs as well as societal virtues, and finally the understandable desire to improve economic and technological status, can be maintained and occasionally improved. The outlook of this essay suggests that solutions will be highly context-dependent, with the overall scheme sketched in this section serving only as a guideline and not a manual.

Our second sub-topic is the way in which meaningful personal communication can be maintained. A writer in Los Angeles complained recently that the only time she has any genuine human contact is when she has an accident on the freeway, and the driver of the other cars starts yelling at her. Modern technology has expanded the kinds of people with whom we can keep contact. We have inexpensive links with people in other parts of the world. On the other hand, communication without personal contact can take away some of the affective qualities that are parts of communications with people for whom we have not only respect, but for whom we care as well. In Singapore families got together within a given apartment-block, and arranged to have readings for the small children every day, with different parents alternating at it. This is also supported by the government. A USA congresswomen when visiting there was heard to say: "Back home we have to pay people to do this." We have already seen that there is evidence for the need of some affection in early childhood in order to engender sensitivity towards the suffering of others. We do not know in what other ways person-to-person communication helps develop sensitivities in humans. One could also argue that within certain conceptions of the good human agent the ability to initiate and respond to personal communication has intrinsic value.

Personal communication can help enrich both individual and communal life. This cannot be ignored and overridden by considerations of speed and efficiency. Any adequate solution within a community to this challenge has to take into consideration individual ethics as well as communal, economic and political needs.

The golden mean in this case, as so often, is going to be highly context-dependent. New modes of communication can be, and are being developed. We must, however, consider against this background the permanent need for personal communication as an essential ingredient in the well functioning individual life pattern.

Our third topic under the heading of the challenge of technology and economics to ethics is the variety of types of cooperation that can evolve in a technologically advanced society. Cooperation has two different morally relevant aspects. We can distinguish different kinds of cooperation, and we can separate different kinds of motives for cooperation. For example, cooperation can be mere coordination. One person's time on the computer can be coordinated with the needs of others so that several people can get enough time on the same machine, provided the temporal segments are well distributed. A second kind of cooperation is working together on the same project. Complex projects require different people playing different roles that add up to the well functioning unit completing joint tasks. This mode requires additional and different capacities from those required for the first kind. Finally, there is also cooperation involving the joint setting of aims for the whole working unit, where at least some of these aims will be communal in the sense of not being reducible to aims of the different participating individuals. Such cooperation is required in a hospital. The overall aim of a well functioning hospital is healing and helping patients to cope with suffering. It may be that this also can be achieved when the individual workers have different individual goals. Maybe in some places most people do the work only to earn enough money for themselves. There is however at least one argument supporting the claim that having a joint aim and this being accepted by the workers makes a difference to how the project fares. The difference emerges when we contrast job performances based solely on work descriptions, i.e. work being done solely within the confines of specific lists enumerating needed performances under specifiable conditions, with work that is related to certain areas of concern, with the general understanding that within that area a person is responsible for whatever may come up, be it predictable or not. Genuine concern for a task that cannot be specified exactly is optimally induced by having made one's own for the overall aim that the whole project has, and this in turn is easier to realize when the overall aim has a moral dimension. This is at least consistent with the aims of the individuals who work on it, and at best can be made an enlargement of values that individuals already have.

Thus we see that at least within the general conception of this essay the kinds of cooperation are to some extent linked to certain motivations, and these are not ethically neutral. In terms of stability and willingness to go beyond the obligatory, a community in which people see reward not merely in financial remuneration, but also in the value of what is being accomplished, e.g. work on outer space exploration, is likely to do better than the ones in which individual economic gain is the dominant motive.[21]

We can understand the notion of cooperation better when we look at its contrasting elements. Cooperation is at times contrasted with lack of cooperation, and at other times with competition. The difference is crucial. Cooperation and competition can co-exist under carefully specified conditions. Cooperation deals with overall success of a project, while within that conceptual space there is room for competition between cooperating units in terms of magnitude and efficiency of work done. The scheme developed here states merely that ultimately the cooperation must take precedence over competitive aspects, in cases of clash. Cooperation contrasted with lack of cooperation is a different matter. Lack of cooperation may have selfishness as its roots, but in other cases it is a function of having different aims. In cases of conflict resolution, getting to the roots of lack of cooperation should utilize this distinction.[22]

These themes can be extended in many directions, and the suggestions would have to be compared to the already existing vast literature on cooperation and the lack of it. These remarks are meant to show that our main theme and specific point about intertwining the individual and the social-political is relevant to the work in that area.

Another type of interweaving is exemplified by the relations between personal and civic friendships. Personal friendship

---

21 Collins and Porras, *Built to Last.*
22 For interesting steps taken in this direction, see J. Zelger's GABEK project, Innsbruck.

admits of kinds (utilitarian, ultimate aim oriented, etc.) as well as degrees. For our purposes we shall concentrate on the friendship built around the mutual interest in trying to exemplify the best character we can have under our circumstances. Personal friendship of this sort involves the following three conditions. 1) Joint pursuit of highest character type. 2) Care, concern with each other's welfare. 3) Personal contact and interaction. Before we turn to the comparison with civic friendship, let us first look briefly at reasons why civic friendship is an important communal value. A brief answer would point to a theme that permeates this book. One cannot lead successful individual and communal lives on contrasts, laws and promises alone. There will always be the unexpected need of a friend or a country that we have not codified. Furthermore, it strengthens personal and communal relations greatly when the whole person, reason and emotion is involved, not only a part of the rational part. Harmoniously unified agents can give each other more and different kinds of support than mere binding by contract.

But clearly in civic friendship we must drop the third condition listed above for individual friendship. The civic reaches way beyond the circle of people we can touch and talk to. Still, 1) and 2) remain. 3) has to be changed into the requirement for some less direct communication.

Here we see then a concept two parts of which are constituents in two wider concepts. There is a difference in the third component. The intertwining is very graphic here, since we see people practicing friendship, at times in their own name, at times representing groups. The skills and abilities required cannot be sharply separated.

3. Bringing About Adequate Intertwining

There must be many ways of accommodating these intertwining in ethical theory. We can safely assume that some of these bridges will be better than others. In this section we will see how one such attempt fares. The two components are the Ethics of Ideals and a community oriented social-political theory. The Ethics of Ideal has at its base two components; adequate overall aim in life and a related character structure that has intrinsic value and is also instrumental for the adequate ideal. Within this theory there is no sharp moral–prudential distinction, and it claims that all of what falls usually under individual ethics can be derived within it. The social–political theory has at its base the thesis that what holds a community together, the "communal ties" should be seen as a semi-normative notion, and should be regarded by the community as one among the values that have top priority. E.g. respect, concern for the welfare of others, trust and care could be construed as such communal ties, and institutional–legal structure would be built on these.

Let us look first at the empirical interdependencies. Kindness and similar virtues can find their proper places in the combined theory sketched. For it will be a part of the kind character that is one of the key components of the individual ethics, but it will be seen also as either constitutive of or empirically helpful towards the establishing and maintaining of ADEQUATE communal ties.

The combined theory also incorporates the second dependency, illustrated by the optimization of a structure like democracy. For the empirical dependency there is the need of the structure in order for it to be effective, to have individuals with certain character traits to be implementing it. Such traits include maintaining values, considering communal goods and not only individual ones, being sensitive to suffering. But these are empirically also linked to any ethically adequate ideal ethics. Hence the interwovenness of the two components. This proposal will not please those who see some political structure as having intrinsic value. For within this combined theory political structures are always instrumental. At their best they will serve what is both in ideal ethics and communal–political ethics the right virtues and ties. However, I fail to see sound arguments for the intrinsic goodness of any political structure; in the absence of such, the benefits of the combined theory seem to outweigh whatever disadvantages some strands of liberal thinking see in it.

The third dependency rests on the putative empirical claim that without some early childhood experiences of warm positive affections a human will not be capable of appreciating the suffering of others later. If this is a necessary empirical condition of a rich moral life, the communal dynamics and structures within the combined theory would attempt to optimize the chances of everyone receiving such affections as a small child. Clearly optimizing chances is all we can do; affections cannot be commanded by law, and cannot be induced by promising benefits.

We turn now to the conceptual dependencies. Friendship based on shared values is both a part of an adequate ideal ethics and also a part of the communal ties of the social theory. In the latter, those aspects of friendship that can be incorporated into "civic friendship" (e.g. not close proximity, intimacy) become parts of the communal ties. Some of the friendship-making characteristics in turn will be constituents of the type or types of character that go with overall aims to form the basis of ideal ethics.

The delineation of the moral domain is an important task of the kind of community in which the communal ties have top value. For basically this delineation determines what should be borders of communities, and what kinds of creatures should be seen as members. This last issue, in turn, brings us to the Ethics of Ideals, for it provides the foundation of conceptions of what an adequate agent is, and this provides guidelines for determining what kinds of creatures should be part of the moral domain.

The problem of priorities cannot be "solved" by any ethical theory, since clashes between individual and communal needs cannot be totally eliminated from human life. Still, when we survey some of the problems faced by outstanding women like Alva Myrdal, the combined theory helps us to attempt to bring the two kinds of needs more into harmony. Indeed we witness today a number of enlightened steps in terms of vacations, work loads, staggered work hours, etc. that seem to move in this direction. Still, there is an underlying conceptual difference that can have practical consequences "in the clutch." The argument behind much of the current humane steps is that in the long run such arrangements improve efficiency. According to the theory of this essay, this predicted contingent state may or may not obtain. But the humane steps have to be taken anyway, for these are dictated by the combination of ideal ethics and the right kind of community oriented political theory.[23]

---

23 Royce interprets the Christian virtue of charity as a communal virtue. Royce, *op. cit.*, 34–35.

Finally, when it comes to facing up to the challenges that new technological and industrial practices bring with them, our combined theory offers at least one way of forging guidelines to create a society that can absorb SOME technological and industrial changes while still keeping a "human face". First, it places constraints on economic and technological expansion (some call it "progress"). It says that dehumanization is much too steep a price to pay for unlimited expansion of technology and industrial efficiency. The specifics need be worked out in various contexts, but at least it is not just compromise between various self-interests of different groups, but a principled way of approaching the problem. Furthermore, the same considerations apply to modes of communication and cooperation. The cry of dehumanization has been heard before, but the theory sketched here makes it have more teeth in terms of articulation, instructions for implementation and adjudication of conflicts—not between the prudential and the moral, but between different conceptions of what our deepest values and commitments should be.[24] Change in this framework is not mere legalistic wrangling but healing;[25] healing psychological as well as physical wounds. This way of looking at ethics has deep historic sources; it is time to draw some more strength from these.[26]

---

24 For earlier argument see Bellah and Associates, *Habits of the Heart*.
25 Loetter, *Injustice, Violence, and Peace*.
26 I am indebted to Rosalind Hursthouse and Fred Miller for many useful suggetions.

Part II

COMMUNAL TIES IN A VALUE-BASED COMMUNITY

INTRODUCTION TO PART II

The arguments in the last chapter of Part I show that we must construe individual and communal ethics as conceptually and empirically intertwined. In part II the intertwining will be documented in more detail, and the chapters also show that within communal structures communal dynamics should underlie whatever laws and institutions are erected. Most modern political scientists and political philosophers will be opposed to these theses. They believe that their key task is to describe and articulate desirable laws and institutions. How people will come to actually adopt these and identify with them is left open as a "mere empirical question." Standard modern political theory considers rights, claims and obligations, and proposes structures within which these can be defined and thus add up to a coherent abstract structure of rules and regulations. In the theory to be articulated in the chapters following it will be argued that we should first think about better and worse communal dynamics. That is to say, we should think about what shared beliefs, values, and attitudes should hold the community together psychologically. We should then fit the legal and institutional structure to the requirements of conceptions of adequate communal dynamics.

For the purposes of the initial discussion we shall regard communal dynamic as the combination of communal activities, shared values, high regard for the ties that bind us together, and communally respected attitudes manifested in interpersonal contact. The introduction serves partly to present the case for regarding sound communal dynamic as the foundation on which laws and institutions should rest, and not the other way around. Laws and institutions by themselves will not function well, if at all, unless certain attitudes and cooperation activities provide the right underpinning. An obvious example is taxation. If many millions conspire not to pay taxes, the system of taxation, no matter how "rational" it seems to its founders, will not work.

In the ensuing chapters we will chart the internal anatomy of a well functioning community. First we will show in what sense the adequate community should be what we will call an Ethical Community (EC) and how such a community must rest on a normative conception of what the communal ties should be. We will also develop criteria for better and worse communal ties, and make explicit some of the salient psychological assumptions that our theory requires. We shall then develop a proposal for what the adequate communal ties should be, and defend this program. At the end we will also show how the proposed tie meets the criteria of adequacy laid down earlier for communal ties, and that such a proof is not circular. In the second chapter it will be shown how the proposed EC, with the tie as described, fits a certain conception of how responsibility and freedom should function in an adequate community. The emphasis will be not on abstract questions about the concepts "freedom" and "responsibility," but on the communally-oriented questions of how responsibility should be assigned to individuals in a community, and how this affects and is affected by conceptions of freedom that will be defended in this essay.

The proposals and notions developed in the first two chapters i.e. chapters IV and V, will then be used to lay a foundation for the concept of justice that is in harmony with what is said about an adequate EC. The main thesis of that chapter is that the foundation of justice is sharing. Sharing is shown to be a universal human attribute, and the problem of justice is represented as the challenge of getting people to want to share many things with many individuals and communities.

Finally, the theory developed also covers, even though only in rough outlines, what attitudes and activities should be forthcoming in an adequate community towards those individuals and groups that are outside the community in question. Justification will be given for humane attitudes towards the "outsider" without abandoning the view that a plurality of communities, political, social and economic, is desirable and should not be thought of as temporary, to be replaced by some mega-community that covers the whole globe with all of its diversity.

We shall now turn to brief sketches of some contemporary tendencies in political philosophy that a theory of a sound community opposes. First, our approach opposes purely legalistic approaches to communal problems. Within such approaches laws are seen as fundamental to specifying acceptable social and political behavior, including ties, aims and activities. These laws are seen as giving stability to a community. Other than occasional reinterpretations, no further need for maintenance is perceived as necessary. This kind of stability is seen as both too rigid and too fragile. If laws are the foundation of communal life, then changes need be accompanied by changes in law. This is both cumbersome, and impractical, since gradual changes cannot be captured fully by static laws. It is an approach that is also too fragile, because once the legal entities break down, there is nothing for the members of a community to fall back on. Laws—if sound—are supported by the attitudes that are the foundations of communal ties and aims. Laws should emerge from these attitudes, and their acceptance and maintenance is fuelled by the persistence of the underlying attitudes. A legal structure needs to be supported by a communal dynamics. We see this today in examples as physically distant from each other as the USA and South Africa. For laws to be effective, respect, trust, understanding and interpersonal relations engendering cooperation are needed. This communal dynamics will be articulated in the subsequent chapters. Apart from its being ineffective, a predominantly legalistic society will have an unsatisfactory communal life. Legalistic attitudes breed a spat of lawsuits, and within such a context distrust reigns supreme. Legalism has negative effects on warm positive attitudes in the community, because it encourages confrontation instead of readiness to compromise. Love grows cold when communal interactions are given solely legalistic outlets.

This essay is also opposed to any kind of monistic determinism, views according to which all important social developments and structures have basically only one kind of underlying cause. Such a view is economic determinism, i.e. the conception that all important political and social changes have exclusively economic underlying causes. This view spawned the slogan that "once we fix the economy, we are over the hump." This outlook is refuted today by facts over and over again. Fanaticism ignores economic advantages, nationalism ignores prospects of financial gain, and forcing economic systems, no matter how "rational," unto countries whose traditions and communal fibers are not compatible with such a system cause a great deal of harm. We find also examples like a poverty stricken part of Calcutta which nevertheless has fine communal life.[1] There are also cases like in Oakland where youths told social workers that they would refrain from crime if they could get a well paying job. Upon further questioning they said that the pay they had in mind was what a local drug dealer would earn. This situation cannot be remedied by economic measures. No community can pay most young people on that level of remuneration, and even if they did, there is no evidence that the youths would not press for more. The situation requires trying to get the youths to rethink their values, help them to strive for realistic economic goals combined with satisfactory relations to their communities. A striking example going against economic determinism is the recent study of the abolishing of slavery in the USA by the economist Robert Fogel.[2] His analysis shows that moral, religious, social, political and economic factors all combined in bringing about this change that had such an impact on American life.

This essay is also opposed to certain types of individualism, including taking the notion of a human individual for granted, and derivatively also the notion of individual basic needs. It construes legal and social structures as at their best mere means to satisfying individual needs. More extreme versions of this view assume that individuals should be allowed to seek ways to meet as many of their needs as possible, and thus the state should be a "minimalist" state. It should interfere with the lives of its citizens as little as possible.[3] This essay opposes such a view on two grounds. First, we shall show that certain elements of close relations, such as friendship and family, can be abstracted and extended to cover large political communities. If it is true that thriving communities have a part of their basic psychological underpinning rooted in those we find in families, then the call for minimalist states loses its force. For in the case of families and friendships the "least com-

---

1 LaPierre, *The City of Joy.*
2 Fogel, *Without Consent or Contract.*
3 Nozick, *Anarchy, State, and Utopia.*

munal effort" view does not work. Secondly, as we have already seen in the first half of this book, there are many morally relevant conceptions of individual human nature, and when we make decisions and act we need to choose between these, implicitly or explicitly. Within a conception, that regards reason the most important part of a human, one kind of decision will be made, and within another one that gives top priorities to emotions, different ones will be implemented. This point can be extended to show that different conceptions of individual nature also affect conceptions of communal ties and aims. For example, if we think of a human as primarily determined in choices and preferences by a drive to maximize gratification, then we obtain a conception of communal life that stresses competitive elements and compromise. If, on the other hand, we conceive of human nature as open to the pursuits of a variety of ends, both cooperative and competitive ones, then we can also think of humans as assigning top priority, e.g., to relations in which the distinguishing marks among individuals are blurred. We can take more narrow conceptions of individuals according to which only their non-relational attributes provide the conceptual pool for essential characteristics, and also a wider conception of an individual that allows for essential features of individuals that are relational.

This essay addresses considerations supporting a wider conception of a human individual, and uses this to show how elements of friendship and their basis can be built into political communities.[4]

Building elements of friendship and other key values into communal life provides what we call communal dynamic; namely the attitudes, aims and types of interactions that constitute the communal aspects of our lives. In the next section it will be shown how adequate communal dynamics should underlie our rules, laws and institutions. Without such a foundation the purely legal and abstract aspects of what makes a well functioning community cannot fulfill its roles.

---

4 Moravcsik, "The Perils of Friendship and Conceptions of the Self."

1. Communal Dynamics and Political Structures

A few years ago I discussed with government officials in Singapore the daunting challenges that this small country faces in view of its diversity, both ethic and religious. The officials expressed fear of the neighboring giants—China and Indonesia—and wondered how their people would be able to stand up to any possible attack. As they put it: "that is when we will find out whether the social glue holds." It is interesting that in their statement the key worry was not the relative small size of their country's armed forces and economy, but "the social glue."

This social glue is one of the several conceptions that fall under what in this essay we call "communal dynamics." Communal dynamics has many aspects. It includes the ways in which people regard each other and interact. It includes the sharing of what is regarded in the community as basic values, and thus also the character types that are seen as to be encouraged in public life and in the educational system. One conception of the communal dynamics is labeled "civic friendship," and dates back to Aristotle.[5] According to this conception the communal dynamics that underlies laws and institutions should include some elements of what Aristotle regarded as the highest form of friendship. This includes sharing what are regarded as intrinsic values. Thus also certain traits of character.

Complete Aristotelian friendship requires physical proximity and causal interaction among the participants. But in the large states of the modern world this would not be possible. Some of us think, nevertheless, that some of the ingredients of Aristotelian friendship can be extracted from the whole, and used as parts of the foundation of communal dynamics today. Trust, cooperation and respect can be grounded in the roots of Aristotelian friendship. This view influences the way in which Communal Ties and communal life are construed in this essay.

Since a communal dynamics can be better or worse, criteria of evaluation are needed in order for a community to exercise ongoing rational critical self-reflection. This chapter will deal with these matters. The main function of this part of the work is to show why com-

---

5 Aristotle, *Nichomachean Ethics*, Book VIII, section 9–11.

munal dynamics should underlie and inform the laws and institutions that are erected in a society. This view clashes with what most political theorists and philosophers today believe. Their view is that laws and institutions should have conceptual as well as practical priority. It is also held that once the appropriate institutions and laws are put in place, the population will become accustomed to these, and in due time develop acceptable communal dynamics as well. For example, some people believe that if democratic rules of government and a fitting legal system are established, then people will come to adopt in their own lives democratic outlook and practices. Thus an adequate voting system, impartial courts, and an educational system that is universal on a minimal level, is supposed to provide the foundation for the development of adequate communal dynamics.

One version of this "modern view" also incorporates a form of behaviorism. It says that once we establish the right laws and institutions, we can train people in terms of behavior how to interact and relate to the state, and that as long as the behavior is rewarded in terms of hedonistic or economic values, a democratic society can function well.

Within this version some suggest that we can evolve non-aggressive behavior by giving the practitioner material rewards, and that eventually this will lead to a non-aggressive person.

The key assumption of this view is the naïve hypothesis that by controlling behavior we can change the internal psychological attributes of humans. Empirical evidence against this hypothesis is overwhelming (Southern Tyrol, Balkan hostilities, African tribal warfare, etc). The difficulty of maintaining this view is well illustrated by what happened at a conference in Stanford. The key problem in Eastern Europe was identified as corruption. One political theoretician suggested that corruption could be reduced by offering monetary rewards to those who stop behaving corruptly. This proposal seems to suggest that the way to get rid of corruption, e.g. taking bribes, is to bribe those taking bribes. I doubt that taking a "superbribe" will change the internal character of those who are corrupt and take bribes. At another occasion a newly rich Russian said on television that "in our country today greed is the prime virtue." But a society in which greed rules will not be able to generate respect for laws, and thus the whole conglomeration expires in chaos.

The main claim of this essay is that adequate communal dynamics is prior to the legal structure and other political institutions. At any given time we need some legal framework in a working society, but the source of improvement and maintenance of the good features must come from the communal dynamics. The laws can only function well if the underlying dynamics supports these.

This claim needs modification. Obviously, we cannot put all of the communal dynamics in place before we have laws and institutions. For example, a part of the communal dynamics is to be willing to try to understand the law, and to abide by it as something beneficial. If there are no laws at all, one can hardly practice this. But SOME parts of the communal dynamics, notably some trust, must precede all legislating. It must permeate even the first attempts to formulate laws, build institutions. Another obvious example is conflict resolution. Initial trust and willingness are necessary prerequisites.

The following are the advantages of the sort of communal dynamics advocated here over national, religious, political loyal ties. First, the latter are exclusionary, regardless of character. You are born Dutch. If that determines your basic loyalties, it is something not within your power to have or not to have. On the other hand, building character is to a large extent in one's own hand. Hence it is a sound source for loyalty, and does not rest on properties that one has involuntarily. Besides, one can have firm ties to nation or church, and still be a thoroughly antisocial person who is only a hindrance in communal matters. Communal dynamics is furthermore such an aim that its realization presupposes some of the virtues it contains. We can install appropriate communal dynamics only if our mode of installment is humane.

There is nothing in this account that prevents power or achievement to be one of our key aims. But these "goods" must be acquired and maintained within the framework of sound communal dynamics. Cooperation above competition remains the guiding light.

As an example, the following would be ingredients in an adequate communal dynamics in some contexts.

1) Capacity to understand the laws and have an interest in these.

2) Interest and capacity for education needed for informed voting, in regard to accountability and knowledge of issues at hand.

3) Trust and respect or concern.

4) Civic friendship.

As we can see, this involves both reason and emotion since it contains partly attitudes in which those two are intertwined. We want a community with cooperation, purposeful lives of members, intelligence and character as background for appropriate laws encapsulating directives needed for individual ideal realization and maintenance of adequate community.

To claim conceptual priority for one thing over another is to claim that the conceptual specification of one thing depends in non-empirical, theoretical ways on the conceptual specification of some other element. Thus first we spell out the three ways in which it is claimed here that the specification of the communal dynamics is conceptually prior to the specification of the legal and institutional structure of a given community.

First, we claim that there is an overlap between the concepts in terms of which one describes the communal dynamics and those that play important roles in describing standard laws and institutions, and the employment of these concepts in communal dynamics has a priority over the employment in the descriptions of laws and institutions. Trust serves well as an example of these conceptual relations. Trust plays ethical roles on three levels. It is a virtue in most theories of individual ethics. Trusting in appropriate circumstances, even when there is not enough evidence to judge reliability, is needed in human character to deal with forced option between trust and distrust, when the choice of the former can lead important cooperative activities.

It is easy to move from the above to seeing that trust is a key element in communal dynamics. (A former Secretary of Defense said at a Ph.D. examination that without initial trust one cannot build a well functioning cooperative decision-making body.) Trust is needed in order to provide interpersonal links in the community that will provide an attitudinal context for the development of respect, approval and other positive attitudes. But trust is also needed in making explicit presuppositions for various laws and institutions. As Tom Tyler pointed out,[6] a legal system defining crime and punishment functions at its best when the citizens have

---

6 Tyler, *Why do People Obey the Law*.

trust in the reasonableness of the laws, and have a basic understanding of these. One could add that without minimal trust in the
laws the system could not function at all. Thus we see that trust
must be a part of a full description of how the law works. But this
trust is not itself generated by laws and rules, but emanates from
an adequate communal dynamics.

We find the same conceptual dependency in connection with
the notion of freedom. This can be seen in the case of so-called
free elections. A certain amount and type of freedom must be a
part of the communal dynamics. Without this responsibility or
respect for an allegedly autonomous person could not arise. Some
of this freedom also becomes part of what is called free elections.
We need to specify what kind of freedom is involved. Freedom
from brainwashing, external force, racist exclusion, etc.? Ultimately the kinds of freedom included in any particular political
context will depend on communal agreement and dynamics.

We also face the question: "for what kinds of persons are we
defining the free elections?" What are minimal qualifications? Age,
intelligence, having served the country? Some modern philosophers think that we define free elections for all creatures that have
the faculty of autonomous rationality. But this complex notion
must be broken down into further constituents. Some of these will
be moral capacities. We must rely on the communal dynamics to
bring out what is seen by the community as in moral contexts the
ability to think about practical questions on "one's own," envisaging all possible alternatives, rank these in terms of value and having the imagination to construct varieties of implementations, taking into account variations in context. There are also philosophers
who believe that free elections are simply, a priori, necessary
ingredients of any adequate social–political structure, and thus
independent of commitment to any communal dynamics. This
view faces considerable difficulties. Would we want "free elections" (now purely structurally defined; human goes to place X,
fills out questionnaire Q, places object in box B, etc.) for people
who are not given a sufficient variety of candidates to choose from,
have been brainwashed or drugged, and do not understand what
elections could be that are not defined simply by divinations?
"Free elections" depend on the electorate being made up at least
partly by those approximating the ideal of FREE persons. There

may be much disagreement on what a free person is; e.g. must it be an individual who knows what responsibility is and how to carry it out well, or some minimal personal freedom must be part of the structure. Without this, election could be just a ritual performed by robots, or robot-like creatures that can move, punch cards, and can place cards in boxes.

The second way in which communal dynamics is conceptually prior to the institutional framework is its shaping the latter. This amounts to conceptions of adequate communal dynamics actually forming and formulating what kind of a legal system and what kinds of political rights and obligations as well as opportunities a given community should maintain. The extent to which such shaping is desirable, and the ways it is supposed to function is a matter of dispute. At this stage only the fact of conceptual dependence is demonstrated. Whether this is good or not, and whether such dependency is acknowledged by the different societies affected is a further issue. For example, free elections in many political theories entail certain levels of education among the citizenry (as suggested by John Dewey). The question then arises as to how a given level and kind of education should shape a given social–political institution. In large parts of South Africa prior to the collapse of Apartheid the citizens did not know what voting was, what responsibilities it brings with it, and what consequences it has. Hence the first election that was attempted dealt only with simple questions about a scheme for a constitution, and not with the complex matters of party politics we see in Western European and North American countries. Furthermore, since there was no other available human resource at hand, the members of the political parties had to take a hand in explaining voting to large segments of the population. This involved a tremendous risk of trust. One had to trust the political parties that they would really instruct people in voting in terms of procedure, and not use the opportunity for brainwashing, and creating many ignorant part-fanatics, and so on.

The communal dynamic in existence can also shape the form of the judicial system. One cannot expect global rules about how to train and certify judges and lawyers. Hence a plurality of communal traditions and opportunities will determine who practices meeting out justice, and what the appropriate procedures should be.

We shall turn now to the third type of priority; namely the priority of choice of communal dynamics over the question of the range of application of laws and institutions. If we have a certain legal system, for what kinds of creatures is it designed? The simple answer: "for humans" in an inadequate response for the following reasons. A constitution constructed under the assumption that some humans have a slave-like mentality and are not capable of creative reasoning will look different from one that assumes creative rational capacities to be universal. Economic theories also tend to be based on different assumptions about human nature. For example, socialistic theories tend to assume strong cooperative capacities spread universally, and equally universally choices indicating high priorities for cooperative activities and less value placed on competitive values. Some versions of capitalism, however, assume a widespread commitment to the priority of competitive values over drives to share and enjoy communal work and profit distribution. The situation is similar to what we discuss in individual ethics as the problem of the range of application of ethical principles. One can opt for some version of categorical imperatives, but this by itself will not specify what the range of application should be; e.g. only friends, only Greeks, only one's own tribe, or anyone with whom we are in contact, or all of humanity. One might object that rules of application could be added to the institutional structures, and thus avoid the priority of the communal dynamics. But this does not work. For if we have rules of application, these will have to be justifiable. And the justifications eventually must reach the communal dynamics. For example, limitations of good conduct to one's friends and the exclusion of one's enemies will eventually be backed by: "but look at how we interact! We just fight and try to dominate." A "reform" movement—such as we see towards the end of Homer's *Iliad*—must rely on deeper layers of interrelatedness and—commonality. For example, pointing out that all those concerned are warriors, facing the same fate, expecting early death, living by the same code for warriors, even if given contextually changing application. A recognition of "we are all in the same boat," not only in classical literature but in modern novels like Albert Camus' *The Plague* can forge a new communal dynamics, with larger groups involved and new attitudes emerging. This will inevitably change the institutions governing law, order, distribution of goods and possession in the community.

A similar example can be given from the treatment of a "free speech" issue in Singapore. At one point pornography appeared on many newspaper/magazine stands. Some people objected to this, others did not. Eventually the government called for a vote on this. The people voted by a considerable majority against allowing the pornography on the stands, and so these were taken off. One must discuss the issue of priorities between minimal limitation on free speech and publication on the one hand, and an environment in which what the community regards as healthy for young people as well as not offensive to others, on the other. It is not plausible to think that the difference will be settled by reference to rules. The debate should be rather conducted within the framework of discussions of what kind of a community the majority wants.

The three aspects of priority introduced also work well in the case of medicine. Practices and institutions of healing and curing involve—among others—the following issues. Is there an agreement among the affected parties that medicine is not just a way of making money, or a way to please people, but has its own built in values, including the construal of health as a final end—in addition to its instrumental values—and that it cannot be reduced merely to what people want or what pleases them? A further and relevant property of health is that it is both needed in spelling out the institutional and legal structure of a variety of institutions (hospitals, etc. related to it), and it is also a key element of communal dynamics, since we specify ethically relevant attributes as caring, concerned, kind and others that are constituents of the communal dynamics of any adequate institute of healing. Furthermore, the communal dynamic will shape the institutions. For if that dynamic stresses the humane qualities of a physician, then the institution will have to provide in its structure stress on clinical instruction rather than concentrating solely on the scientific and technological aspects of healing. Furthermore, in medical schools there is the well-known struggle over the relationship between the orientation towards research and the interest in healing individuals with not only "interesting" but also everyday illnesses.

Finally, in the case of medicine too, the question of range of application of the rules and opportunities arises, not only in terms of whether access to healing should be a matter of who can pay, but also in terms of age, and the question whether predictable further duration of life should enter in the extent of the effort made to heal and prolong life.

Someone might object and claim that the dependencies and relations claimed above hold only in the "good" communities, but bad communities can survive on a minimal level even if the relation between institutional structure and communal dynamics is not considered. If we think of the links in causal terms, then such a claim collapses right away. For example ignoring the plight of the poor leads to the state of mind: "if they don't work, we don't sleep."

Furthermore, the conceptual links in cases like hospitals and schools must be present since they play a role in how we define these institutions. The possible ignoring of the links seems more imaginable in the case of the political units. To be sure, we must grant the possibility of the existence of communities without the links mentioned above, but that is because these are communities without a complete political theory. At a minimal level a complete political theory requires a sketch of laws and institutions, a statement about the relation between the institutions and communal dynamics and, if deemed relevant, a description of what an adequate communal dynamics would be. A political theory that does not meet these demands turns out to be incoherent. If possible conflicts between the proposed abstract structures and the predictable communal dynamics are not settled by the theory in terms of justified priority relations, then the theory is incomplete.

Other aspects of incompleteness include justification solely in simplistic terms like "God wants it this way." Such a claim would have to include an account of the nature of deity that is invoked in the justification. Or in other cases the institutional structure includes means and opportunities for torture, and the projected dynamics is simply fear. Fear is a very fragile communal tie. It can break as soon as the political situation changes, and the external pressure on citizens that pushed them together is no longer there.

It seems, then, that any political or communal theory should confront the challenge of claimed conceptual priority in the three senses articulated above. Accepting the priority of the communal dynamics allows us to include it among the final aims of a joint individual–social ethics. We can also construe various proposals of political structure as means to the achievement of a certain communal interaction and level of welfare.

Viewing political structures in this way is hardly popular today. Many persons regard their own favorite political or economic theory and ensuing structures as ends in themselves. There are, however, great advantages to the view advocated in this paper. For if political structures are means to final human ends, then we need not be so dogmatically rigid, and in our discussions with others who hold on to different political and economic structures we can treat the differences as different means to a common end. We agree on what we want a community to be like, and then see the institutional proposals as suggestions for appropriate means. Within such a framework for dialogue we could also entertain the hypothesis that in different cultures at different stages, some political–economic structure might be better than others, and perhaps there is no political–economic theory that is the best for all societies. On a modest scale, if we do hold on to certain features and not complete descriptions of the communal dynamics as needed in any adequate societal structure, then we can have an objective grounding of our ethics, with contextual and even in some cases relativistic conceptions of institutional implementation. Let us look at this in terms of a few examples.

One of these is the recent change in political and economic structures in Russia. Very crudely, during communism the state took care of individual citizens through its institutions. Individual initiative and related responsibility was scoffed at. Unfortunately this is being replaced with institutions within which free individual initiative is allowed to spread without barriers, and without any official link, or link via an adequate communal dynamics, to responsibility. (E.g. such responsibility would lead to trying to keep the gap between the wealthiest and the poorest from becoming wider.)

Given the priorities explicated above, such an approach is thoroughly misguided. An attempt to create adequate communal dynamics would be concerned with showing first in small steps how individual initiative can be, and should be, combined with responsibility. Relying on such practices as already in action, such as family ties, one could show how, even outside of family, in healthy interactions individuals should show concern for other individuals. (Such moves have been encouraged by some foreign investments.)

There used to be a "Messianic" element in political theory such as communism that said that "in the long run, the system will work." To this J.M. Keynes replied: "in the long run we are all dead." But one can detect similar "Messianic" elements in current moves to spread capitalism and democracy. Obvious obstacles are shrugged off as "temporary." There is no sound evidence for any of these futuristic predictions; in fact, some of my colleagues in our economics department pointed out that as of now there is no good empirical evidence to support the claim that there MUST BE a way in which a socialist–communist society can be transformed into a capitalist–democratic one. Given the outlook and proposals of this paper, the choice should NOT be represented as between the shopworn dichotomies of communism–capitalism, democracy–police state. It is more in line with this essay to consider four factors: some personal/political freedom, some form of justice in court, some level of security, and some level of quality of life, including not only economic well-being, but also the opportunities of achieving pride in one's work and being able to construe it as contributing to the community in objectively sound ways. The communal dynamics can be seen partly as relating to these four factors as we shall show shortly.

It is then a further empirical question as to which of these combinations can be realized in which country, depending on variations in historical processes, cultural factors, current communal dynamics and other such factors. The view I am laying out in this paper remains AGNOSTIC with regards to what will happen "in the long run," and with regard to how much similarity should be aimed at concerning institutional frameworks between different countries.

The second example is the stream of changes taking place in China. Outsiders want to promote capitalism, again without the component of responsibility, and try to rely on some version of Human Rights doctrine to help inject more humaneness in various political–legal interactions. This is a typical case of not considering the current communal dynamics, 5000 years of history, and hoping that bringing in new structure will by itself solve key problems. An alternative way would be to start with the conception of the family as a right and relatively self-sufficient unit, and then gradually show how the dependencies that the traditional family illustrates are needed today in larger units. In this way the kinds of relations typical in a well functioning family can become the focus of attention, rather than the concrete structure of the family by itself. Such extensions, or arguments of similar sorts that take something good from the existing communal dynamics, try to expand and reshape it and use it as a part of the underlying communal dynamics for new structures, are likely to be more successful in effecting healthy social–political change than the institutional change based Western approaches. In the course of such work one can also clarify such notions as looking up to elders for advice. In my teaching in Singapore I was confronted with the students' questions as to why they should follow the advice of elders when these are not familiar with modern technology. In reply I pointed out that there is much that technology can teach us but there are also other types of questions, such as which values and virtues are likely to be long-lasting, and which ones provide the basis of loyalty and of finding meaning in our lives. These are questions that technology does not answer, but under usual circumstances the elders are in a better position to answer than most others. Similarly, whether the young offspring should or should not become a physician is a question concerning which input can be provided by different types of people, but on some questions concerning the humane qualities needed in the practicing physician, the elders still have a lot to contribute.

These examples show that changes in the communal dynamics can contribute a great deal to facilitate sound changes in society, and that it is most unlikely that mere institutional and legal changes can bring these changes in the communal dynamic about.

The four factors: freedom, security, justice, and quality of life, including pride in work and accomplishments, need different ways of interrelation and fixing proportions and priorities. In some small countries, sandwiched between two "giants," security seems more important to people than certain aspects of freedom. In other countries that are large, and have no fear of external forces, security is less critical, and there is more stress on individual free-

dom. It is senseless to ask: "Who is right?" Priorities and proportions must match the circumstances and historical traditions.

In some societies that are changing from extreme autocratic
rule to a more representative legal system justice will seem more
important than mere quality of life. In other societies the emphasis will be the other way around.

We can relate the four ingredients to ingredients of a sound
communal dynamics in the following way.

In deciding how much and what kind of freedom (free
from...what? Free to do what?), the underlying communal dynamic should include respect, and thus a basic agreement on what is
to be respected in people and on what ground, need be considered
as well. Having this kind of communal dynamics does not give us
a decision procedure on circumscribing freedom, but it creates
some of the structure and the needed underlying attitude and outlook for the negotiations.

The same considerations apply to security. Arrangements for
security can be made on a more self-centered basis, as the "walled
camps" of expensive groups of houses outside of San Francisco
show. Quite different structures become available if members of
the community possess another element of the adequate underlying communal dynamic, namely concern for the welfare of the
other members. This underlying element can guide the development of such diverse arrangements as neighborhood watch, police
forces working together with various welfare organizations, and the
development of agreement on what is being punished, if needed,
and why.

The third ingredient, justice, also admits of a variety of conceptions and implementations, with the proviso that probably in
different cultural and economic contexts different judicial structures will be the most desirable ones. A system of justice does not
work well in a community unless people understand it and respect
it, and have developed trust in the various elements entrusted with
administering and enforcing laws. So trust and respect in the communal dynamics are needed as the background for developing and
maintaining justice.

Finally, in developing a consensus on what should be included under the rubric of quality of life in a given community, and
which ingredients need special stress, it makes a great deal of dif-

ference whether the quality (qualities) are construed purely in individualistic terms (what each individual should have) or partly in terms of what constitutes the communal good, specified in ways in which this cannot be reduced to mere sums of individual happiness. The following serve as illustrations.

A community may want to build a hospital. Hospitals are typically designed to deal with illnesses of various types, not only those widespread among the builders of the institution. Furthermore, these public structures are designed to serve an indefinite number and kinds of people; not only the community as it exists at the time of building. Thus we can look at the hospital and its staff and their functioning as serving both individual and irreducibly communal aims.

Similar things can be said about schools and education. Schools too are built and staffed with an indeterminate future generation in mind and with needs to be served that may become evident only a long time after the construction.

It should be noted that not all communal aims are as laudable as our two examples. For example, assuring that a given state will become and remain a great power in a certain region can be a communal aim. In such cases the problem is not that the members of the community have communal aims, but that these are misguided. It is difficult to see how one can argue that having maximum power in the hands of a few in a region will create a happier and more cooperative community. The motives for such communal aim are more likely to be greed or unjustified insecurity.

These remarks, then, suffice to show the extent to which—for better or worse communal dynamics in all three of the senses specified—is conceptually prior to institutions and laws that serve to define the legal status of the society.

2. What is to be Done?

It is a common mistake in moral and political philosophy to consider the question of what are better or worse individual or communal ethics in terms of how one would build a society "from scratch." We rarely face such challenges. To some extent one might think of the origin of the United States that way, if we abstract from the people who already lived here at the time of the arrival of the Pilgrims. People from diverse parts of the world came to "neutral ground" to start something new that was to serve all of these humans and successive generations. Even in this case we do not start from "scratch" since the people coming already had communal experiences and had most likely various conceptions of how to live together and relate to each other. Still, new constitution had to be written and law established.

In practical context we consider a society "in mid-stream," already having laws, institutions, and some kind of communal dynamics, no matter how incoherent. The realistic questions center on: how to transform what there is into something better. Perhaps theoreticians mistake at times the claims of objectivity for the claims of "looking at things from the outside." Objectivity claims that we should attempt to articulate our recommendations from as neutral and unprejudiced standpoint as possible. But one can be inside a community and insist that by any reasonable objective point of view there is a desperate need to improve the medical service.

Chapter IV

DEVELOPING ADEQUATE COMMUNAL TIES

The introduction showed that adequate communal dynamic must underlie the rules and regulations of a thriving community. In this chapter we give a more detailed analysis of what an adequate communal dynamic is. This analysis shows that at the core of the adequate dynamic we find communal ties. That is to say, among the cognitive and emotional elements that a critical mass in a community should share, the most important elements are those that function as binding the community together. There may be many other elements in a communal dynamic: shared activities, regard for different but compatible values, favorite leisure activities and others. Every community must manifest some cooperation. This chapter argues for the basis of cooperation to be cognitive and emotive elements that enable us to view each other as members of the same community, and shape the modes of cooperation and attitudes that we have towards each other as members of that community. At times fear and suspicion play large roles in holding a community together. The view of this chapter is that such communities are built on quicksand. Fear is directed typically against some external element. Such elements can come and go, thus providing a very fragile basis for the communal cooperation. The same holds for financial rewards binding people together. These have a very contingent mode of being. The rewards can disappear overnight, and the community ends in strife and chaos.

The main proposal is, then, that the key elements of the communal dynamic should be certain cooperative values and attitudes. A community based on this can be construed as a value-based community, for the ties that bind it are certain normative attitudes and conceptions. The contrast between a value-based community, a species of which is the community based on adequate communal ties, and the standard community based on laws, rules and institutions is a key to our approach. At the same time, we should stress that membership is a matter of degrees in the value-based case, and there is an overlap between the two types. Some communities are based both on adequate communal ties and on institutions that are equally important but at the same time in harmony with the ties.

In order to see the difference, let us take two extreme cases from both types. A paradigmatic case for the value-based community is the early Christian community. (Other, secular examples that come to mind are the reading groups focusing on interpreting classical texts that function in various English and American universities.) In these communities key values are shared voluntarily. These values include both shared aims in term of what is to be accomplished, and in terms of the ties that determine our modes of cooperation and the constraints of internal competition. Some rules and procedures develop in order to keep the functioning regular and predictable. But these are of limited importance and could be changed without touching the essence of the community. The same applies to our religious example from an early stage at which politics, earthly power, have not yet infiltrated the communal structure—as far as one can tell. The aims in terms of achievement are harmonious with the ties that bind the community. There are procedures, but as we see from what we know of this group, the procedures (who does what menial work) are of limited importance and could be changed without any major rearrangement of aims and ties.

A typical standard community is the early Roman Empire. It was held together by laws and rules, and the fear of the population from those in power. In some periods there was a common worship of the emperor, but there is no evidence that this was voluntary or sincere. Maybe the ruling class was held together partly by pride, but that is hardly a durable tie. It can change with any political upheaval. In this respect it is very different from trust or respect.

In some modern states or social communities people work for a mixture of both types. The degree of success in such enterprises is not up to this essay to determine. There are also other candidates for what holds a group together. For example political views, aims for producing certain goods, religious wars. All of these are woefully fragile in comparison with what in this chapter we see as genuine ties. Most importantly, if these items become values by themselves they do not determine the natures of interaction in a community. Efficiency can leave a group constantly fighting with each other and religious warlords are no more likely to be humane and caring than non-religious ones.

Finally, in these introductory remarks it must be stressed that in many communities we need both virtues as ties and laws as rules, but the key point of this essay is the matter of conceptual priority. The rules are mere means—at their best—to the harmonious functioning of the communities in accordance with the cooperative communal ties. Trust must come first, efficiency and power distribution second.

One might object that this could hardly be an adequate analysis of a typical political community since sharing values by itself does not require construing ourselves as being regulated by laws. And indeed, as defined one can sketch a value-based community that cuts across political or economic boundaries. At the same time, in thinking about political units one should keep in mind that being a political unit and being a value-based community can coincide. At least we can aim at such coincidence, and since that is a matter of approximation, the realization of such a coincidence can become a matter of development taking up years or even decades. For example, one would hope that South Africa will embark on such a journey.

In order to place the notion of a value-based community in proper focus, several points need to be cleared up. First, some philosophers like M. Walzer and D. Bell have in their political philosophies placed the normal legally defined community into the group of central ethically relevant philosophical conceptions.[1] For example, if the law-based community within which one happens to find oneself is oriented either towards a purely legalistic conception of what defines membership, or it is oriented towards shallow values of self-interest, one could ignore the demands of that community in favor of adhering to the norms of the value-based community to which one belongs. The two authors mentioned are at times labeled "communitarians." The same label is applied to

---

1 Bell, *Communitarianism and its Critics*; and Walzer, *Spheres of Justice*.

Etzione.[2] However his theory still takes the individual as the onto-logically fundamental element in adequate conceptions of political communities. Our theory regards the individual and the community as equally fundamental. Each has its claims and potentialities. The two—as we saw earlier—are intertwined. Within our theory neither has foundational priority.

In bringing into the discussion the value-based community we tried to answer the question, aired already in the introduction, of why not just stick with legally defined communities.

We then sketched a conception of adequate communal dynamics within which that dynamic is construed as embodying or striving to embody a value-based community. Finally, in this chapter we also need to show why a value-based community should center on adequate communal ties. This conception contains the claim that societies can be changed by direct intervention in fundamental ways. Before we define "value-based community," we need to spend some space on considering social change, its varieties, its possibility and its limitations.

It may seem obviously true that communities and societies can change in various ways, but our theory also requires that we humans can change societies by conscious reflection and choice. The possibilities of this dimension are at times judged much too optimistically. For example, it is assumed by many people today that one can change any society based on Marxist social and economic principles into a capitalist society. But in fact this has never been done before. Nobody can be sure that it can be done. It is also unclear whether economic structures themselves can be changed without doing a great deal of damage to other aspects of communal life. Furthermore, already existing aspects of communal life in a given society, together with traditions and cultural values, might make drastic transitions less feasible. Even if feasible, we do not know what realistic predictions for a time-span for such changes might be. The extent to which people can change their society depends, not surprisingly, on psychological rather than economic factors.[3] In one society, such as South Africa, the prospects of change, achieved gradually, might be better because

---

2 Etzione, *Rights and the Common Good*.
3 Fogel, *Without Consent or Contract*.

in that society there are a large number of people who have patience and understand the complexities of their situation. In other countries where traditions and other psychological factors do not engender an atmosphere of patience, like in many East-European countries, the prospects for the gradual evolution and development of new types of communal life and structures might be more dim.

Adding to a law-based community an appropriate underlying dynamics is not an all-or-nothing affair. It cannot be done "once and for all." Moving in that direction is partly a matter of conscious resolution, and maintaining such a status is partly a matter of conscious vigilance.

In these respects mere laws and regulations differ from attitudes, or combinations of laws and attitudes. Laws can be changed more quickly, and more drastically; e.g. abolishing the legal backing for slavery. But the attitudes needed to make the laws effective and help transform society often take much more time and effort. Furthermore, a thriving community requires stability. This cannot be merely a matter of keeping certain laws intact. With changes in cultural contexts, laws necessarily change their meaning whether we like it or not. (E.g. consider the meaning of "property" as Locke used this word, with its meaning applied today to the thorny issue of whether one computer company in California "stole" ideas from another.) Hence the underlying stability must be founded on basic ethical attitudes that can endure even through periods in which either laws or their interpretation undergo considerable change. Both the human ability and need to plan, and the challenge of carrying out responsibilities well, require stability in our individual and social lives. These reflections need to be taken into consideration as we ponder the philosophic problems of how much change is desirable for the community.

We turn now to the definition of the value-based community.

1. Definition of the Value-based Community

DEF.: A valued-based community consists of a collection of humans associated by some tie or ties that are thought by these humans to have both instrumental value and value as ends in themselves. Members of this community partake of cooperative activities in order to realize something that is thought by the members to have some value, and for the realization of which such association is necessary.

Ideally one could construe a religion without a clerical hierarchical structure, as such a community. Members could be widely dispersed across national and geographical boundaries, and only the sharing of certain religious and ethical ideals, including ideals of how to relate to each other, would tie them together. One can think along similar lines of a community of physicians, across political boundaries, who are dedicated to the development and maintenance of humane caring attitudes in medicine. In this case too, the nature of the shared aim dictates a certain set of attitudes and interactions among the practitioners.

This kind of a community differs from one specified purely in terms of procedural values.[4] For while certain procedures may instill certain values in people, in some cases this does not happen, or even if it happened, after a while the procedures remain but without the underlying attitudes.

Our notion of a value-based community is both wider and more narrow than the usual everyday notion of a community. It is more narrow, since there may be communities that are tied not by shared values but only by laws about certain modes of conduct and cooperation that have been handed down through centuries and the rationale of which has been forgotten or ignored. For example, mere fear can hold together—temporarily—a community and its obedience to laws, without members sharing any significant part of what we called in chapter I. ideals. Countries or other political communities disintegrate at times because the citizens fail to share any significant values.

At the same time our notion is also wider than the usual one. For essentially it is on shared values that determine individual and community-oriented aspirations, and it does not say anything about legal or ceremonial ties that we typically associate with communities. The reason for this is that our theory regards the notion of a value-based community as fundamental in a normative sense. This is what various collections of humans should try to

4 Hampshire, *Innocence and Experience.*

embody. This proposal does not deny that there are differences between various kinds of communities—in our sense—and that the different concepts of what a community is also have different problems and challenges. Our claim is that if the community is an adequate value-based community, then it will find it easier to cope with specific problems, adding to our account more specific demands for certain attitudes and rules.

Within our account individuals and communities have equally fundamental ontological status. There is no room in this theory for reductionistic theses, either favoring individual or states. Equally important valuational statements are made about both kinds, and these are semantically not reducible to the other either way. Individuals have to decide ultimately how much importance they assign to their intellectual endeavors, and communities need decide what kind of a school they want to build. A communal decision is not treated in the work as a mere sum of individual decisions, in the same way in which a declaration of war is not a sum of individual decisions.

Within a value-based community both individuals and communities have value, as final ends. Within such communities the quality of our interactions and the attitudes that we have towards each other are among the things we cherish most. Such communities can also give us the best hope for providing some of the most sought after items in the world today, such as security, friendly relations, and the appropriate framework for developing what we called in the first half of the book adequate individual life-ideals.

The definition presents being a value-based community as a matter of degrees. For it provides room for such questions as: how widely are values shared? How well developed are the communal ties? To what extent do the existing institutions have underlying human attitudes? Furthermore, being such a community is not something we can establish once and for all. Sharing values and maintaining ties is a constant stream of activities. Maintenance can deteriorate, and what was valuable can be lost without millions becoming aware of this. To be sure, maintaining a legal framework also requires maintenance. E.g. we need to modify, reinterpret laws, and consider new areas of implementation. This can be seen even in such simple cases as traffic laws. But far more of a total effort, involving intellectual as well as emotional factors, is required for the maintenance of attitudes such as those that constitute adequate communal ties.

The fact that being such a community is a matter of degrees should not be confused with the other feature of our definition, namely that it provides room for evaluations of whether a community is better or worse. For not all ties are equally adequate, and the same goes for communal activities and aims. A community may have a clear commitment to communal ties and aims, and to these having final value, but it may have an inadequate conception of what an adequate communal tie is, or what is a desirable aim for a community to have. For example, a society might believe that increase in material goods for all will decrease tensions built around religious or ethnic differences, and this belief can be shown to be false by subsequent developments. Alternatively, we might assume that extended communal dialogue would impede economic progress, and then find out that in fact such correlation does not hold in many cases.[5] Slow economic changes accompanied by much attention to the qualities of communal life might bring more lasting results than pushing a strange and new economic structure on people, awakening new tensions and frustrations that eventually negate whatever economic progress was achieved.

In our examination of values, value maintenance and contextual implementation as involved in value-based community theory, we will need the following distinctions among values.

a) General values, such as trust, honesty, and caring attitude.

b) Constituents of values; e.g. what should count as constituent of trust within domains, such as relations between neighbors or international arms control.

c) Contextual specifications of values, such as describing what should count as being dressed so as to help maintain health, in Tanzania, and Yellowknife, Canada.

d) Values as means, in contrast with being unqualified general values, and constituents.

Equality as such, for example, is a general value. Agreement on this entails the acceptance of treating humans as equals in

---

5 Dasgupta, "Well-being and the Extent of its Realization in Poor Countries."

appropriate ways and with respect to the appropriate parameters, and the conviction that this is both a final and instrumental good. This characterization shows the need to go on to contextual specifications. In a given context, what are appropriate ways, and parameters? These differ depending on whether we are dealing with hospitals, schools, or political units. Furthermore, even on that level we need to distinguish between different cultural and historical contexts. Cutting across the distinction between the general and the more specific and contextual is the distinction between value and constituent. Intelligence is often assumed to be valuable, but we need to settle on what the constituents of intelligence are. E.g. only inductive reasoning, or also practical reasoning? Is reasoning about values included, and also creativity? Finally, there is a familiar distinction between ends and means, ultimately also involving the distinction between final and instrumental value. The complexities of this dichotomy have been discussed in the last century in an outstanding way by John Dewey, and the results of this work will be utilized in subsequent chapters.

The first part of the definition says that both a value-based community as such, and adequate communal ties are human final ends.[6] This does not exclude their also having instrumental value. In the ethics of Plato and Aristotle a discussion of some item having intrinsic value is linked to showing that these also have instrumental value. A value-based community has the obvious instrumental value that it can function as the underlying element for the legal system of a regular political community. It has also other obvious instrumental values for families, friendships and other communal entities.

It has value as an ultimate human end, because it serves as the basis for justifying different proposed values and relationships among members of a community. At the same time, it itself does not depend for justification on some further level of goodness. The question: "why should we base our laws on ethical considerations?" does not admit of an answer in terms of further justifications. One can point to factors such as self-respect, autonomy, self-determinations, all of which are involved in construing the value-based community as we do here. But these values are not "higher"

---

6 I am indebted on this point to K. Korsgaard.

than what constitutes a value-based community. They are interrelated with the notions that define the latter type of community. Humans who want to have opportunities to reconsider and revise their basic values, as life goes on, want their laws and institutions to rest on a value-based community, so that norms will determine customs and not the other way around.

As an alternative one might suggest that communal structures have only instrumental values. They provide values of various sorts, safety, opportunity to increase wealth, etc. for the individuals who are the members. This purely instrumental role is rejected already by what we said at the end of the first part and the introduction to the second part of this work. If, as suggested, individual and communal values are as intertwined as was presented, then we cannot cut out conceptually an allegedly purely communal realm of value and construe this as purely instrumental. Within our conception both individual and community are on equal ontological and moral footing. Hence the communal structures are not merely of instrumental value to the individuals, and the individuals are not of merely instrumental value to the state or other political unit.

The following argument supports considering the communal ties as not only key components in a communal dynamic, but also to serve as parts of what are ultimate human ends.

Ties need not be construed as intrinsic. One might think of a tie in purely utilitarian terms. For example, business contracts have often that flavor. But we are still faced what William James would have called a forced option. We will have SOME kind of relationship that figures crucially in our interactions with others. Should we not decide on the qualities of these interactions? Nobody is completely indifferent towards such questions as to whether his relations to others is based on fear and mistrust, or mutual hedonistic advantage, based on mutual advantage, or including some aspect that we can see as being an end; such as respect, care, or love.

We will be committed to some conception of our ties with others, even if we refuse to think about it, and exemplify this or that relation without much forethought. We might be moved to opt for cooperative relations within which the emotional and intellectual autonomy of the participants are preserved as much as possible. The ground for this would be that we would consider what reaction our choice of a tie will evoke from others. This is not the same as a Kantian command to universalize. It is simply a prudential guideline. If you behave this way, how will you like it if people follow suit? Such considerations help us to opt for respect and not manipulating others, expressing positive emotion and not just narrowly self-centered attitudes.

This line of reasoning can lead us to opting for ties that show respect for others, and for ascribing the value of ends to these attitudes.

Another line of reasoning starts with the analogy between individual character and communal character. As we saw in the first part, we did not define the good person solely in terms of aims, but also in terms of character. The intuition underlying this choice is that it is not only your aims that matter in life, but given that there are typically many ways to well chosen aims, the way you feel, think and act while you work toward your aim also matters. Character determines how I act as an individual towards other individuals, and what psychological characteristics I want to build up in myself.

Analogously, a community can have aims, but will also have some typical ways in which members behave in communal matters towards each other, and the way the community behaves towards others. Needless to say, these matters of conduct—if these are to be genuinely expressing ourselves—must have appropriate attitudes underlying them.

Thus the choice of tie should be a matter of finding one that we can construe as an end itself, just as we construe individual character that way. Furthermore, the nature of the tie typically determines in part what our attitude and actions towards others and other communities should be. Openness and trust in a community provides at least prima facie grounds for trying to expand these attitudes also towards those outside our community. Since interaction with other communities can hardly be avoided, the same consideration of what we can expect in terms of how our attitudes and actions will affect the other communities applies here too, and should move us towards the cooperative and kind, rather than the merely combative stances.

These considerations show the crucial importance for a community to reflect on what seem to be the ties that bind us together and influence how we treat other communities. The intertwining of the individual and communal also plays an important role here with regard to the learning process. Given appropriate individual attitudes, these can also be used to permeate the communal ones. Likewise, in reverse, an understanding of the kindness and consideration that governs our communal activities can also have an impact on the acts and attitudes of the individuals. These considerations back the claims about what should be included among our ends expressed in the first part of the definition.

Ranking adequate communal ties at the top of our value hierarchy has important consequences for our communal practices, and these consequences mirror some that emerge in the Ethics of Ideals explained earlier. Just as there are clear clashes between adequate individual ideals and the demands of efficiency, so there will be conflicts between the adequate communal ties and the demands of political or communal efficiency. John Rawls stated in his well-known book on justice that fairness must always take priority over efficiency.[7] This statement alone could be used as the foundation of devastating attacks on the social and political lives of most countries today. It says something not at all complimentary about the spirit of our times that Rawls' statement was not taken in this way.

We can enlarge Rawls' point by saying that whatever our conception of the best in human character is, be it fairness in a Kantian frame or our highest ideals in the ethics of this book, it should dominate over matters of efficiency.

Turning to communal ethics, within the value-based community the analogue to character is the nature of the communal dynamics, and in particular the communal tie that determines our attitudes and modes of cooperation among ourselves and in relation to other communities. As Rawls' dictum, this conclusion too could be the basis of a thorough social and political critique that would affect most countries.

The second part of the definition introduces the notion of communal activities. These are activities within which the individual contributions are intertwined and the result can be attribut-

---

7 Rawls, *A Theory of Justice*, section 13.

ed to the community as an agent over and above the sum of its individual members. Some obvious examples in our world are the modernization of society, the forming and implementation of environmental policies, the forming and maintenance of educational institutions, and the maintenance of practices of healing. Within a value-based community communal activities are essential parts of the communal dynamics, in addition to the activities of individual members or groups of these.

Communal activities have aims. This is built into the definition by the third part. These aims are aims of the community and not just the sum of the aims of the members. Communal aims are not the mere compromises between individual or local interest that characterize communities so often. The communal aims presuppose the viability of the notion of the common good as not merely the sum of individual goods.

The development of communal aims and activities requires communal participation. This can take a variety of forms. Loners who fly planes to carry the sick to faraway hospitals do not contribute typically to explicit dialog and discussion of where the community stands, and where it should go. But with their contribution to communal well-being, and their example of a useful lifestyle embodying so many admirable character traits, they too add an important ingredient to communal dynamics out of which consensus should emerge. Good members of a community may differ from each other both in the extent to which they participate in conscious communal reflection and in the ways they contribute to such activities. But as we saw, there are reasons why some conscious communal dialogue about aims and values must take place. This raises the question of a "critical mass" that needs to carry on dialogue. There is no general rule about this. The critical mass will vary depending on the nature of the community, the practical context, etc. Such dialogue should be based on seeking out contributions from members without violating their privacy. Communal discussions degenerate into noise-making contests when those volunteering output are given free hand over those who are by nature less gregarious and less ready to express explicitly formulated views. Furthermore, some issues need expertise. In these cases trust must develop between groups with more expertise and the community at large.

To end, let us stress that an ethical community demands neither conformity within the community nor gregariousness. The implementation and development of adequate communal aims can be helped just as much by those who prefer solitude as by those who need frequent close social contact. A fine example of the former is pilots who work for the Public Health Service at Navajo or Hopi reservations. Their job involves the difficult flying challenge of landing in difficult places on a reservation, loading into the small planes at times gravely ill people, taking off again without causing the ill too much discomfort, and landing at the public health center with the patient still in a relatively adequate condition.

These people want to have the challenge of the difficulty. They are their own bosses in many ways, and contribute to what they can plainly see as the public good. Our theory regards these as vital elements in an adequate society, no less so than the more gregarious who join larger organizations and feel good in the presence of larger crowds.

This discussion of the value-based community and the desirability of its being based on certain attitudinal ties presupposes certain theses in moral psychology. For we saw that in a sound value-based community both individuals and the community set not only instrumental goods and ends that turn into means, but also final ends. We also saw the need to assume the importance of warm affections in a thriving community, be it a hospital, or a crew cooperating on a joint project. Finally, we also see in the articulation of such a community the need to posit types of cooperation that do not rest on mere self-interest.

In view of this, the following moral psychological assumptions are made explicit as required by our theory.

1) It is a necessary truth for the theory that aim setting and aim developing be a part of the communal dynamic. It is an empirical hypothesis that such processes can and do take place in the human psyche.

2) Humans should, and often do, cultivate warm positive feelings towards others, and being the recipient of such feelings has a great influence on moral development.

Humans have the desire to share some items with some people. Thus one of the key tasks of a theory of ideals and value-based communities must be to sketch ways in which this sharing can be expanded, both in terms of the types of items to be shared and in terms of the participants in the sharing.

The first condition contradicts such views as psychological hedonism according to which humans are constructed in such a way that a fundamental desire for pleasure informs all of their practical reasoning. In our theory it is necessary that individuals and communities define themselves, and develop final ends that have not only instrumental but also non-instrumental value. The empirical hypothesis that this can take place and is often practiced by humans rests partly on the denial that a purely mechanistic explanation of humans adopting values, and centering their lives on certain goals, is either necessary or desirable, or backed by empirical evidence. Phenomenological evidence supports the first condition, and since there is no a priori objection to it that could not be refuted—e.g. "the myth of the priority of mechanistic explanation"—and the paucity of empirical evidence supports the rejection of this condition, we should embrace it on the pragmatic ground that anything that fits an adequate normative conception and is neither conceptually absurd nor implausible on empirical grounds should be adopted.

The second condition has its roots within our theory in recent reports by psychiatrists and educational psychologists,[8] according to which experiencing some emotional warmth emanating from someone in the immediate environment early in life is an empirically necessary condition for developing sensitivity towards the suffering of others later on. Within our analysis an adequate communal dynamic is not merely a matter of activity emanating from purely rational reflection. It is a combination of the cognitive and the affective. It is not merely the claim that some emotions facilitate cooperation, but the stronger claim that having certain emotions, and also being able to direct these towards humans outside the immediate surroundings, enables us to understand and deal with others that on the basis of pure reason would not be possible.

Sympathy, love, devotion and care are some of the examples belonging to this category of feelings. It is something sought in family relationships as well as in relations like that between physician and patient. Social problems are at times ascribed to chil-

---

8 Damon, *The Moral Child.*

dren on account of their being emotionally deprived. Philosophically this is a difficult category, since it seems to be basic, not
admitting articulation in terms of definitions. "Warm" functions
here admittedly as a metaphor, not admitting of rigorous literal
characterization. This conceptual difficulty, however, has not prevented philosophers and psychologists from seing the enormous
practical role that such emotions play in human interactions.[9] For
example, maintenance and reinforcement of mental health is
facilitated by receiving emotional warmth from others, and such
warmth also helps with the adequacy of various human interactions. In spite of the definitional difficulty we communicate quite
well about these phenomena, and developed ways to engendering such warmth.

The third condition brings out the importance of sharing for
the theory of this book. Sharing emerges already on the fundamental level, found on both the individual and the communal
level, of sharing values. The thesis that a sound aim-setting and
then a sound communal aim development rest on the non-instrumental value of character in the one case and the communal
dynamic in the other, implies that humans should be ready and in
fact eager to share values with each other. For such sharing will
bring with it the attitudes needed to construct individual character
and communal ties.

From sharing values we move on to sharing experiences seen
as having good consequences or ingredients. These will include
intellectual companionship or sharing of objets/experiences that
have aesthetic value.

We already see these types of sharing at the level of early
childhood. Small children want to show their parents things seen
by them as instances of beauty, or e.g. in offering to share toys, we
see spontaneous efforts to share with a restricted group what is
deemed to be enjoyable.

We see these psychological features developing and maturing
as humans move from childhood to adulthood. Our theory, however, in order to be an adequate foundation for individual and
communal ethics, must also deal with the need and challenge to
share material goods such as food and money.

---

9 For an extended discussion of caring see Noddings, *Caring*.

On one level we can account for such cooperation as self-oriented. As the proverb says: "when they don't eat, we don't sleep." In a society in which sharing is widespread there is likely to be less frustration, enmity, anger, and thus most likely less violence. At this state we want to ask ourselves the question: "do we not want to live in a community in which sharing is widespread?" This is only a very general question. Even if the answer opts for a sharing community, we need to specify the details of such arrangements. We shall see guidelines for this in chapter VI.

Our theory, however, requires in its psychological foundation not only enlightened egoistic sharing but also viewing sharing as not a burden, and indeed, in many contexts as fulfilling activity. We shall see below the philosophical anthropology that underlies positing the reality of such attitudes in a community.

The nature of the underlying communal dynamics and the foundation for adequate communal ties will be spelled out by our account of what a communal tie is, and what criteria of adequacy this notion carries with it. We have already defined the notion of a value-based community. We shall define the notion of a communal tie for this kind of community, with the understanding that being such a community can be a matter of degrees rather than an all-or-nothing division. It has also been stated above that conventional rules and laws can accompany a political structure, where this is seen as the more superficial element in the complex.

2. Definition of a Communal Tie

A communal tie in a value-based community, and thus in a community for which some shared values and some form of cooperation is presupposed, determines essential modes of cooperation and of interpersonal activities in communal matters.

This determination is effected by having certain psychological ingredients, centering on certain values, underlying the appropriate cooperative activities.

The tie must contain psychological ingredients that work towards the maintenance of the community bound by the tie posited. As mentioned already in our definition of the value-based community, the tie must be regarded by the participants as being an end in itself, not having merely instrumental value.

Let us reflect on this definition. First, one might ask why mere cooperation, regardless of people's motives and reasons, is not enough. Maybe the cooperation rests on a contract, maybe on force, maybe on economic incentives? Our reply is that such cooperation is not only fragile at any state, but also contains nothing on which one can base hope for persistence. Such cooperation does not involve the human psyche; it merely tries to inculcate certain behavioral patterns by appeal to physical comfort.

The definition mentions modes of cooperation but at this stage leaves the possible modes wide open. For example, mere habit of obeying laws, identification with an ethic or racial, or religious group would qualify. But when in the next section we turn criteria of adequacy, and present a concrete proposal, this latitude will become drastically cut. Thus this definition says only that the tie needs a psychological grounding. It leaves room for considering better or worse ties. Ties need not be either perfect or bad. In actual practice, there is room for gradations, and these can be outlined along different dimensions. It may also be the case that in different cultures in different contexts one ingredient of the tie is more important than another. The matter of maintenance is of vital concern in our theory. Different values and psychological elements have greater or lesser survival value in matters of cooperation. As the saying goes: "you cannot buy friends." A slogan that may be banal, but is—judging by conduct—not well understood by those responsible for international politics. Some psychological factors may be very intense for shorter periods of time, but have little lasting impact. This is the case in which demagogues sway a crowd.

Aristotle thought that agreement on what is good character, and then joint attempts at realization gives a foundation for persistent bonds. This suggestion is as helpful as efforts to reach some consensus on "character." Some ingredients seem to have the required power. One of these is overcoming frustration. Even when we have good ties installed, impatience and demand for instant success can ruin a community. Overcoming frustration is a very basic ethical value, even if it does not make frequent appearances in books on ethics. We should add also, that in many cases the challenge is to overcome JUSTIFIED frustration and resentment. Presumably this is accomplished when the agent can keep in mind the most important aims and bonds, and this helps him to "look beyond" the injustice at hand, reach for the realization of the more important aims, and let the redress of immediate injustice rest.

The tie applies to many different kinds of value-based communities. Some, like families, are biologically defined as well, some in political terms, and some in idealogical terms. Cooperation in these communities does not always require the same psychological capacities. One might wonder why not list loyalty as an overarching value that helps the persistence of a community with sound ties. But loyalty by itself need not be viewed as a good thing. There is loyalty to good causes, to good friends, communities, and other such social units. But there is also loyalty to criminals, politically power-hungry individuals, abusive family members and the like. There is no reason to suppose that these are desirable character traits, since the consequence of such links is likely to be quite damaging for the agent and for others affected. This holds even if we construe "damage" in the most idealistic and enlightened viewpoint of self-interest.

This is the reason why we do not find loyalty listed by Plato as a virtue. He judges loyalties with their object glued on. Loyalty to Goodness, Beauty, and the like is a good trait, while loyalty to tyrants, sophists, etc. is not. A modern moral philosopher might disagree and attempt to separate loyalty as such from its objects. Thus misguided loyalty would have a good component, and a bad one, involving mistaken judgment concerning the object. Plato and Aristotle seem to treat loyalty "adverbially," like "fast" or "slow." There is nothing good about being fast or slow as such. Goodness and lack of it depends on what it is that we do fast or slowly.

Loyalty is also a bad thing when exclusive loyalty to one cause blinds the person from seeing other compatible objects worthy of loyalty. John Dewey remarks that it is good for a person to be a member of different compatible groups, with different aims affecting different aspects of life, so that the person lives a well balanced life and does not become a political, religious, class-conscious etc. fanatic.

With these general remarks in mind, let us consider the definition clause by clause. The first condition spells out that the communal tie should determine how, for example, desire for profit, cultivation of rationality and drive for increased knowledge, and good will, should blend in a thriving community. Being able to make a living is a necessary condition of adequate survival in modern communities, but attention to the communal tie should place this need as only one among many. To an extent, there is a minimal level at which income is needed, but increasing this should not become an obsession, especially if it is the means to increase harm for others. Again, if the tie includes mutual concern for the welfare of others, then the dominant values in the community cannot be purely competitive. Much of the external goods that the cooperation among others achieved by having this tie could also be reached without the strong demands made on the internal moral psychology that our formulation of this condition makes. But this seems to be one of the advantages of this theory. The second condition demands a way of living and interacting with other humans that makes the cooperative part not a burden, or mere external good, but as rooted in basic concerns, orientation and attitude in the individual. For it places at the foundational level certain attitudes that are cornerstones of both cooperation and of self-improvement. And it places at the center of communal ethical discussion such questions as "what qualities in a human warrant respect? What qualities warrant trust? Concern?" Theses are more manageable and while having an objective conceptual core, these are also more amenable to contextual interpretation.

The third condition confronts us with the task of specifying among desirable psychological ingredients those that are likely to help the community with its values to survive. Some forms of inner conviction are more likely to help persistence than mere fear from outside authorities. But the convictions cannot center primarily on competitive values. Being the most successful salesman, musician, politician or architect are values that do not last, and like being the "best gun in the West" such competitive aims lead always to inner insecurity and thus fear. Cultivating feelings and attitudes of worth are more likely to help persistence, because these can be based on inner criteria that do not depend on popularity among what at a time happens to be our environment. Purposefulness is an important ingredient in meeting condition 3. It helps to unify one's life, and if the aims are well selected, then this unified life will survive upheavals caused by external factors.

Finally, persistence is facilitated if the members are bent on maintaining those attributes that enable them to be conscious, reflective participants in communal life. This is the self-reflexive aspect of our theory. We tend to satisfy the demands of the theory when we try to be good theory formulators and implementers.

In addition to the factors and aspects mentioned, our theory needs to defend the claim that the character traits like respect, concern or care and the intellectual components we reviewed should be seen as enabling conditions rather than constraints and restrictions. One cannot characterize formally an item as an enabling or a restraining condition as such. For in a rigorous formalism we would have a domain A, and a function that divides it. The divided parts can be called B and B-; the choice of which is positive and which is negative is arbitrary. While one can look at respect and cooperation as enabling conditions because they enable us to build harmonious communities, the same attributes can also be construed as constraints, for they curtail strong self-oriented competitive drives for success and acquisition of goods. At times people invoke the notion of human nature, and claim that the cooperative attributes express salient elements of human nature. But this requires an argument that greed, aggression, and similar attributes do not express deep elements of human nature, or at least not the "good" elements. This leads to problems of how to define "good" in this context without begging questions.

Our approach is to treat what is enabling or constraining as a relational predicate. Thus in our work we list selfishness, hedonism, paternalism, drive for power and a few more similar attributes, and say that with respect to these the adequate communal tie is constraining. Then list attributes like being respectful, cooperative, concerned with the welfare of others, and describe the theory as being enabling with regard to these items.

This leaves us with a normative decision concerning what a good theory of individual and social etches should construe as enabling and what constraints it should contain. The answer to that demand is contained in our arguments for what our theory conceives as adequate individual ideals and communal ties. In our stressing that these are normative ethical issues we call attention to the fact that there is nothing that is in some basic sense "repressing." Psychology cannot tell us what counts as repressing or enabling except in reference to its describing a conception of human nature, and any such description relevant to the issue of repression will have to contain ineliminably normative elements.

At this point let us turn to criteria of adequacy for communal ties.

3. Criteria of Evaluation for Communal Ties

The tie should be an important enabling condition for the necessary communal interactions that lead to the formulation and maintenance of communal aims.

1) The tie, with its roots in both reason and emotion, should allow for and facilitate the development of individual ideals as defined in this theory—and it should be in harmony with the approximately adequate ones.

2) The tie should play a key role in creating a value system within which the dominant values include cooperative ones.

3) The tie should be either based on, or at least be compatible with the three morally relevant psychological universals posited in this theory.

4) The tie should contribute to the stability of the community without forcing on members a rigid code of practices.

Intuitively, we can construe the first criterion as playing a key role in forging the right context in which a community can formulate reasonable and justifiable aims that members are likely to adopt. The second condition creates harmony between individual and communal aims, as prescribed by the argument of Chapter III. The third condition states that the tie must not rely solely on elements like fear or competitive tension, and the fourth ones makes sure that the conception of the tie is not psychologically unrealistic. Finally, the tie should guarantee stability in the community insofar as external conditions allow this.

Even a quick glance should convince us that these criteria leave open room for a wide variety of candidates for communal tie. There are different ways of creating an adequate communal atmosphere, individual and communal aims can be reconciled in a number of ways, and many conceptions of a tie can be psychologically realistic. Finally a tie without power to assure some stability is not a "tie" in any practical sense.

After a discussion of the criteria, our own favorite candidate will be presented, and it will be argued that it is adequate and superior to a wide range of alternatives.

The first criterion is justified by the consideration that we will need much communal interaction in a normative community to discuss activities, aims, and interpersonal attitudes, and that not all kinds of ties are equally conducive to create the right psychological back ground for this, such as listening to other people, be willing to consider new alternatives, justify positions, and consider the common good.

Obvious candidates for meeting condition I, would be trust, ability to compromise, seeing what seem at first sight as ultimate ends, as in fact means to some end one shares in common with our opponents—as Dewey suggested—and being able to suppress resentment for the sake of higher values. Even a cursory glance will show us that these items are not on the same level of fundamentality. Trust is a fundamental attitude. But the ability to compromise is a complex attitude, specified here on the surface level. A number of different attitudes can underlie it. For example, belief that a partial victory now can create an atmosphere in which significant changes can be effected later. Or healthy skepticism towards one's own ideas, and thus envisaging as real possibility one's failure.

The second criterion is meant to rule out the ties binding certain fanatic communities, or workaholic orientation in places of work. It does raise the difficult question of how far we can in practice harmonize individual interest, based on individual ideals, and communal interest, based on a conception of the communal good. In our theory the two should be intertwined. In practice conflicts can arise. Hence the problem of priorities. As we saw in our treatment of this issue in part I, there is no simple general answer to the question of which set of interest should have priority. As already frequently stressed in this essay, ethical theory provides guidelines, not decision procedures.

This condition also links the communal tie to the individual ideals discussed in the first part. The "roots" of the tie are certain basic attitudes. As we have seen, these combine reason and emotion. E.g. for trust we need a certain cognitive judgment, and then an accompanying emotion that cannot be identified apart from the judgment that gave its rise. Since the adequate ideals include cooperative attitudes, a natural link is provided between these ideals and adequate communal ties. Furthermore, the development of adequate ideals is greatly facilitated by the agent being in a value-based community with adequate communal dynamic. Adequate ideas are likely to develop in contexts in which the participants have respect for each other, and encourage in each other autonomous thinking and the emergence of autonomy.

The third criterion ensures that in an adequate normative community cooperation will be based on non-competitive values, and not be merely the result of compromises achieved in an atmosphere of constant competitive pressure. If the communal tie has final value, as was argued above, then the mode of cooperation it ensures should also be seen as having such value. This means that the mode should reflect non-competitive virtues.

What leads to an adequate underlying psychological structure? Many ideas can be derived from what both in classical and modern times we call "Civic Friendship."[10] Elements of this can be projected beyond the small tight circle of people we tend to call good friends.[11] Concern for the welfare of others, for example, need not be restricted to a small circle. Awareness that people geographically far removed from us can affect some of our vital interests can become the basis of concern with the welfare of humans with whom we have only indirect contact.

Another source of maintenance is what J. Royce called "loyalty to a cause."[12] Royce does not mean by this loyalty to any fanatic cause. As he develops the notion of loyalty to a cause, this becomes the kind of loyalty that can expand from attitude towards mere cause to attitude towards those sharing the cause. There are loyalties that, unfortunately, end as in the case of Jonestown. But others can end with communities as described in D. LaPierre's *City of Joy*.[13] Communities of the latter kind can face hardship and adversity without the "social glue" dissolving, because the content of the cause to which they are committed demands appropriate ties of care, respect, and concern.

---

10 Aristotle, *Nichomachean Ethics*, Book IX.
11 Schwarzenbach, "On Civic Friendship."
12 Royce, *The Philosophy of Loyalty*.
13 LaPierre, *The City of Joy*.

Some ties will not help bring about persistence. For example, when the tie resolves around prestige and power in the community, or too much stress on rights and not enough on enabling conditions. For example, one may have a voting system within which everyone has a right to vote, but a large percentage of those qualified cannot vote because they have no means and opportunities to go the appropriate place and structure where the voting is to take place. In general, even if the aim is well intentioned, a mode of implementation that leads to much frustration and enmity in the community can end up doing more harm than good. At times a less than perfect system of justice need be tolerated if any realistic implementation in that context would lead to frustration and violence on a large scale.

Inadequate communal ties could thwart the development of good ideals. For example, in a community in which everyone is trained to see his or her worth strictly in the respect or lack of such that the others express towards the agent, good ideal planning becomes very difficult. The same applies to a "cold community" in which members are not experiencing the expression of warm positive emotions in the first few years of their lives.

Another source of poor life planning is a fanatic community. Such a community takes away the sense of self-improvement that participants should feel free to experience as they journey on various paths of towards these overall aims.

Still other contexts in which the community does not foster a healthy development of the combination of the self and other directed attitudes are illustrated in Book VI of the *Iliad*, where (lines 45–65) a warrior is about to show clemency towards his foe and is promptly chastised by his brother for being so soft and not administering justice, which is perceived there as a "help your friends, harm your enemies" principle.

The expression "value system" is ambiguous. One might mean to refer merely to an abstract structure, namely a description of what values humans should have in a context, and how these should be related. But the same term can also denote a "functioning value system" that is a communal life that moves along in accordance with certain ideals, principles, and conventions. Developing such a living system can take a long time. After development comes the equally difficult challenge of maintenance.

At times the maintenance of values requires a martyr. But in most cases a bit of understanding, trust, empathy, cheerfulness and readiness to help others by facilitating their psychological healing goes a long way. This sketch of the everyday complexities of a functioning value system shows why it needs an appropriate communal tie. Such a tie will hold people together both while they build the value system and while they are trying to maintain what is already, not only in words but also deeds, in flow. The building up of the value system requires cooperation. The same can be said about maintenance. An individual by himself cannot maintain a system of values for a community. Hence the requirement that the tie should ensure that among the ends pursued several should be cooperative and not competitive, and that broad outlines of types of cooperation should set the constraints for the exercise of the competitive ones.

It would be a real mistake to try to squeeze all of the types of cooperation needed into one concept such as fairness. Other factors include, in different contexts, degrees of willingness to share goods, extending responsibilities to new areas of joint work and build up trust. None of these can be reduced to fairness; though according to some moralists fairness must accompany all of these tie ingredients.

This proposal does not prescribe equality. It would inject enough of the sound communal tie so that people aiming at a high level of welfare would not do so at the expense of others. But once they meet that condition, the competitiveness of working for a higher standard of living could be exercised, and the mere fact that inequalities would result would not be a blemish on the community. Of course this needs to be qualified by the caveat that different communities with different traditions have a variety of views on mere equality. For example, many Russians would rather have a lower standard of living but only minimal inequalities, while in other traditions larger inequalities are not viewed as a negative aspect of public life as long as everyone's standard is higher in that arrangement than it would be with smaller inequalities. The fourth criterion ensures that adequate communal ties have appropriate psychological foundations. Within our framework there is no special moral sense of good or duty and related motivational sources as in Kantian ethics. But in our theory what others see as unique moral structures can also be derived with an empirically satisfactory psychological background. This condition deals with the adequacy of communal ties and the moral psychology that underlies the notion of a sound value-based community. We spelled out three pillars for the theory of communal ties and related communal dynamic. Herewith a few remarks showing how these underlie some of our requirements for adequate communal life, and what it would be like to have communal ties that are incompatible with this moral psychology.

First, setting non-instrumental, final ends for ourselves and for our communities is such a deep-seated and essential ingredient in our conception of the life of thriving individuals and communities, that it is difficult to imagine a value-based community without it. Our theory ascribes a certain autonomy to individuals and communities. This autonomy is not a mere matter of rights to do this or avoid that, but also the ascription to each agent of the ability and challenge of seeing ultimate ends for a whole life or reasonable parts of it. It also ascribes to the agents the ability to participate in ongoing free reconsiderations of aims and implementations. The freedom involved here is that of rational deliberation not determined by external forces or internal psychological compulsions.

Thus a communal tie that involves unconditional and non-deliberative submission to alleged authority violate this criterion of adequacy. Thus various cults, ideologies that force adherents into thoughtless submission, and alike, are ruled out. We have to admit that satisfying this criterion is a matter of degrees, and that in our age of deliberate manipulation of so-called information it is not easy to draw a line between what is and what is not an acceptable mode of persuasion. But just because a line cannot be drawn sharply, that does not mean that we should not do our best and draw it in context as well as we can.

The second pillar creates difficulties for communal planning. It is one thing to say that we proclaim the need for everyone being linked from time to time to others via warm affective attitudes, but it is quite different to state how a community can help to engender such feelings. This criterion is not meant to be a recipe for the "touchy-feely" society. It is meant rule out societal interactions that in every way tend to reduce the thinking feeling person to a robot-like creature who is taught to react to everything with calculations of utility and regard such as dominating over any feelings such as love, compassion, sympathy and the like. This criterion is difficult to meet also in many cases in which there is no conscious effort to stifle warm affection, but the parameters for human interaction are set in such a way as to minimize the possibility of expressing such feelings. A society can lapse into such a state without anyone planning this. Indeed, it might take an "awakening" to realize that we are lapsing into such a state, called at times "dehumanization." Thus the condition demands quite a lot of the community at large, and also of the individual participants. On the positive side, a conscious realization and implementation of the principle that wealth requires responsibility and compassion tends to help create the atmosphere in which warm feelings are likely to emerge.

The relation between the third pillar and adequate communal ties is intuitively obvious. After all, what good is a tie if it does not tie us together?

Tying us together brings stability and our fifth criterion. What is stability? How does is differ from stagnation? When is it not oppressive?

To meet the condition of stability involves using our rational faculty. For in the practical context rationality entails planning and the development of the right attitudes. But both of these activities require time. We need a certain level of the unchanging in order for planning to be realistic. We must assume that certain factors will remain fixed over the time for which we plan. If everything changes all the time, we cannot predict, consider future alternative, and life becomes chaotic.

Likewise, cooperative activities take time, and we need enough confidence in certain elements in our society and ourselves to remain constant if the activities are to be planned well and the actions actually lead to the desired aim. We also need a degree of stability in order for hope to make sense, and a human life without hope is a disastrous thing.

Friendship and trust enter into varieties of adequate communal ties, and these too require some stability in society in terms of values, external circumstances and political institutions.

Let us now turn to elements that can destroy stability or make it undesirable. One of these is stagnation. The economy or political life can stagnate. When political life stagnates, it becomes boring. This is a real danger for a society, since boredom with, for example, democratic institutions and procedures can facilitate the emergence of demagogues who in turn can turn into dictators.

Stagnation is at times contrasted with change. We must, however, distinguish superficial from deep changes. For example, the persistence of trust and mutual respect in a community are deep elements, and change in these is undesirable. Changes on the more superficial, e.g. technological level are acceptable, even beneficial, provided that these do not damage the underlying communal dynamic.

The kind of stability a thriving community needs is not to be confused with rigidity of laws and institutions. In fact, overly rigid legal systems tend to work against stability. For these are likely to be more specific and thus in the storms of historical change more brittle than less rigid more elastic rules.

The kind of stability that is an ideal ingredient in a communal tie is what we might call dynamic equilibrium. That is to say, a balance between opposing forces that, when checked and modified, can supplement each other. This could also apply to economics. If humans could find a raw material that meets most of their needs, is available to everyone, and is not energy that exists only in some limited way on the planet, then the relationship between desirable communal ties and economic competition could be much closer than what it is now.

4. Proposed Adequate Communal Tie

1) Members of the community respect each other.
2) Members of the community have concern for each other's welfare, and for each other's conception of their respective welfare.
3) Members of the community trust each other in matters deemed to be involving communal issues.
4) Members of the community have a caring attitude towards each other.

In surveying this proposal we must answer the question: In what sense do these ingredients constitute a tie? We think normally of what ties together a community as either legal bonds, or familial relations, workplace, or other social institutions. So could we not see these as somehow basic, and think of the four factors listed above as additional elements, supplementing and strengthening the communal ties? We need also consider the suggestions that a collection of people scattered geographically could have the attitudes listed without forming a community. Do we form a community every time we respect and trust each other? In answer we must remind ourselves that the Communal Ties proposed are to apply to an ethical community in the sense defined above. In such a community cooperative work and shared intentions are already presupposed. This answers the second question: yes, we can have these attitudes outside communities, but the attitudes become very important in the context in which we spell out HOW certain cooperative tasks should be carried out by agents, and what attitudes we expect to be thriving among these agents.

The first question can be viewed in the following way. To be sure, there are political, economic, social, biological and religious concerns that can mould a community. Our theory says that it is not necessary for an adequate community to have these legal–institutional ties. Furthermore, when a community combines what we describe as adequate ties with the other structures mentioned, the proposed communal tie should be seen as most fundamental. That is to say that the political and economic factors may change, and so can our views on what is significant about biological bonds. But the Tie, with its four ingredients should provide the foundations for what will hold people together when engaged in cooperative activities. It remains unchanging in its basic content, while the other factors can undergo drastic change.

As to the need for some legal foundation, this is felt to be a factor because in social–political ethics we look at the state or city as paradigmatic of the communities about which we theorize. But this is misleading. There are communities without legal trappings, and some of these are of central importance in our lives. One of these is friendship. There are no laws regulating who can be friends with whom, or what the basis of a friendship will be. Yet not only does our theory apply to friendship, but some of the ingredients of friendship are good candidates to be built into the fabric of communities of all sorts.

There are other groups, built around a joint interest or mission. The Society of Artificial Intelligence Researchers for Public Responsibility is a fine example of this group. These reflections show that communities based on shared values and cooperation make sense even without legal structure. Furthermore, it makes sense to construe the ties of such communities as centering on the nature of the social life and codes of cooperation that we expect from an adequate community.

Having thus shown the feasibility of the kind of communal tie that we posit as basic, we need to consider why our choice should have this privileged position. In defense of our choice let us briefly sketch popular alternatives.

One alternative is to suggest a combination of specified rights, claims, privileges and responsibilities articulated explicitly and let adherence to these be the basic communal tie. This suggestion is incompatible with what is presented in this work as a community that is also an ethical community and has adequate ties. Mere adherence to a legalistic structure is neither good nor bad. The decisive questions concern the grounds of such adherence. It could be a communal dynamic that resembles to a large extent what is proposed in our theory. Or it could be a fear-driven attitude that leaves the population open to adhering eventually to a different legal structure promulgated by a dictator or small group of adventurers. Furthermore, it would be a real loss if a community adopted such a scheme, and then turned a deaf ear to proposals of how to improve the communal dynamics, just because the proposal runs against the grain of the existing legalistic structure.

While structures as the one sketched create too much rigidity in the community, other possible alternatives, such as love or benevolence leave too many communal values and processes undetermined. Neither love nor benevolence guarantee respect for others, and yet without this element the members do not have the status of an autonomous decision making agent. That notion, however, is crucial to being able to choose and live the life emerging from an adequate Ideal, in our sense. Similar objections apply to benevolence. Benevolence may be a good additional element in the communal dynamics, but it is not a substitute for the kind of cooperation dictated by our four ingredients of the tie.

Finally, one might urge responsibility as a key tie. But responsibility is seen within our theory as a separate underlying notion. Responsibility, as we shall see in the next chapter, permeates all of communal life within an adequate ethical community with adequate ties. But, in our view, it needs to be grounded on other, more fundamental notions. It cannot serve as a self-sufficient basic ground for insuring the right kind of cooperation between autonomous agents.

We still need, however, to take up, in this chapter, the promise made earlier that the proposed tie will be shown to comply with the criteria for adequate ties listed earlier. It will also be shown that the criteria were not set up to imply analytically that only our proposed tie will be adequate. In other words the specification of the criteria and the proposed tie do not form a conceptual circle.

In order to carry out this defense, we will look at the ingredients of the adequate tie in more detail.

The four conditions are expressed in what linguists call the generic construction.[14] To say that "members...do this or that" is like saying "beavers build dams;" we do not mean necessarily most beavers or even all but that this is the natural expected standard by which we define the "healthy beaver." The same applies to the use of "members" in this context. There must be a critical mass of members who meet these conditions. The critical mass will have changes in members and need not be exactly identical across the four conditions. The exact determination of this critical mass across contexts and conditions is impossible. It is not just a question of numbers, but also of kinds. Maybe the collection of humans not meeting one of the conditions is not large numerically, but make up a distinct group in terms of age, ethnicity or some such politically salient characteristic. Under those circumstances the community is in trouble. Furthermore, a member satisfying one of the conditions is a matter of degrees. If there is a loss in trust, or some kind of trust is not built up, how much trust are we talking about? Is the loss of trust primarily directed to the government, or to fellow citizens?

It might seem that for different types of communities, one or the other condition should be more important. This is mislead-

---

14 Moravcsik, "Generiticity and Linguistic Competence."

ing. To be sure, perhaps for some units, like a family, care comes easier and more naturally than respect, and the other way around for political units. But at a fundamental level all four ingredients must play roles in a thriving community. A family with much love and care but not enough respect, and thus not enough stress on character, will have difficulties facing challenges requiring a clear conception of what the basic values and aims are for the unit, and will fare even worse when changing contexts also require justification for the upholding of these values, e.g. that the qualities of our human interactions are more important by and large than economic progress. Conversely, a political unit within which there is sufficient shared respect but not enough of the warm affective qualities like care and trust will "grow cold," with mere legalism attempting eventually to replace a healthy communal dynamics.

These four ingredients cannot be derived from our definition of an ethical community, since we can share values and have communal activities and aims without respect, care, trust, and interest in the welfare of another. E.g. our shared value could be the spreading of a certain political ideology. Furthermore, the four ingredients are conceptually independent of each other. Respect does not entail interest in welfare. I can respect a great composer but have no interest in her welfare. Nor does it entail trust or care. Some people with respect-warranting attributes, like certain conductors, are not trustworthy and we need not care for them. Likewise, none of the other three ingredients entail respect. We can take interest paternalistically, trust, and care for people whom we may be fond of but do not respect.

Again, taking an interest in the welfare of another does not entail either care or trust. The latter are warm positive affective qualities, and we can take interest in others without these. Conversely, we can have these affective qualities without taking an interest in the welfare of the object of affection, as it happens—unfortunately—all too often. Finally, trust and care do not entail each other. We care often for people we do not trust, and trust by itself need not lead to caring.

The four ingredients are ends in themselves. They are parts of a good character that one wants apart from consequences. For these are basic ingredients of conceptions of an ethical individual agent, or a communal agent that one takes as a starting point in

working out schemes of values. The ingredients include both quality-dependent and direct attitudes, for both individual and community, thus covering all of what is needed to have a stable psychological and sociological structure with which to find meaning
in life and face challenges. The fact that all four have value does
not mean that in given contexts one may not have priority over the
other. Such priorities can be set by shifting demands on which
characteristic needs special stress in this or that social context. At
times wisdom is heavily in demand, at others it is carefully articulated concern for the welfare of a neglected group. Respect and
concern for the welfare of others are quality-dependent attitudes.
I.e. we direct these towards others in virtue of some characteristic
that they have. We cannot just go around respecting people,
regardless of what we think of their character. A kind of trust and
care, on the other hand, are direct attitudes. We can direct these
towards other humans apart from the qualities they have. The
qualities can be relevant in two ways. Either these function as
grounds for deserving a certain attitude being directed towards the
possessor, or as grounds for evoking concern or sympathy with the
possessor on the basis of the plight he or she is in. At times both
kinds of quality dependencies play parts in the development of
attitudes that are parts of communal ties.

We shall now turn to a justification of the four candidates as
ingredients, and at the end will also review them as meeting the
conditions of adequacy laid down above for communal ties.

Respect can have a variety of kinds of objects. We can have
respect for the wisdom of some sage. But the application relevant
to the theory of ties is that of humans. Respect in the sense used
in this context is an attitude towards humans. It is not merely
activity. E.g. one could specify "honoring your father and mother"—within some traditions—solely in terms of activity. But
respect for humans of the sort that goes into our communal tie
involves having an attitude involving cognitive and affective qualities. It assigns to its object non-instrumental value. It construes
the object, i.e. the human deserving it, as a partially self-deter-
mining entity, capable of exercising options among alternatives.

Within our theory the key issue is not how much respect one
shows, but the reasons for the respect. These need to revolve
around the rationality and character of the object.

In a recent paper S. Darwal distinguishes two kinds of respect.[15] One of these coincides roughly with the quality-dependent kind of respect that is a part of our desirable communal tie. The other, called "respect of recognition," is not dependent on qualities that demand desert.

In our framework there is no conceptual room for the second kind of respect. The community is held together by values. Sharing in these is the basis of respect. The sharing of values must be the determining factor, since "membership" even if strengthened by legal links, is based primarily on the actual or potential participation of the cultivation of certain values, and interactions.

Respect in a community lays the foundation for ascribing some value to each individual, as an end and some autonomy to them as decision-makers. For while we may find someone useful on account of instrumental values, respect implies that the object of this attitude has also qualities that have intrinsic merit. Presumably we work towards the realization of adequate ideals of those to whom we ascribe intrinsic value. Thus this ingredient establishes a domain of members whose life we respect and try to help. Furthermore, respecting people for intrinsic values implies that we respect also them for the development of these values. One cannot be brainwashed into being intellectually curious or honest. These qualities need be developed self-consciously and hence on the basis of some autonomy. Respect based on the recognition of such autonomy is important for a community, for it engenders an attitude in communal discussions that enables us to regard each member as a potential participant, and as someone worth listening to.

This ingredient brings with it the need to make an effort to reach at least partial agreement on what are respect-warranting attitudes. Respecting someone for his wealth can be shown to be less justifiable than respecting someone on the basis of character. A community in which there is mutual respect but on the basis of very diverse qualities is a fragile community, for the elements in this diversity can change with the change of contingent matters, and thus threaten the maintenance of respect. Agreement on the

---

15 Darwall, "Two Kinds of Respect."

respect-warranting qualities brings with it the effort to maintain these qualities in the community.

We can have better or worse reasons to respect someone, and since the possession of the typical respect-warranting attitude is a matter of degrees, we can respect someone more or less. We respect persons within different roles for different reasons. Traditionally, however, philosophers assumed that there are general "all-purpose" respect-warranting qualities as well. Hence the list of excellences in the ethics of a Plato or Aristotle.

As noted before individual and communal ideals are interrelated. Developing adequate individual life ideals involves making assumptions about what kind of a community would be conducive to the development of these. In turn, specifying an ideal community brings with it assumptions about desirable character traits in members of such communities. Hence selection of respect as an ingredient in an adequate tie already has implications for individual welfare. The second ingredient, concern for the welfare of others, is a constructive way of putting respect to work.

Concern for the welfare of others is demanded by the fact that in a community we make decisions about the welfare of others, and should be concerned what our actions affect. Such concern need not lead to egalitarianism. One way of formulating the concern suggests that when deciding to make changes or to stick to the status quo in a community those affected most by such matters should have crucial say in the decision. For example, a wealthy attorney in Atherton insisted a while ago that we must maintain our basic civil liberties, even though at times "we must pay the price for that." In particular, he insisted, we must maintain current restrictions on police activities, even if this means giving up some security. The main difficulty with this position is that if we keep the status quo, the wealthy attorney does not pay any price at all. He sits in his safe and wealthy neighborhood. The brunt of the price paid is borne mostly by the poor black mothers in East Palo Alto, only a few miles away from Atherton, who would like to have some hope for their children, and thus would like to be able to send them to school without constant fear, and be able to wait for them at the end of the day without trembling when the child is ten minutes late returning. Under these circumstances the community should be willing to curtail civic liberties such as being exempt from sudden searches, etc. since such sacrifice would lead to significant and badly needed improvement in the welfare of some of the least advantaged.

A typical way in which concern for the welfare of individuals can be manifested in a community is the implementation of systems of education. The following example shows the need for concern with communal ties, and not just with raising average knowledge. The Massai in Kenya are a nomadic tribe. Part of the tribe was told by Western organizations, designed to offer help, that they should settle down so that a schoolhouse can be built for the children. This move would destroy their way of life and with that a lot of the moral fabric of the community. For such fabric is often built on institutions that cannot be transferred easily from one context to another. However, other alternatives suggest themselves when we keep in mind the proposed ingredient for the tie. For one could train Massai teachers who would then travel with various parts of the tribe, and teach the children during their wanderings, thus not destroying their way of life.

The two ingredients defended so far, respect and concern with individual welfare, place constraints on how far the community should invade privacy. To be sure, the exact kinds and amounts of privacy to be reserved for individuals should vary from context to context. But the two ingredients ensure that considerations of adequate individual ideals and opportunities for self-improvements will be used as parts of the guideline for drawing the distinction between the private and the public domain.

Are respect and concern for the welfare of other individuals jointly necessary and sufficient for an adequate tie? Why add the other two proposed ingredients?

The first two conditions represent quality-dependent attitudes, and are thus tied to practical reasoning, in which we justify how we feel and act towards others, in terms of reason.

The last two ingredients represent attitudes that we need to carry the communal tie in cases in which the rational structure is in turmoil. There may be a crisis in values, or in the geographical distribution of members, thus making dialogue more difficult.

We also need the last two ingredients because these shape fundamental attitudes that humans need to express. The capacity to have direct attitudes is just as crucial to the emotional development of a human as the rational capacities. The two conditions channel the direct attitudes into appropriate paths. Furthermore, the development and maintenance of the direct attitudes is helped if it comes at a stage that had the thriving of quality-dependent attitudes. Having respected people and had concern for them helps to develop trust and care even when the quality-dependent ones do not function well. If these do function well, then the direct attitudes are an important supplement, thus engaging the whole human personality, not just a part linked to reasoning. We have already seen in the case of the juvenile criminals how important early direct positive warm attitudes are in the moral development of humans. We need to develop trust in a community with adequate tie, in the face of uncertainty about individual performances.

Trust comes in various kinds.[16] We have general expectations of members of the community that they will behave in certain predictable ways in human interactions. Thus, for example, I trust other drivers up to a point on highways, and the people I meet on the street. This trust is based only on regular of behavior and minimal cooperative attitudes, without any specific motive assumed. Needless to say, without this minimum a society could not function. We could not walk on the streets, and could not drive to work.

There is also trust that demands more of agent and object. Such is trust in specific individuals based on these having certain qualities, e.g. reliability, or honesty. Under ideal circumstances we should have enough evidence about members of a normative community so that we can all trust each other on such quality-dependent basis. In fact, we often lack such information about others. E.g. we see members of our communities perform their jobs responsibly and with sensitivity in more restricted contexts such as their business, or other professional occupations. We see them exercise self-restraint in a circle of friends, we see them calm in a family crisis. These items help to build up conceptions of reliability. But a modern community will be typically too large to allow us to gather this kind of evidence about many people with whom we participate in communal activities and decision making. In these cases a "leap of faith" is forced on us. For distrust is just as much a matter of faith, i.e. choice beyond rational evidence, as

---

16 I am indebted for discussion of trust to Tim Haeg.

trust. We need to choose between two direct attitudes. Hope in the value of our project and community will often push us towards the positive step, but such steps are never without risk and danger. Furthermore, there is a fundamental quality needed for the maintenance of a thriving community, namely, constancy of character. I.e. the person who respects others will continue to do so, the person who cares for others will maintain that attitude, etc. This fundamental characteristic underlies all others that enter into matters of trust, such as keeping promises, agreements, and other bases of cooperation. Yet what would be sufficient for ascribing this to others? Trust in the sense of faith enters the picture at this point again, namely trust that is directed at specific people, even when sound credentials in terms of character are lacking. We are often forced into situations in which trust or distrust of this sort need be manifested. For example, a river needs to be cleaned up, and any one country contributing to pollution or cleaning up does not have enough information about communal attitudes of the other. In such cases we might go ahead and trust with the hope that all of the relevant agencies will develop the attitude that "we are in the same boat" with respect to the problem at hand. Such direct trust should not be described as irrational. When forced with direct trust or distrust, there may be various reasons for adopting the former. For example, it will lead to the increase of probability that cooperation will start, or help strengthen other ingredients of an adequate communal tie.

We need to consider reasons of what is good, not merely right in such contexts. For trust is an attitude. It contains a belief that we should behave and cooperate in certain ways. It also contains a feeling towards the other. But we cannot be obligated to feel this way or that way. Hence we cannot have an obligation to trust. There are, however, circumstances that help develop this attitude.

For example, previous work in a community bound by the adequate communal tie would engender the kind of atmosphere in which direct trust can develop. Once we are used to working with people with whom we share values, respect, and mutual concern, we might be willing to take the "leap" and trust others even in contexts in which the fulfillment of the other conditions cannot be taken for granted. Of course, events can take place that would destroy direct trust. Even that need not be a permanent condition. But this brings up the problem of forgiveness, and this phenomenon is beyond the confines of this essay.

There is also "the trusting person" as we describe him in everyday use. This is someone whose naivete leads him often to misplaced trust. This kind of person should not be confused with the individual we have just considered, namely someone who on the basis of conscious reflection and understanding the risks opts for the positive attitude of trusting individuals in contexts forcing options, with the hope that this by itself will either lead to the trusted person rising to the occasion, or lead to more positive interactions at other times in contexts in which others can know that we are willing to take these moral chances.

Since we are dealing here with direct trust that does not assume sharing of values prior to the trust being extended, we need not think of this attitude as limited to members of ethical communities. Extending trust outside the community can have beneficial results, even if at times it turns out not to be rewarding in the short run. For example, exclusionistic stances in a community are often the result of insecurity and mistrust, rather than purity of belief. In other cases distrust towards what is inside of people leads to excessive reliance on external factors like compulsory initiation rituals or other external signs of membership. In religious contexts, mystery rites and rituals are likely to emerge when there is much skepticism about confessional content. In secular contexts we see similar phenomena. When people inside themselves doubt that their accumulation of wealth really deserves respect, they are likely to form clubs and other associations with rigidly defined external signs of membership. While such signs are not bad in themselves, when these become ends and not just means, the form replaces content. Concentrating on ritual and external criteria of membership is no substitute for devotion to ideals that require both the intellect and emotion to cooperate, and since such matters are not on the surface, also require trust.

Direct trust could also be viewed as unconditional trust in the sense that it does not depend on desirable character traits already exhibited. But such trust can be short-lived or lasting a long time. It can be direct and then withdrawn at the first sign of the object not living up to it. Alternatively, it can be lasting when combined with forgiveness that blends in this context with faith and hope. The long-lasting trust is easier to develop in an ethical community in which the ingredients discussed above are already at least partly in place as parts of what binds us together. Respect and concern for others is likely to engender hope and trust. Alternatively, other direct attitudes like love might have the same effect.

We shall now turn to the fourth ingredient, care. Care is a direct attitude. We direct it towards people even when they do not possess qualities showing desert of some sort. Furthermore, it is an attitude that radiates warm affective qualities towards the objects. We see it functioning in relations like friendship and ones uniting families. Its absence leaves the relevant community in a cold atmosphere in which the danger surfaces of the participants becoming emotionally deprived. It is also an important part of the relation between physician and patient, and can be an ingredient in other important relationships such as teacher-student, fellow worker, or fellow member of a religious group. The loyalty that results from relations involving quality-dependent attitudes like respect depends on the maintenance of certain good qualities. The loyalty of caring is unconditional, and thus not dependent on continued meeting of standards for a good human. Can we predict that unconditional care will continue no matter what? We can say that the caring did not depend on commitment to desirable character traits and the presence of these in the object. But care can be at times killed in people by the total degeneration of the object. Since it is predominantly a feeling, we have no complete voluntary control over it. Famous examples abound on both sides of this issue. There is Lara in "Dr. Zhivago" whose love and care for her husband is killed by his becoming an executioner. But there is also King David whose love and care for his son Absolom is not extinguished no matter what evil deeds Absolom perpetrates. How many times does love and care forgive? There seems to be no general answer to this question.

This special warmth and loyalty that caring adds to the adequate communal tie is important, for it will help the tie not to disintegrate in cases of social and political turmoil, when values are questioned and rejected, and the putative fact that members share values becomes problematical. For example, during World War II, changes in army occupation also often meant changes in regime.

Hence for an interim period the "policemen moved off the corner" and with him any legal structure or institution. Under those circumstances while some people keep, others lose all moral bearings and abuse others as well as the property of others. Some humans continue to cooperate and be decent to each other, simply some on the basis of retained quality-dependent attitudes, others on the basis of direct attitudes developed earlier. This direct attitude makes it easier to hope that a new value-oriented community can be built up again. Assimilar situation arises when people are taken out of rural contexts and pushed into an industrial urban framework. The drastically different social and economic context can shake values in some. Yet direct attitudes among family members or neighbors can help decent human relations to survive, and be the ground for eventual reuniting on the basis of values worked out.[17]

Care creates an atmosphere of receptiveness within which participants in communal discussions are less likely to take rigid dogmatic stances, and be more receptive to alternate implementations schemes and compromise. Care typically develops in contexts in which the partners have close personal contacts. But interdependence recognized, or a feeling that we are "in the same boat" as after an earthquake, or as in Albert Camus' *The Plague*, can also be the basis of caring even if the participants do not know each other directly.[18] Let us now review how the proposed tie meets the criteria of evaluation set forth earlier.

The first criterion prescribes that the communal tie should function, among other things, as an enabling condition for sound communal aim setting, and maintaining of values. The ingredients of the proposed tie seem to fit this requirement well. Mutual respect goes hand in hand with individual autonomy. For respect is directed at humans in view of some non-instrumental value that they possess. There is nothing wrong with relations built on mutual utility. But such relations are not long lasting, because they depend on external circumstances. The tie meeting the first criterion is deeper, for it rests on human characteristics that depend less on external factors.

---

17 An interesting illustration is provided by Walker's *The Color Purple*.
18 For an extended discussion of caring see Noddings, *Caring*.

The second ingredient brings out something essential in what should be the nature of our interactions with others. These interactions at times tend to be purely manipulative, or at least with only our benefit in mind. The ingredient of concern does not ask for altruism, though that too can meet the challenge. It asks for some non-selfish orientation towards others. Joining others in a fight for a cause can be non-selfish. It need not be altruistic.

Without some non-egoistic attitude communities will fail to measure up to the adequate community, with adequate communal dynamic and ties. There are communities that are built on compromises between different self-interests of individual members or of groups of members. But, as we saw earlier, what is in our interest is conceived by us to a large extent in view of what kind of a person we take ourselves to want to be. Long lasting and deep loyalties are not likely to emerge in a community that is based only on self-interest, even if there are institutional devices built into the structure for exchanges leading to compromise. If we happen to agree on what is good for ourselves and the community, this consensus should be built on some ethical foundation. Our tie is an example of such.

Trust is one of the cornerstones of activities forming or maintaining aims in a community. This trust can be based in a belief about the stability of the character of others, as well as on a general effort to maintain the values specified by the other ingredients.

The importance of care is based on empirical considerations. The first criterion demands that adequate atmosphere be created for certain communal activities. These will typically involve sensitivity towards the suffering of others, and this, in turn, seems to rest partly on empirical conditions insuring early exposure to being cared for. It is a capacity that humans need to cultivate if they are to fulfill all aspects of their nature. Its exercise helps a friendly atmosphere for aim setting and maintaining.

As we turn to the second criterion we can see it, superficially, as the demand that a community should be good for the development of good persons. But reflection on the details of the criterion and the tie shows it to be more than that. Our characterization of a good person included an account of a good agent, and additional conditions relating to being a person. The second criterion for good communal ties deals with the social aspects of human nature and their shared aims, activities, and feelings. There is an overlap between the two topics. This should be obvious since it has been argued before that we cannot completely separate individual and social ethics. But overlap does not mean identity, nor is there here a circularity. The overall conception of a community bound by respect concern, trust, and care places constraints as well as spells out enabling conditions for the communal dynamics that, we argued, must underlie any legal and institutional structure. One might think that the delineation of the adequate individual ideals serves as a constraint on what a community should be like. But this is a misleading picture. One could just as well construe the communal tie as placing constraints on the range of adequate individual ideals. A more informative way to view the relation between the individual and the communal criteria in this context is to represent them as mutually supportive. Even if someone claimed that the abilities of respect, concern, trust, and care should be a part of every adequate individual ideal, spelling out what it entails for communal activities, sharing of values, and feelings is an additional task. To be respectful towards individuals is to accept the claim of their autonomy. To share respect in a community requires additional attitudes and skills of implementation. Having an adequate individual ideal will also facilitate humans to become good members of a community with adequate ties, but it does not assure this with certainty.

In Plato's political theory two levels of harmony are posited. There is the harmony of a community, and the harmony within individual agents who are the members. But one can envisage communal harmony in different ways. One can accept Plato's basic claim, and have different ideas on what an adequate communal harmony is from the one he entertained.

The same applies on the individual level. The second criterion articulates a demand on the communal dynamic. At the same time, it must be dependent on criteria for individual ideals, else we do not know with what the ties are supposed to harmonize.

Criterion three asserts that the adequate tie must play a key role in cooperation and cooperative attitudes being among the final, not merely instrumental, values of the community. One might ask: why should the ties play this role? Why should this not be a distinct condition in social ethics? Our reply points to the fact that according to this criterion the tie should function as specifying a mode of cooperation. There are many different ways of cooperating, with a variety of possible motives. Our chosen tie adds up to a mode of cooperation. We should cooperate not only out of fear, or purely utilitarian considerations, or on the basis of an independent moral imperative, not grounded in adequate human psychology, but on the basis of mutual respect, concern, trust, and care. The difference between such communal cooperation and others is like the difference in medicine between genuine healing, with care and concern for the patient as the key factors, in contrast with just doing a job, exhibiting mere caring behavior, and similar such extraneous motives. This criterion points to cooperation of a certain kind as a human challenge and mode of self-fulfillment, rather then a burden to be grudgingly borne.

Criterion four reminds us that within our theory the adequate tie represents certain attitudes among humans, and not just legal structures. Hence the adequate tie must be based on a realistic psychology. This cuts two ways. The psychology must be realistic and not demand unrealistically high standards of inner and external lives. At the same time, it should be an empirically supportable psychology rich enough to show the possibility of expressing beliefs and attitudes posited by our theory, and not be conceptually boxed in because of possible conflicts with fashionable philosophical reductionist programs. This primarily concerns doctrines in the philosophy of mind.

It is easy to show that the proposed tie meets the fourth criterion. The first psychological condition states that setting aims as ends and not merely as means is a conceptually and empirically viable human condition. The first ingredient in the proposed communal tie is based on this hypothesis. Mutual respect entails construing oneself and others in the community as having not only instrumental but also non-instrumental value. For genuine respect is based on attributing to the human object of this attitude some degree of autonomy. The other ingredients do not entail the adequacy of the first psychological claim, but are compatible with it.

The second psychological thesis does not demand the third and fourth ingredient of the proposed tie, but can serve as an empirical underpinning. The tie assumes that there are genuine direct attitudes expressed by humans among each other. This includes care and trust. The second psychological assumption posits on empirical ground the possibility of such attitudes.

The posited tie does not assert what the third psychological assumption says, but is very congenial to it. Trust, and care, lay a very natural foundation for sharing. This applies both for sharing values, ideals, or material goods. Thus we see that the proposed tie with all of its ingredients is at no point in conflict with the three psychological conditions, and at some points is closely connected with some of these.

In order to avoid the semblance of circularity we need to point out that there are other communal tie proposals that could meet the psychological conditions laid down and hence satisfy criterion four. For example, a combination of mutually expected utility and benevolence could satisfy this criterion. The argument for the superiority of our proposal does not rest on claiming that all other proposals are psychologically less well grounded. Rather, the justification of the tie is that is presents a more solid and hence potentially enduing tie, and involves a larger range of human capacities, both cognitive and affective, than the alternative just mentioned, or others listed earlier.

The fifth criterion brings out salient differences between different types of possible ties. An adequate community must have some degree of stability. Without some stability in what we can assume can persist, what we can assume will be believed, and what will move people planning, prediction, and lasting interactions are not possible. Thus the stability that this criteria demands is not in terms of superficial practices and institutional gestures such as etiquette, types of entertainment, level of economic welfare, and similar customs and habits. There must be stability in some fundamental beliefs and attitudes.

The proposed communal tie meets this criterion exceptionally well. For respect, concern, trust, and care can survive in spite of fluctuations in wealth, changes in modes of production or political power. Furthermore, if our emphasis is on respect and the other ingredients, society is not in danger of atrophy. For these ties do not demand rigid rules and customs. Respect, trust, or care cannot be defined even contextually in terms of rules and regulations. Certain rituals might be helpful in reminding people of the communal tie, or calling attention to some features of the tie.

Hence the value of mourning those who died in battle, or a feast centered on love and good will. But these institutions can change in form, and leave the basic values intact. A purely legalistic way of specifying ties lacks the flexibility to adjust to new contexts that one based on respect, concern, and trust has.

Within a certain range, aims can change, practices can vary, and laws need rewriting or interpretation. If we have a tie with the listed ingredients, an adequate community will survive changes and can adopt a critical stance towards proposed changes, adopting some, rejecting others, without lapsing into the absurdity of regarding every arbitrarily surfaced change "progress."

Skeptical readers might wonder what is really important in this proposal. After all, everyone agrees that life is easier when people agree on some values thus facilitating cooperation. In traditional views and in the view proposed in this chapter a community is made up of individuals with their own values, and communal–political institutions with their own laws and regulations. What does this theory do apart from stressing how much better things go if some important values are also shared in the community?

The response relies heavily on the notion of *priority*. The communal spirit and its intertwining with cultivation of the proper individual ideals is more fundamental than the mere working out of laws and negotiating conflicting individual interests. We see this in many cases in which substantial changes occur, and the law as well as activity of the law enforcing agents are suspended. The value-based community will survive, the merely legalistic, or material goods oriented societies will not.

In our theory the basic elements of the communal tie are neutral between varieties of political, economic and personal values. These change often, even if some changes are more drastic than others. The value-based community with the adequate tie will survive these changes far more easily than the merely conventional society. Stress on priorities brings with it "layered" thinking. Much is true about us, but some truths are more fundamental than others. Who we should be, and how we should construe the most fundamental relationships we have with others are more fundamental matters than nationality, taste in economic systems, and admiration of technology. These things can change while the basic structure remains. This is the insight that our theory attempts to capture. Thus within our scheme we can construe the ties that bind as the ties that build, rather than the ties that chain us. The difference between these two views determines to a large extent the underlying moral psychology of a collection of individuals. Which view will be appropriate is determined partly by the nature of the communal tie proposed. Our theory sketches the nature of appropriate and adequate ties, and the kinds of individual psychologies and choices of ideals that go with such communal structure and are also worth pursuing as what is fulfilling for the individual.

This theory is fundamentally incompatible with any structure within which a part of the population becomes disadvantaged, or driven away on the ground that doing this enables the government to bring some important goods to the remaining population. Within our theory adding benefits in such a way that this denies to others participation in a thriving community is much too high a price to pay.

In conclusion, it should be stressed that the criteria reviewed admit of a variety of candidates as adequate. The essay does not claim that our choice is the only one meeting the standards, but rather that it meets these better than other candidates that one might consider. For example, a religious or ethical code on exhortations can meet the criteria in a minimal sense. So can mythologies centered on non-aggressive patriotism. But in terms of engaging the whole human psychological structure without monopolizing any one part, and linking the tie to the basic conditions of good community planning and selection of individual ideal, it is difficult to think of a proposal that would surpass or even equal the one articulated in this chapter.

Chapter V

FREEDOM, RESPONSIBILITY, AND WORK IN COMMUNAL LIFE

In the previous chapter we discussed a key ingredient in a well functioning community, namely the ties that should hold it together. In the first part of the book we sketched adequate ethical ideals. Combining these two notions, we reach a conception of a human with the right ideals living in a community that has appropriate communal ties, and holds these in high esteem. So we can place the good individual into a community with the right ties or form. In this chapter we sketch some of the content of the good community, not only in terms of individuals, but in particular in terms of three essential conditions that give a part of the communal content of a community. These are freedom, responsibility, and work. Without some freedom we cannot build an adequate ideal, and carrying out in practice such an ideal requires responsibility for the consequences of this implementation with regards to other human beings affected. Finally, some kind of work is needed both for sustaining the community and for supplying yet another aspect of fulfillment for the individual. In most modern communities work takes place within some political structure. Hence we must say something about how our theory affects what should be said about political structures.

An enormous amount has been written on each of these topics. Freedom, responsibility, political structure and work have been subjects for many books and other treaties for centuries in a variety of cultures. In this chapter many of the topics handled in many treaties on political theory will be left untouched. The main aim of this chapter is to explain how the conception of the good agent and good community affects issues that belong to political theory.

Freedom and responsibility have two aspects. Metaphysical problems are involved in both notions. At the same time, we must

also confront the problems emerging in trying to formulate guidelines for how these notions should be embedded in communal life.
This essay does not claim to answer metaphysical questions.
Hence in the first section we will give only a brief review of some
of the main questions, and formulate a pragmatic stand on the
basis of which we shall proceed to discuss the communal issues in
this chapter, under the assumption that freedom and responsibility, at least as interpreted here, have adequate rational foundation,
so that we can dismiss the purely logical possibility of these being
illusory as not affecting our work.

After the brief metaphysical survey we move on to dealing
with questions like: "How should freedom function in a sound
community?" "How should freedom be encouraged and
assigned?" "What should be the relation between freedom and
responsibility?" "How should responsibility be assigned in a good
community?" "What are the criteria for responsibilities well carried out?" "To what extent should freedom be assigned on the
basis of a member having carried out some responsibilities well?"

On the surface freedom seems to clash with responsibility. If
one takes on responsibilities, then one is constrained in terms of
what one can do. The same consideration applies to the relation
between freedom and work. We even contrast in some contexts
freedom as "free time" with work. In this chapter an attempt is
made to convince the reader that in a value-based community with
the members having or striving for the right ideals, and the community having adequate ties, these clashes can be disarmed.
Responsibility can be construed as an enabling condition in many
contexts, and work of the appropriate kind can be a part of the fulfillment of the human potential and not a mere means to earn a
living. One can misinterpret our suggestions. First the suggestions
are not meant to apply only to a utopia in which individual ideals,
communal ties and communal dynamics are perfect, whatever that
may mean. Rather, the normative notions just mentioned can
function as guidelines, and thus a community that tries to approximate the idealized states sketched should function with the
notions of freedom, responsibility, and work outlines in this chapter as further guidelines.

After the treatment of metaphysical issues in the first section
we turn in the second section to freedom. Freedom is typically

linked to rights. Specifying a set of rights can be turned into a list of freedoms. The rights and associated responsibilities then add up to a demand that other members of the community should not hinder, and in fact in some cases enable, the agent in question to exercise the freedoms encompassed by his or her rights. One could see this as one of the responsibilities of the members of the community and indeed the communal structure as such. But this suggests, of course that the individual whose rights we are supposed to protect has also his responsibilities to the community. In this way we can see strong conceptual and empirical links between freedom and responsibility. This is one of the main themes of sections 2 and 3. Spelling out the link turns out to involve a variety of qualifications and modifications.

After the section on freedom in a sound community we turn to responsibility. We show that the simplistic formula of "x is responsible for y" needs the addition "for community C in virtue of x's possessing qualities Q1...QN." In the chapter each of the argument places and their appropriate holders will be discussed. Justifications will also be given for the scheme, and the normative proposals of how to fill the "gaps." No magical formula will be presented that would give a decision procedure for specific fillings for all contexts, but we will see how attention to adequate individual ideals and communal ties can help with the tasks of specification. It will also be shown how in our conception freedom is always in some way conditional. This part of the argument will be opposed by many who call themselves liberal. The proposal will be seen to be softened by the claim that is a part of our view according to which the conditions on freedom may in some contexts be referring to human potentialities rather than actual human performance. But for many contexts, the relation between freedom and some form of accountability in a community is quite firm. This suggests that we do not have freedoms on a "once and for all" assignment basis, but have our freedoms and our performances subject to periodic review.

Having responsibility tied to communal authorities and our freedoms and rights linked to communal context suggests that a section should deal with appropriate authorities for exercising the power to assign and review. These matters are handled in most societies in political contexts. Hence section 4 deals with the nature of political units, and how our conception of a healthy community should have an impact on what we regard as appropriate in political structures as well as how much latitude such considerations leave. Philosophers often start their political theories with questions like: "why should people gather together in political units?" or "why should an individual join society?" Our section does not raise or answer such questions. Given the pragmatist tone of this book, we simply assume that humans in typical contexts are born into a society, and that for most the question about "joining" reduces itself to whether they want to be in the society into which they are born, or try to join another one. Thus the basic questions of political theory are not about how one would construct an ideal society with concrete suggestions about laws and political institutions, but rather about how and on the basis of what criteria we can improve upon this or that society. In this respect proposals like ours about communal ties serve very well. For a society can have our proposed good tie to various degrees, with better or worse implementations, and with more or less communal consent. Plenty of room for improvement there—and also plenty of room for decline.

The section points to many things that one would want in a good society, such as safety, the opportunity to earn a living, and join others in cooperative enterprises as well as the possibility of forming non-utilitarian lasting friendships, and some system of law. The section divides such requirements into the basic essentials and the ones that are good to have but cannot always be realized.

We do not argue for any one system such as democracy, communism, dictatorship, or meritocracy being the ideal system for all human societies. We have already argued that a mere abstract structure cannot be our final end. The final end is a certain communal dynamics. At most one could argue that a certain political structure is the best means towards that end for all societies. The section does not take a stand on this, except for urging tolerance and against the premature denunciation of systems on the ground that they would not work in one's own culture.

One could look at political life the way some of us view natural languages.[1] There maybe a common core—in our theory specified in terms of communal dynamic—and a variety of contextual

---

1 Chomsky, *Aspects of the Theory of Syntax.*

differences. In the spirit of John Dewey we could look in this framework at differences in political idealogy not as disagreements about final ends, but about means to an end of adequate communal dynamics, about which we have at least overlapping conceptions.

The section sketches four components as essential maintaining some freedom and responsibility for all, offering some security for all, offering a way to make a living, and instituting a system of justice to handle criminality and the distribution of goods.

These conditions are very general allowing for much variety in contexts, and in implementation. How much and what kind of freedom do people need and want in a specific cultural context and tradition? How will attention to security impact on freedom in a given context? Does a good system of distributive justice conflict in some contexts with the effort to give everyone opportunities to make a living that is suitable for that individual?

The specification also allows us to suggest that in some small countries sandwiched between giants it makes sense to stress more defense, even if this takes some toll on individual liberty, while in large and powerful countries the matter of security may be less urgent, and thus there is more room for individualism. We shall also see how the ingredients of good communal ties such as respect, concern, and trust, as well as care, can have an impact on the way we interpret the four conditions on the political unit in a given context.

Political units are organized around certain needs, and while some of these may be permanent, others change with time and context. Hence, a key issue in political theory should be how to change a community for better conditions. One might call this the ethics of social change, and it will be touched upon in this section, though the topic deserves a separate book. When considering the feasibility of a proposed change, benefit–cost analysis need be applied. For example, we might want to change certain cultural traditions in order to allow more impact for certain economic demand. But it may turn out to be the case that in fact, some of these cultural traditions are tied—empirically, not conceptually—to important moral values in the community and their destruction would result in a chaotic situation concerning communal dynamics.

Many of the problems involved with sketching conditions for good political units that are compatible with good communal ties, the sharing of values demanded by the value-based community, and the necessities of the survival of the political unit, are interwoven with what one assumes about work done in the community. Hence the fifth section deals with work. Again, the essay is concerned with communal dynamics and ethical dimensions of working conditions on an abstract and thus flexible level. The section presents a proposal, and also shows how one can relate this with the ingredients of good communal ties, and a sound view on political units. The notion of justice too affects both our conceptions of a good state and good work and working conditions. This is left, however, for the next and last chapter.

1. Metaphysical Considerations of Freedom and Responsibility

Our ordinary conception of freedom is, roughly, that the free person can do whatever he or she wants. Everyone understands that since our actions impact on the actions of others, some restrictions on freedom need be in place. Hence we deal with different freedoms in different aspects of our lives.

From a philosophical point of view our first sentence is already problematic. What do we mean by "want" and by "can" in this context? Philosophers tend to start with defining different kinds of autonomy. For example we have intellectual autonomy when nothing external or internal determines or at least hinders our normal considerations of alternatives, deliberation, and choice to take place. Of course this is just a first step. Philosophers have different conceptions about what our "normal" decision making and thinking really is. In some versions of freedom it is linked to willing. Hence the label "free will problem." Presumably we are free when our will is free. But that leads to the difficult question of what will really is, and whether a scientifically adequate psychology should use or avoid voluntaristic concepts.

The autonomy sketched so briefly above is also seen as needing some clarification with regards to determinism and indeterminism. These relationships are also objects of a wide variety of opinions and theories.[2]

---

2 A good collection of relevant work is in Berovsky ed. *Free Will and Determinism.*

Still other philosophers do not think that we need to take stances with regards to these options, and concentrate on characterizing freedom as depending on a unique notion of "can" as it occurs in our initial sentence. For example John L. Austin thought that someone acts freely if and only if he could have helped doing what he did.[3] Detailed analysis of this proposal is beyond the scope of this essay. One, however, can link Austin's view as a modern variation of Aristotle's view on this topic.[4] According to Aristotle we act freely (at times translated as "voluntarily") if and only if the source of our action lies within ourselves, and nothing external hinders in this. Of course, we need to refine what "external" and "internal" mean in this context. A reasonable and sympathetic interpretation would render this as the claim that what is not determined either by external factors such a coercion, or internal forces such as kleptomania and other obsessions, is what we do freely and are thus responsible for. One can accept this, without specifying what "source" means in that context. Philosophers disagree on that, but we can leave that matter undecided. We freely do those things the source of which is our nature or a part of it. For Aristotle human nature includes deliberation and choice that is not illusory. Aristotle has a non-mechanistic view of human nature.[5] He holds that "at our best" we are capable of thinking through problems, considering alternatives, deliberate, and choose in such a way that the chosen action can be seen as "our own" and is something for which we are responsible.

To place this stance into proper perspective let us consider William James conception of this issue.[6] As a good pragmatist, James points out that as human agents interacting with other humans we cannot help but regard ourselves and other humans as having freedom of decision in my contexts. One can attempt a thought experiment. What would it be like to wake up one morning and decide that we no longer believe that humans have freedom and responsibility? Is such a situation at all conceivable? Could we go on with even the minimal level of human interac-

3 Austin, *Philosophical Papers*, essays 6 and 7.
4 Aristotle, *Nichomachean Ethics*, Book III.
5 Code and Moravcsik, "Explaining Various Forms of Living," essay 8.
6 James, *Pragmatism and Other Essays*.

tions? Later Jean-Paul Sartre put the same point in a more dramatic statement. He claimed that humans are "condemned to freedom." The key claim is still the same. We cannot help but think of ourselves as people who praise, blame, demand responsible conduct from others and ourselves.

From outside pragmatism and existentialism one can comment that none of this PROVES the non-illusoriness of freedom and choice. But we can also say that nothing so far in any of the debates we referred to above proves the illusoriness either. Thus we might as well get on with the task of formulating conceptions of freedom and responsibility in our communities as well as we can. So-called ultimate problems with free will are in the same boat as problems about showing, (proving?) that the world is not just one entity and our pluralistic conception of it an unavoidable illusion. We may never be able to understand fully the human state of exercising freedom. That may require forging concepts, types of causation, etc. That is beyond human understanding.[7]

Given this stance, we need to consider what distribution of permissions and enabling conditions for freedom are best suited to human communities, aiming at some shared values, are striving for adequate communal ties. The proposals of the sections on freedom and responsibility can also be applied, with modifications, to communities that according to our view function inadequately. Our exercise of freedom is bound to affect other humans. Considering the consequences of this, and also with the welfare of those affected in mind is responsibility. Our section on that topic considers how responsibility should be ascribed in a community, and what it takes to carry out responsibilities well.

There are different kinds of responsibilities. One might want to define in general what it is for someone to be responsible for deeds and condition, in a general moral sense of this notion. This can then serve as a guide for assignments of responsibilities in communities. But we cannot say unqualifiedly that only those who are morally responsible can be held for payment of damage to property. For example, there may be a shipment of goods from Minneapolis to New Orleans, and the shipment is damaged without the possibility of pointing to agents as responsible for this. The

---

7 Point made by Chomsky in conversation.

court will still decide on who should pay what kind of reparation, even if only on pragmatic grounds. We can label this as legal responsibility.[8] We need to separate from all of this a sense in which we describe someone as a responsible person, meaning that he is good at carrying out responsibilities assigned to him.[9]

Freedom needs to be acknowledged in a community in order for it to have an impact on how communal affairs are managed. This is not a trivial observation, since in different communities different kinds of freedom will be in focus. For example, there are communities in which the issue of freedom of and from religion does not arise. Everyone is brought up to worship some object or spirit, and issues of atheism or divergence of religious dogma simply do not arise. For modern societies a different issue arises. Let us consider the freedom of invention. Is it a basic right for humans to be inventing new artifacts of any kind? Does society have rights to constrain the inventor so that he will consider the consequences of his invention for other members of the community? How far do the rights and claims of the community go, and how far can we constrain human creativity? Again, in many cultures this question might not arise. It is more likely to arise in modern technologically advanced communities in which technology may be invented that has clearly foreseeable damaging consequences, or consequences that might be very damaging, but nobody can tell even probabilistically.

The upshot of all of this is that freedom and responsibility in actual life require interpersonal activities for implementation, and ways in which this will be carried out requires communal acknowledgement.[10]

In the following section suggestions are made about appropriateness with regard to political structures, and also with regard to work. We show how the discussions of all of the previous sections in this chapter as well as the other chapters bear on these crucial communal structures and activities. For all of this the pragmatic, and metaphysically neutral, notion of freedom in the Aristotelian sense suffices.

---

8 This issue was raised by H. L. A. Hart in a seminar he gave at Harvard.
9 I am indebted for clarification of these issues to Prof. R. Kleinknecht.
10 I am indebted to Andria Chow for clarification of these matters.

2. Freedom

In this section we will discuss how freedom functions optimally in a sound community, and what its links are to responsibility. First we need to distinguish freedom from various obstruction, and freedom as an enabling condition to liberate us and thus enable us to pursue and fulfill a variety of aims.[11] For example, we might need a law that prohibits a class of citizens being prevented from voting. On the positive side, that means that they have the right to vote. But this is not yet an enabling condition. We might also need laws that enable people of various kinds who might not be able to go to a voting station, or do not understand the language of the voting sheet, or simply do not know what the point of voting is, to receive the required assistance.

Within communal life, these kinds of freedom emerge in a variety of contexts. Thus we need provisions that spell out "freedom from" and "freedom to" for a variety of contexts. We cannot do this for all possible contexts. This is where the communal tie enters the picture. We need to trust each other so that the relevant citizens and authorities will manifest concern for the two kinds of freedom, even if it might take some time before these matters can be codified.

Apart from spelling out the varieties of freedom members of the community are to enjoy, we need to deal with the problem of setting priorities for cases in which exercise of freedom by different parties clash. A frequently occurring context for this is labor dispute. Often it is assumed by one party that efficiency and drive for profit should have priority, and by the other that the opportunities for all workers to make a decent living should receive primary consideration. Such clashes are settled optimally by negotiation. Conflicts between important rights and freedoms can hardly be settled by calling one of them fundamental and part of a minimal set of freedoms. This can be illustrated by a conversation between President Reagan and Michail Gorbachov. Reagan said that voting is a human right, to which Gorbachov replied that the right to work is a human right. There must be other elements that need be brought into such debates, besides that of human right.

---

11 Berlin, "Two Concepts of Liberty."

For one can imagine two sides endlessly "bumping heads" one insisting that only this, and the other that only that should be called a human right.

We started with a consideration of metaphysical debates about freedom. In those discussions one can treat freedom as a descriptive term. But we can see now that as soon as we begin considering the actual communal situations in which we need to consider the value of this or that kind of freedom, and establish some comparative standards, we are dealing with freedom as a partly normative term. "I should have this or that kind of freedom" can mean that I am qualified to be entrusted with this or that freedom, or it can mean that it is in the interest of the community that I should be entrusted with the freedom at issue. Optimally, the two demands coincide, but this is often not the case.

Another way to get at the normativity of freedom is to consider that freedom is not the same as arbitrariness or randomness. Freedom is what a human under normal conditions and not considering various contextual factors should have in the way of possibilities to choose. In this way freedom in its partly descriptive and partly normative role resembles health. This too designates not a condition to be specified in purely descriptive terms but one that we regard as state of the normal well functioning human. Normality and sound functioning are not concepts that can be given a purely non-normative analysis.

So far we considered ways of injecting into communal life various factors that give us freedoms from possible interference and also enabling conditions. But we also need to consider how much freedom we should assume as due to humans outside our communities. For we should also treat the outsider with respect and that involves ascribing to him or her the right to certain freedoms. This stance is also compatible with maintaining that the amount of care and concern we owe to people will not be invariant across humanity, regardless of how much contact and interactions we had with them.

S. Darwall proposed that we have two kinds of respect for others.[12] One is a kind of basic respect or recognition, with basic rights, and the other the respects that we have in various degrees

---

12 Darwall, "Two Kinds of Respect."

for various members of society in various contexts. In the theory
of this essay the former kind of respect, and thus recognition of
freedom, does not exit. No freedom or assignment of responsibility is categorical: all of it is always conditional. But there will be
contexts in which we meet stranger, or humans we know but about
whom we have little if any information concerning reliability. In
these cases we can still consider potential reliability and thus
potential responsibility in the treatment of their freedoms. Thus
we can assign something that resembles what others call basic
freedoms or human rights, in our theory. But we add the important proviso that such assignments, like the contextual ones, are
open to revision if new relevant evidence warrants this. Should all
humans be regarded as having this kind of freedom deserving
potential? Within our theory, that is an empirical question. We
might want to start with that assumption, but empirical evidence
can surface—from everyday experience or genetics—that will
change any reasonable stance.

In view of these considerations let us distinguish two applications of freedom.

There is a general objective and non-contextual notion of
individual freedom:

x is free to do y is if x is a position in which the action to be
performed originates from his own human nature. This is, of
course idealized, since external conditions can interfere with normal functioning.

Secondly, there is the freedom that we utilize in assigning and
protecting freedoms within a given community. This freedom is to
be characterized as:

x is free to do y in community C in view of C's decision based
on x's having qualities $Q1...QN$. Conceptually the first characterization should have priority. That is to say that if an agent does not
measure up to that general condition, then the community should
not assign freedom to him. On the other hand, the general condition should also work as a stimulant on the community. If someone meets it, then the burden lies on the community to justify any
decision that would take away or curtail the freedom. This conceptual relation prevents our viewing the judgment of the given
community as the final word. Within our framework it is possible
to say that x is free, and should have freedom, even if the commu-

nity denies this. There are two sources of freedom assignment. One is the objective general characterization of freedom, the other the considerations of the clashes in the community of freedoms and the needs of the community.

One can think of freedom in a community in two ways. One is to assume that everyone qualified in terms of capacities should be free, and restrictions should be imposed only if this is within the basic interests of the community, and judgments to that have been given justifications.

This might seem an enlightened position. Unfortunately it does not work, because as we have seen freedom should also be treated as an enabling condition. Thus apart from a "no interference unless absolutely necessary" policy we also need a policy on how and when to work towards enabling conditions. For example, some of our educational and health policies are of this nature. These freedoms based on enabling conditions do not come without cost. Thus in each of these cases a benefit–cost analyses need be carried out. But, as we have seen, these analyses cannot be completely utilitarian, since good communal ties prevent this. Some of the costs involve comparing some final ends against others in terms of importance. In case of enabling conditions the conceptions of the community of what are adequate ethical ideals must enter the deliberations. For one can construct enabling conditions for a variety of different tasks, opportunities, and states of enjoyment. Every community must face the question of which of these are doable within a given context for a given community, and can be judged, justifiably, as worthy of pursuit.

In political contexts the tension between freedom and rights on the one hand, and constraints on the other is phrased as the contrast between the private realm and the domain within which the state can—should— interfere. But in modern societies this contrast is of very limited utility. The state–private contrast fares best in societies in which the private marks out a domain that contains activities not, or not much, affecting other people. The more interdependence we have in a society, the less the dichotomy has utility. Thus when used in these contexts "private" becomes a semi-normative concept. It does not simply denote what is within the legal rights of an individual, but what SHOULD be regarded as private in the sense that the government should not regulate it, even if there is some interdependence between the citizen in question and the rest of the community. In carving out domains of the private, communal ties should enter. For one of these is trust. No matter in how much detail we specify what people must and must not do as we try to eliminate harm that individual undertakings can cause to others, there will always remain the uncodifiable element, since at no time in history can we specify completely the class of possible human actions. We must talk in this context about natural or physical possibility. As for the infinite class of logically possible actions, there is not much that we can do, or should try to do concerning it.

We see, then that any actual representation of freedom in communal activities and individual undertakings within communal or simply interactive setting needs to deal with the issues of how the exercise of freedom will enrich human life, how the exercise of one should be allowed to affect the welfare of others, how it affects the distribution of goods in the community, and how much unlegislated latitude it leaves in the community. As we can see, the key terms of "enrich," "welfare," "distribution of goods" have normative layers in their meanings. Furthermore, these terms need be assigned on the basis of the kind of ethical considerations that go into communal dynamics building and tie, and ideal buildings, and not merely on the basis of duties and utilities. The value of our choice for communal tie as ingredient can also be shown in practical circumstances. At a doctoral dissertation examination that centered on formal approaches to strategy construction and consensus building, a former Secretary of Defense who was a part of the supervisory committee spoke up and said that none of these formal devices will work unless there is initially among the participants of the project a basic trust.[13] It is comforting to note that from time to time philosophical reflection and practical experience, even by "non-humanists" who deal mainly with technocrats, can coincide to this extent.

In conclusion we should take up the issue that will have been on the mind of many readers. It will be objected that these pages of remarks on freedom are superficial, do not deal with complex

---

13 This is an account of an actual Ph.D. examination at Stanford University. The author was one of the committee members.

technical details of decision-making, and do not amount to a "theory." We are accustomed in so-called Western cultures to discuss freedom in terms of rights, claims, duties, obligations, and similar other legalistic notions. The pages of this section scarcely contribute to that voluminous literature. In response it should be stressed that this section had a less sweeping but equally important aim. This is to show that no matter how industrious we are in formulating systems of rights and duties and modes of calculations for utility, we will have an incomplete conception of how freedom should function unless we include discussions of ethical individual ideals, communal ties, and conception of communal dynamics. As we shall see in the next section, the inclusion of discussion of responsibility is an equally important part of the whole enterprise of specifying the challenges and obstacles of discussions of freedom, both in terms of common conceptual core and contextual variety.

3. Responsibility

Our discussion of freedom leads to the discussion of responsibility, since we saw above how appropriate handling of one's freedom entails looking at the consequences of what we freely do, and to have concern for the welfare of those who are affected by the proposed consequences. To some extent, the enabling conditions involving freedom are assigned to us in well functioning communities with a view on how well we recognized our responsibilities and how well we carry these out. At the same time, just as one might claim that humans have basic freedoms not depending on merit, so it could be claimed that humans should be able to take upon themselves some basic responsibilities, even if such undertakings are not given on the basis of proven reliability. To sort out some of the different types of responsibilities and their functioning in our social lives, let us consider the following three sentences:

1) x is responsible for y.
2) x is responsible for y because the community assigned this to x on the basis of x's having qualities Q1...Qn.
3) x is responsible for y, though the community does not acknowledge this.

1) represents what we might call moral responsibility. To sep-

arate it from what we called legal responsibility. Moral responsibility is based on the agent's having alternate possibilities. To be sure some modifications are needed for an explicit account, but that is beyond the scope of this work.[14]

2) specifies the functioning of responsibility in a community.[15] In the optimal cases there is a clear dependence of 2) on 1). For a community should not regard something as a responsibility of someone if the projected activity does not qualify as a possible responsibility for the agent in sense 1). 2) is a very general scheme, and it has to be filled out in different ways with regard to different tasks and jobs in life; such as profession, family, political, and others. (2) also brings up the challenge of coordinating the freedoms and responsibilities of members of the community, and set up priorities in terms what will be assigned and protected to which members.[16]

3) Brings up issues like civil rights, the right to be free from unjust persecutions, and similar potential restrictions. A well functioning community must always be on guard against mistakes it might commit that fall into the category covered by 3). But on the other hand awareness of such possible mistakes should not deter us from the recognition of incompatibilities, and the need to coordinate freedom and responsibility among members of the community.

At times people are tempted to link freedom and responsibility together too closely, as in:

4) no freedom and responsibility should be given or allowed to anyone in any context unless it can be shown that the freedom will be used responsibly.

Such a link is untenable. As in the case of freedom, in the case of responsibility too we must allow for human potential for carrying out responsibilities, and thus grant freedom even in some cases in which strong evidence of the ability and design for carrying out responsibility well cannot be found. We should also realize that mistakes in carrying out responsibilities in a few cases is

---

14 Frankfurt, "Alternate Responsibilities and Responsibility."
15 My fourfold pace-holder analysis resembles in some ways to Baier, "Types of Responsibility."
16 Feinberg, "The Moral and Legal Responsibility of the Bad Samaritan."

not sufficient for denying freedom; or at least this should be our guide for action in extreme cases of violations. In place of 4) we should adopt the milder

> 5) acknowledging some freedoms for a particular x should be made partly on the basis of considerations of the prospects of how in the exercise of the proposed freedom x would exercise that freedom responsibly.

We must, however, be willing to extend some similar principle to those who are outside the community in question. Just as one is willing to extend the ingredients of a good communal tie to outsiders who share with us at least some of our values, in the case of freedom and responsibility too, we must exercise similar extensions. The human potential to exercise freedom and to do this responsibly should be recognized in all of those humans who possess the relevant normal capacities. In doing so, we exercise one of the key elements among the four we listed as ingredients of a good communal tie, namely trust. This trust however does not amount to an unconditional command. It is subject to reconsideration in cases in which new evidence emerges. For example, it may be false that the people of Uganda at a given time are not ready for democratic political functioning, but assessing the truth of this claim is an empirical task. One cannot reject claims of this sort a priori.

Let us now separately consider the elements that fit the various argument places in our scheme 2): agent, action to be performed, community and warranting qualities. Agents have many different responsibilities in different contexts. But the following important condition applies across the board. A responsibility carried out well cannot be reduced to a set of duties. Let us consider the responsibilities of the operator of a train from Landquart to Davos. No list of expected problems and hence precautions to be taken can exhaust the responsibility well considered. We can never spell out completely all of the contingencies a train might encounter. This case, as well as standard cases of parental responsibility, shows that responsibility well considered will always be broader and more flexible than any set of duties specified.

There can be no "job description"—a recent favorite administrative device—for being a parent. It requires a commitment to do whatever turns out to be needed in the only partly predictable life of a child. To be sure, within that relation duties—on both sides—can be specified, but the framework is provided by the communal ties and the sense of responsibility that goes with this relation and ties. Responsibility well carried out requires a flexible readiness. Reality tends to outstrip imagination.

The second argument place specifies the range of responsibility. A promising way of specifying scope—anticipated to some extent by Aristotle—is based on the insight that though we have no direct conscious control over certain beliefs and feelings, there is much that we can do to bring ourselves into psychological states within which we will have certain beliefs and feelings, or can succeed in maintaining these, if we already possess them. For example, though one cannot choose to be angry or not angry, one can do a great deal to bring oneself into states in which the anger is likely to stop, or states in which anger at this or that is likely to arise. E.g. not acting on anger, trying to remain calm, reminding oneself of bad consequences of expressed anger, etc. can be useful in such a context. Or, to take another example, one cannot force oneself to be sympathetic towards someone, but one can do a great deal that will facilitate the emergence of such an attitude. Within this approach we can be responsible for beliefs and attitudes, though in a derivative way. Our actions form the primary range, and some of these will also be linked to bringing under this cover certain beliefs and feelings. The complete range of actions, feelings, and beliefs constitute an ontologically heterogeneous set. Some, like worshipping, have to be interpreted intentionally, others like watering plants admit of extensional analysis. In this respect what we can be responsible for mirrors in its ontological variety the kind, event, in general.

We now come to the third argument place. This is divided into two sub-classes. At times we are responsible to communal institutions or agents that assign responsibility to us. Hospitals, political units, courts, are obvious examples. Employers of various sorts also form an interesting group. There are, however, contexts in which we are responsible only to those affected. This could happen, for example, when someone makes a mistake during a steep climb. Furthermore, the two aspects can coincide. For example, fellow citizens of a political unit may be both the communal agents, assigning a responsibility and also those affected by what we are about to do. More difficult cases arise when the interests of the institution that assigns the responsibility and those of the affected do not coincide. For example, a health insurance company might assign responsibility to the physician in such a way that this conflicts with what is in the best interest of the patients. The possibility of such conflicts brings out a key feature of communal life, namely institutionalizing the constant review of responsibility assignments in a community, and the need to harmonize what seem at first glance conflicting interests. At this point someone might wonder if the third argument slot might not remain empty in certain cases. Don't we sometimes have responsibilities without there being any special group to which we owe the relation of having this responsibility? Within the ethics of this essay such a situation cannot arise, since there will always be some group that can fill the third argument place. In these cases too, the agent should have responsibility warranting qualities. It is a flaw in the network of human relations if agents affect the interests of others and lack the qualities that would be required in order for them to carry out their tasks responsibly.

Responsibility warranting qualities, the occupants of the fourth argument place, come in various kinds. First, we must distinguish minimal qualities that are required for someone to have the responsibility at all, from those the possession of which enables the agent to carry out the responsibility very well. For various roles there is the minimally responsible agent and the good agent. Secondly, we need to consider the warranting qualities over and over again in connection with different roles. For the responsible physician caring may be crucial while for the responsible lawyer other more aggressive qualities might be necessary. (We need to separate qualities involved in simply doing something like healing, or arguing in court, from those qualities that are needed in order to do those things responsibly, though there are—one hopes—overlaps between these classes.)

Responsibility warranting qualities admit of two levels. There may be some very general qualitative specifications such as reliability, understanding the task, being concerned with the welfare of others, and others. But even these need to be specified over and over again in context. For example, what counts in this specific context as understanding the task? The task may be being the train engineer on a specific run, or being the chief surgeon in a specific

operation. These complexities should remind us that as with freedom so also with responsibilities we should consider not only
kinds but also degrees.

We tend to assume that the key question is how to protect
freedoms and the rights of people to take on responsibilities. But
especially in the case of responsibility it is often an equally daunting task to convince people that they should take on responsibilities. This becomes very clear in the cases in which people are
relieved of certain pressures that limited their freedom. It takes
much political savvy to remind citizens immediately that with the
release from certain "chains" come new responsibilities. If one can
call attention to the need to build good communal ties in the new
context, this might help to bridge the gap between feeling
repressed and feeling—unrealistically—that in the new condition
everyone can act any way they feel like. Under conditions of
repression trust and care erode. Not paying attention to the need
to rebuild such ingredients of the communal tie can lead to chaos
that is replaced all too often in history by repressive measures, and
the circle keeps moving around. How can we engender or evoke
within a community the process of people trying to take on
responsibility?

First, there are rational arguments for taking on responsibility. Taking responsibility for the consequences of one's action is
important for individual rational decisions about how to implement values. For such decisions typically involve planning. Planning involves considering possible alternatives and assigning values to these, in the light of one's fundamental value commitments.
Not taking responsibility for my actions within the individual context results in some of the alternatives becoming not predictable
on the basis of my usual rational deliberative procedures. This
hurts my chances for implementing chosen values.

Hence carrying out responsibility is an important ingredient
in individual and communal planning and deliberation. However,
this argument by itself will not be very effective unless conditions
are provided that facilitate taking on responsibility. Two of these
are: certain amounts of stability and security. The security in the
political and economic sphere involves being safe from criminals,
dishonest adventures, etc. For without such security we cannot
expect the emergence of responsible entrepreneurs and thus fair

competition cannot develop. For example, developing small businesses need be protected from marauding gangs, and competition need be protected from those who by force and cheating would deprive competition from its presumably salutary effects.

Stability is also required as a condition facilitating the emergence of responsibility among members of a community. For without some degree of stability we cannot make reasonably safe predictions about the future. But without such predictions planning is not feasible. We have seen, however, that being responsible entails tracing the consequences of one's actions. In a world of uncertain future, how could one trace possible consequences, and thus how could one choose and plan responsibly? Reflection on the condition of stability leads us however to a question we also need to ask in connection with security. How much security, how much stability, and of what kinds? For example we might have too much security in a police state in which crime is almost non-existent, but so are possibilities for choice and initiative. Alternately, in an effort to gain stability we might create conditions that could be better described as stagnation. We need to make these important decisions about kinds of amounts of stability and security over and over again, depending on psychological, sociological and economic context. There can be no abstract general formula for these decisions, for what is perceived as stability will be partly a matter of variant psychological conditions. We are talking here about psychological motivations for taking on responsibility, and this is more a function of how humans—in various traditions, circumstances—perceive the world rather than a matter of how the world is, in an objective sense. As in the case of the relation between freedom and responsibility, so here too we encounter a practical but not conceptual circle. Reaching decisions about appropriate security and stability is partly a matter of having a sound community within which such questions can be discussed rationally, but having such a community is partly a matter of having some degree of responsibility.

Working out the development of freedom and responsibility is a daunting task in countries that undergo considerable changes in social, political, and economic structures. A good example is the recent development of Russia. Within their former framework, responsibility, and being responsible meant loyally following the instructions of the Party and the government. With the changes came necessarily the reconceptualization of responsibility. But the immediate need to replace the old conception with a new one was not seen by the leadership. The big change was interpreted by many citizens as from the state in which they could not do what they wanted to a state of affairs in which they could do as they pleased. This shallow interpretation was bound to push the country to the edge of chaos.

Within our theory, the development should be gradual. With each newly gained freedom people should be taught to take on the related responsibilities. One cannot do this with a narrowly materialistic reward system. For example, it will not do to bribe people so that they will not take bribes any more. At this juncture our doctrine of good communal ties comes into play. Taking on responsibility with the newly gained freedom helps to create as communal tie a bond with the ingredients of respect, concern, trust, and care. Taking on responsibility and interpreting the actions of others in the same vein brings with it respect. Respect need not bring concern for others but can facilitate such a development. In an atmosphere in which respect and concern are seen as key virtues trust develops further. And trust is badly needed in a development that involves so heavily assigning responsibilities to people. Even with these ways of attempting to transform society there is no guarantee of success. But the chances are better than trying to work with a combination of crude economic determinism and the promise of more freedom without stressing the linked responsibilities. We need also to be concerned with what conceptions most members of the community will have of what counts as responsibilities well carried out. Are the standards simply matters of what most people think? In contexts in which responsibility has not been examined well, it is highly questionable that a mere majority vote can deal with this task successfully There should be a communal consensus that efforts should be made to arrive at conceptions of well carried out responsibilities for which objective justifications can be given. A well functioning community should always be ready to reevaluate their aims and thus also their conceptions of adequate ties.[17]

---

17 Taylor, "Responsibility for Self."

The above may sound too cut and dry. Thus we should keep in mind that responsibility, like freedom, admits not only of variety of kinds but also of degrees. Neither in the development of a sound community nor in its efforts at maintenance can one expect perfection.

When we consider this complication, we can see also how infelicitous it is to construe the problem to be about free will. Within that formulation it is tempting to think of the issue in yes/no frames. "Is the will free?" Suggest a zero/one answer. But within the framework endorsed in this essay there is much more room for the more or less and the success that is related to kinds, or species, and does not rest on a single overall solution.

Thus these brief remarks should show that working out the problems of responsibilities in a community, like many of the other problems we sketched, rests not on a fundamentally legalistic framework, but rather on sound communal dynamics. This, in turn, can be worked out much better in small rather than large communities.

Thus it will be objected that our theory favors small communities, and when dealing with problems that cut across such communities, it favors federations rather than huge conglomerates. Today there are trends both in politics and in economics towards the large units as to what is desirable. But the push is mostly economic, and we should remind ourselves that economic determinism has already been rejected in this essay, and that communal ties can be hurt by wiping out small units. The biggest danger in erecting large political or economic units is corruption. A small community can live quite happily, even in poverty.[18] In larger communities it is difficult to create trust and care for others.

Thus our hypothesis: the larger the community the more likelihood of corruption increases.

The following considerations support this thesis. First, the larger the community, the less clear the lines of accountability will be. But lax systems of accountability create great temptation towards corruption. Secondly, we saw the need for the development and sharing of certain direct attitudes (trust, care), but without these contacts will become impersonal, and in that atmo-

---

18 LaPierre, *City of Joy*.

sphere corruption thrives. Thirdly, responsibility will be assigned more and more to large committees, and that brings the danger of individuals not feeling or being thought of having specific responsibilities.

None of these considerations are decisive. But, as in other cases, when we consider the advantages of large units for economic reasons, we should conduct a benefit–cost analysis along the lines suggested before, to see how the advantages fare when compared to the advantages of communal ties and adequate individual ideals within small units, and the damage that the large organizations can cause either via corruption or by other means to the basics of well lives individual and communal lives.

4. Political Units

One might think it absurd to write a few pages on a topic on which thousands of pages have been written over millennia. But, as in the case of the other topics in this chapter, we shall restrict ourselves to showing how reflections on individual ideals and sound communal ties as well as dynamics in general affect political thought. We have argued already that individual and communal ethics cannot be done in complete separation, and that in political theory the legal structure should be seen as the super-architect is, requiring a sound underlying communal dynamics. These interdependencies should make it natural that our theory should have some conditions of adequacy imposed on political life.

We have seen already some link between the theory of this book and political theory. For we have seen considerations in favor of small political units, even if these interact within federations. The objections to large economical and political units stem from our conception of healthy communal dynamics, and thus run against current positive assessments of the larger structures on account of efficiency.

Before showing how our theory affects what a conception of a well functioning political unit should be, let us sketch two preliminaries. Our theory is meant to apply to all kinds of communities, such as family, social associations, and others. Thus a reason must be given for singling out political and economic units for special considerations. The defense for this move starts with the observation that respect, concern, trust, and care can be engendered and maintained much easier in communities like family and friendship than in political units like a state. Hence more elaborate treatments are needed to show that some of these ingredients can also function in a state, and their presence should be seen as a constraint on what a well functioning state should be. Secondly, it is easier to convince people that families and circles of friends are natural units than to persuade them of this applying also to states and economic units.

Much ink has been spilled on the question of whether political and economic ties are natural or just arbitrary social constructions, superimposed on the lives of groups. Our answer to this dilemma starts with distinguishing the question of whether being in some state or other is a natural ingredient of the human condition, and the question about whether any given form of a state is to be seen as natural. Our answer is that the first kind of participation is natural, the second is not.

To understand this reply we should compare being a part of some political and economic unity with being a part of some linguistic community. Intelligent thought development and communication depends of having competence in at least one language. Many linguists believe that the ability to master a language is an innate human factor.[19] At the same time, we also acknowledge the variety of structures and semantic units that emerge in any given language, and the fact that within some general constraints, as of now yet not well understood, these have their causes in contingent local conditions. One can think of participation in a political economic unit along the same lines. It is a part of human nature to be a member of some such unit. But the particular structures of any given political unit are mostly the result of contingent external factors, and can be changed by the participants. We are born into linguistic and political communities. Hence within our theory it makes no sense to ask such questions as: "why should I be a member of political Units?" or "what is the justification of being and remaining an element within political units?" For the analogous question about linguistic communities makes no sense either. We can attempt to change,

---

19 Chomsky, *Cartesian Linguistics.*

improve, and extend a natural language, but it makes no sense to suggest that we should withdraw from using language.[20] Hence the typical philosophic question that our theory addresses is: "now that we find ourselves in mid-stream, what would make our political and economic life better, and what is likely to lead to deterioration?" Related to this issue is the question: "what activities and aspects of human interaction are likely to help with the maintenance of what we regard as good communal dynamics and good laws?" For example, it is easy to see how our articulation of the proposed good communal tie provides guidelines for maintaining a healthy community. The guidelines suggest working on the persistence of respect, concern, trust and care. Within a community in which these attitudes are widespread it will be relatively easy to formulate laws that people respect and obey, and institutional structures that are likely to persist.

The communal tie and criteria for good communal dynamics are the basic core of our theory. Sound implementations admit of a wide variety, and are relative to historical, cultural, and ideological contexts. In analogy with this line of thinking we should look for elements that in a very general sense all political units should contain. We can then add to this core variations in implementation and contextual characterizations of what would count as a good realization in this or that context.

The following four conditions are proposed as the core demands on political and economic units from the point of view of demands for adequate ties and communal dynamics. (For the sake of simplifying the account we shall deal here only with the political aspects. But it is easy to draft analogues for economic units, which often coincide with the political ones.)

1) Every member should have some freedom and associated responsibility assigned and protected by the community.
2) A certain level, and kind, of security should be enjoyed by all members, both with respect to internal and external matters.
3) Every adult member should have some opportunity to make a living minimally on a level determined by external circumstances and communal consensus.

---

20 Moravcsik, *Thought and Language*, chapter 3.

4) The community should have a system of justice for handling criminal cases and the distribution of goods. What counts as good should be determined by objective conditions and communal consensus. The system of justice must be in some indirect way accountable to the community.

The following provides justification for selecting these four conditions. Condition 1) has a conceptual link to our proposed communal tie. For one of the ingredients of that tie is respect for others. But without enjoying some amount of freedom, one cannot show respect for others. Respect is the choice to treat others as ends in themselves. If we lack freedom and are forced into respect-behavior, that is not genuine respect. It does not organize one's thinking and attitudes in the way in which genuine respect for others does.

2) and 3) provide the basic conditions for survival, obviously needed for anyone to practice the attitudes and interactions required by the tie. Both of these conditions are left vague and general. For fixing the appropriate level of security and the standard for minimal subsistence are highly cultural-relative and contextual matters. One cannot fix security for all and against any criminals and external foes. One must estimate probabilities of crimes of various sorts, and the international situation. Even after that, since in the modern world security costs a lot of money, benefit–cost analysis must be applied.

4) is the political analogue to the ingredient of concern for others in the communal tie. To be sure, people may have other motives for wanting a system of justice. But that is irrelevant to our investigation. For understanding the relation between the four conditions, and the tie, all we need to do is to show how at least one strong push for a fair judicial system comes from an ingredient of the tie.

Conceptually viewed, the four conditions are distinct and not incompatible. But when facing the empirical world, conflict can arise in several places. For example, in a capitalist society there can be conflict between 1) and 3). As stated, 3) does not place limits on the pursuit of making a living. But 1) can do that; for unlimited pursuit of wealth often does require treating some people as means only and not as ends as well. There can be conflicts between 1) and 3) in terms of work and opportunity to vote. The former is an expression of respect for all adults. The latter may clash with certain demands of taxation to cover the expenses of enabling everyone to vote. As we saw Reagan said to Gorbachov that voting is a human right. Gorbachov replied that the opportunity to work is a human right.

Political context is also effective in determining how much freedom and how much security a country should have. A small country like Singapore, sandwiched between two giants, China and Indonesia, is more security conscious and is willing to sacrifice some individual liberties. A big wealthy county like the USA leans towards less concern with security and more with minimizing limitations on individual freedom.

There are dangers associated with each condition. Too much freedom in the hands of some members can lead to the domination these can exercise over the majority. Contrarily, freedom by the majority without limits can lead to the tyranny of the majority over minorities. Others theories will appeal to human rights and similar fundamental obligations. Our theory appeals to the whole community seeing how domination and abuse either way will destroy the good communal ties, and thus will lead to a less adequate way of living, even if a few have more money and power than they might otherwise.

So in cases in which domination threatens, our theory does make an ethical judgment. But in cases like the difference between the different weighing of security and freedom, as in the USA and Singapore, it makes no sense to ask: "which is right?" The two systems are erected to respond to different needs. Of course, someone might still criticize either the USA or Singapore by saying that even after the needs are considered and recognized, there is still room for disagreeing with how this or that institution functions in the respective countries. But that is not a judgment in principle between freedom and security.

Intuitions can also differ on the relative importance of communal decisions being made wisely or left to majority vote. These two after all can conflict. An informal survey among a group of American college students showed that they prefer the states in which much is left to majority vote, even if it is less efficient, to a system in which there is less room for voting and more is handled by people shown to be competent experts in this or that area. A similar questionnaire among students in Singapore brought the opposite result in preference. As long as both systems are tied to accountability of some sort, our theory does not regard one or the other as superior terms.

Another example involves intuitions about equality. In some countries certain inequalities are deemed acceptable as long as everyone is better off under that system than they would be in any empirically possible purely egalitarian system. In Russia, however, a large part of the population is willing to live on a less prosperous level as long as nobody is getting a larger share of the good than the rest of the population. One cannot simply dismiss this as envy and then label that as irrational. It is quite likely that in the minds of many people egalitarianism in economic matters is tied to their self-esteem. One might deplore this conception of self-esteem and suggest an educational process that helps people to anchor their self-esteem on sounder grounds. But that is irrelevant to the point under investigation. As long as there is this way of construing self-esteem, egalitarian trends will have to be given more weight than in other, less egalitarian countries, even if this means less material wealth in the affected communities.

These remarks are not meant as the beginning of a substitute for political theories like democracy or a police state. Nor are these meant as a substitute for talking about rights and obligations by state and citizen. But the remarks and conditions are meant to show that no matter what ideology and system a group wants to follow, our theory demands that respect be shown to conditions of good communal ties and dynamics. This brief section shows how the impact of such demands can affect the structures and institutions we build. They function as constraints against mere materialism and purely legal foundations, but as we saw the four conditions as stated also encourage a more pluralistic outlook and a less antagonistic stance towards those who find ways to meet the four conditions that are different from the ones we use in our own society. Different structures that can be seen as means towards the same end are more likely to be negotiable, than different structures that are construed by the different parties as ends in themselves.

5. Work in a Good Community

Our comments on the relations between value-based communities with good communal ties and aspects of political units brought up the topic of the necessity to make a living. In typical societies this involves work. In the remarks that follow we shall see what our theory has to say in the way of both constraints and enabling conditions for work. It is a mistake to think of work as always connected with making a living. This is not due solely to the science fiction examples of societies in which people need not earn a living. Since we deal with the typical society, we shall ignore these possibilities. The more important philosophical point is that work may also be involved in projects that are not linked to material reward. One might produce a work of art and not expect any material rewards for it. Or one might work for charities and be proud of accomplishments, without receiving any monetary reward. Thus though we will deal with work while having in mind making a living, our general conception of work will involve more than that.

Modern societies institutionalize making a living. Hence the motion of having a job emerges. Most jobs involve not only work but working for someone or some institution. Hence in assessing how jobs should be formulated in a healthy society we need to keep in mind not only qualities of the work expected, but also relationships to those for whom the work is done. Furthermore, we need to relate the notion of work with employment. This we see in various contrasts. Such as: working and not working, having or not having a job, and employment contrasted with being unemployed. We will also take up the contrast between working on a job and leisure time. It would be most unfortunate if we construed vacation and leisure as necessarily not involving work and thus pride of accomplishment.

Finally, we should note that work, or having a job, cannot be defined purely in terms of observational properties, and that what we regard as work will be highly context dependent. What counts as work in an office in Houston may not count as work among laborers in the Philippines.[21]

---

21 The difficulties of persuading some people in the Far East that just sitting at a desk and thinking should also count as work was narrated to the author by a Stanford volunteer worker in East Asia.

These observations can be captured by the following definition of work. "Work is appropriate activity with efforts leading to some state of affairs or product with the result counting as an achievement hence a source of pride, and the end being considered to be of some value by the community."

This definition gives us a skeleton of meaning, with important gaps left to be filled in by context. What is an appropriate activity depends on cultural context. So do other notions involved such as achievement, considered to be of value, and pride.

So far we have talked about work as what enables us to accomplish something and in many contexts to earn for us a living. There is, however, another strain in Western culture that is made explicit by Aristotle.[22] This concept has its roots in Greek etymology. The word "ergon" can mean "work," but it can also mean "function" or "functioning." Exploiting this one can construe work as a natural human function. It should be some conscious effort on our part that results in fulfilling a part of our human potential. In the animal world this is easy to illustrate. Beavers build dams, spiders weave webs, other animals dig burrows. It would be difficult in an industrial society to make all work a part of fulfilling the human potential. But since this is a matter of degrees, we can aim at a partial meeting of this condition. Ignoring it completely results in work that some theoreticians call "alienation." We shall see how aspects of the good society in our theory help to capture some of the intuitions behind this Aristotelian notion.

Before looking at other details and our general proposal we should note that though the account of work given here is primarily for the value-based good society, it is meant to apply also to other communities that do not meet such high standards, or meet those only partially. One demand that emerges from our discussion so far is that labor and work should be humane. This can be applied universally, but with the proviso that what counts as "humane" will depend partly on the cultural context of the community. The work "partly" should be stressed, for our analysis does not entail that "anything goes." For example, everyone should agree that child labor as practiced in the 19th century—as in mines—is inhumane and should not have been tolerated. But we

---

22 Aristotle, *Nichomachean Ethics*, I. 7.

must keep in mind that in 5–100 years people living then will have most likely similar views about some of our practices. For example, it is most probable that they will view as inhumane thousands and thousands bending over a computer all day long, ruining their eyes, ruining their backs, and ending up with serious wrist problems. If we are to apply our Communal Tie proposal rigorously, then such practices should be halted. It is unrealistic, however, to expect that a practice on which so much of our current technology depends can be wiped out in one fell swoop. This, however should not prevent us from working towards the gradual elimination of this and similar practices. Humanizing the working place should be at least of equal importance if not more, than the construction of machines that promise more speed in performance.

There are already efforts made, for example, in the automobile industry to make working conditions more humane and more in line with what are parts of fulfilling the human potential.[23]

With these considerations providing the background, let us turn to conditions that should characterize work in a well functioning society.

Work must:

(1) enable the worker to make a living, where this is necessary.

(2) enable the worker to take pride in what he or she accomplished.

(3) enable the worker to see what he does as contributing something positive to the goods of others and to the good of the community.

Condition 1) is stated in this way so as not to prohibit counting something as work that meets the definition given above, but is not linked to making a living. The bite of 1) is that when people need to make a living, the work available in the community should be such as to enable them to do that. One could label the first condition as the "survival condition." The second condition is linked to some form of self-esteem that all humans should be able to have. Pride itself need not be good. There is false pride, excessive pride, and other misfirings of this characteristic. But the pride that

---

23 Frithjoff Bergmann's work in the Detriot area with humanizing work in factories is relevant.

comes from work well done is a precious commodity, and every human should be able to enjoy it.

So far we have survival and self-esteem as parts of people working on a job. The third condition demands that the work done should be interpretable as not just satisfying the worker's whim and that of the employer, but can be seen as leading to something that we can regard as objectively good, be it shelter, medicine, educational items or spiritual values. Some work will be more some less oriented towards the community. But some relation to the communal good should be kept in mind, else we inject another random element and one capable of creating chaos into the communal life.

Let us now consider the case in which only the third of our conditions characterizes work. The deficiencies of such a conception include one shared by the conception we just considered, namely that nothing guarantees or even tends to promote good quality work or product. Judging what is in the interest of the community—without additional factors providing conceptual background—tends to degenerate into judging just what members of the community happen to desire. Hence the likelihood of the emergence of low quality work and products. Another problem is that judging work and products solely in terms of whether these contribute to what the public thinks is desirable is unlikely to stimulate competition and industriousness. For in such a system there is no incentive built in, once we fulfill the minimum and find ourselves judged in some sense useful. Hence a stagnating egalitarianism is likely to emerge. Job security regardless of quality of work is not conducive to creativity, effort, or taking initiative.

It seems, then, that we need some combination of both the first and the third conditions of our scheme as necessary ingredients in this normative conception of work.

We will now consider why the second condition is also necessary. First, without it creativity, pride in one's work, and self-esteem based on more than power or prestige will not emerge. Secondly, the quality of work and product—apart from issues of craftsmanship—will also suffer. For only profit and utility, not the satisfaction of having created something that has also non-utilitarian goodness, will fuel the activities.

It will be objected that in technologically oriented societies the second condition is unlikely to be implemented on a large scale. Too much of the work demanded by technology from the least skilled is routine and leads to boredom. But facing a challenge is not a good reason for removing necessary conditions of adequacy. We should view this condition as indicating a guideline that needs to be considered as we plan the nature of different types of work in our communities. We need to be creative about how we try to turn the routine into the worthwhile and interesting. Also, the contrast between the interesting and the boring is to some extent "in the eye of the beholder." What seems to one boring and monotonous might not seem so to someone else who found ways of introducing some psychologically stimulating element into what seems flat to others. Ignoring this condition will in the long run lead to more social upheaval and more psychological problems about work than squabbles of the 19th century variety about ownership.

Today the problem of how to exclude or minimize demeaning work; i.e. work that nobody should be doing, is not related to ownership. It is a problem for management, and requires ethical and psychological input, not merely economical ones. The ethical dimension has two aspects. One should protect individuals from circumstances in which they are forced to perform labor that does not give them enough profit and cannot be viewed as giving them pride, or not even self esteem. E.g. work for others that they themselves could do quite well, and should be a matter of the private sphere. Hence the vanishing in some cultures of servants. The other dimension is the danger that certain kinds of work will cause individuals to lose sensitivity and other capacities needed for participation in communal life. This work makes humans "brutish." Unfortunately, these are not essential conditions, but constituents of an ideal to be approximated. Striving for this ideal, however, is an essential part in trying to meet today our key three conditions.

Finally, we can see that work meeting only the second of our conditions will not be satisfactory, since there is nothing built into it guaranteeing or making it likely that what is produced can bring profit to the worker or be in any way useful to the community. These considerations support the inclusion of all three ingredients into the communal desideratum for work.

Superficially, one might link the conception of work governed by condition 1) only to capitalism, and the one governed by condition 3) only to socialism. But this is misleading. Capitalism and socialism are seen within this framework as two extreme alternatives covering up a wide variety of possible structures. Versions of capitalism can come with the addendum that wealth is also a responsibility, or that capitalism with adequate individual ideals for participants will bring with it also meeting condition 2). Similar considerations apply to socialism. It need not be restricted to just meeting condition 3). It could include condition 2), it could propose various ways of combining 1) and 3). Just as our reflections on freedom and responsibility do not end up supporting unconditionally either democracy or non-democratic systems within the nomenclature of current jargon, so this scheme ends up taking not only a pragmatic stance towards slogans in economic theory, but suggests possibilities for much more subtle and pluralistic classifications of possible schemes in politics.

These considerations about work also provide additional fuel against economic determinism.[24] For the three conditions together suggest that criteria for more or less adequate working arrangements will be only partly economic. Work is one of the key elements in any conception of socio–economic structure, and we see that it is a function of economic, ethical, and psychological factors, as one would expect of any important ingredient in our communal and economic life. The same purely economic structure will have quite different consequences depending on the conception of work within which it is embedded. And such conceptions depend to some extent on what are seen as desirable working conditions, i.e. communal ties of some sorts.

The conception developed immediately raises the question: how much of the meeting of each of the three conditions is desirable, and in what mixture? How much profit, and what kind; and what kinds of incentives for being able to take pride in one's work, and how is this to be balanced with social utility? As in the case of analogous questions about freedom, responsibility and self-discipline, here too the answer has to remain contextual and pragmatic.

There are many constraints that constitute cultural context. Historical traditions, the art of the culture, the difficulty of economic survival, the status of religion in the community, and many

---

24 See also Fogel, *Without Consent or Contracts.*

other such factors fill out the notion of context. In the case of work a delineation of what in our context is worth regarding as acceptable work, we need to balance the "three C's:" coping, competition and cooperation. Looking at the criteria for good communal ties, and what a value-based society should be like will not solve all of our problems, but can be a significant input. The four ingredients that make up our favorite communal tie can be constituents also in a working place as these would partly govern the relationships and interaction among workers. In determining the communal tie for a community we ignored power relationships and placed at the foundational level our four ingredients. The same considerations that supported that move can also be used to do the same thing in the case of work.

Efficiency cannot dominate the determination of the work we do and demand. For example, there is a movement to construct two tunnels under the Alps in order to speed the transportation of goods from one side of the Alps to the other. But this would quite likely cause a great deal of harm to the environment, and much damage to the cultures of the social units within which the population in the affected areas live. Thus in this case the concerns aired in this book could intervene in very direct, practical ways.

In summary, we see that as with many of the other key concepts of this book, the notion of work also requires much contextual filling to complete the concept that is defined partly by a core. We see also that the key notions in a discussion of work are going to be normative. Respect is to value someone for good characteristics, and work is to do things with effort that are worthwhile and help other to cope. We saw that we cannot construe our conditions on work as necessary because in some contests that could not be carried out. But we can regard them as guidelines showing us what we should approximate.

The characterization of work in this section is neither capitalistic nor socialistic. It cuts across that dichotomy that we inherited from the 19th century, and specifies aims towards which either theory can be a means in a given context. Still better, perhaps the desiderata laid out here will stimulate some to come up with new economic and political alternatives.

Chapter VI

THE ROOTS OF JUSTICE: SHARING AND GOOD TIES

Humans have needs. Meeting these require both non-material and material goods. In different stages of history we find a variety of ways in which goods are distributed. Not all ways are equally good. Hence the focus of this chapter on better and worse ways of distribution. Our account will rely on some of the material presented in the previous chapters. This material includes the account of good communal ties, and appropriate ways in which responsibility is to be assigned and carried out in a well functioning community. Still, even if applied to our sketch of social and political structure and work, from this material alone we could not derive the account of justice proposed here. A key feature of this chapter is the introduction of the concept of sharing as a crucial cornerstone in the foundation of an adequate theory of justice.

Distributive justice differs from criminal law. The latter is a battleground for corrective and retributive theories. We shall not touch on that controversy at all. The whole discussion will be limited to certain aspects of distributive justice. An enormous body of literature has developed about distributive justice. Our theory touches only on some aspect of justice. In fact, towards the end it will be suggested that philosophical contributions to theories of justice need be limited to providing foundations and guidelines for how institutions of justice should function. Many other parts of justice should not be seen as legitimate subject for philosophy to take up.

In recent years fairness has been a central concept in philosophic proposals about what justice is.[1] In this respect the theory of this chapter differs from mainstream ethical theory. Fairness obviously must play some role in adequate distribution practices,

---

1 Rawls, *A Theory of Justice.*

but we will try to show that the concept cannot bear the conceptual burden that making it the basic foundational notion would
require.

Thus in this chapter we will start with a discussion of fairness
and its link to rationality and justice. After that discussion we will
introduce the notion of sharing, and show in our analysis of it why
it should be seen as the conceptual and psychological key to an
explication of criteria for well functioning distributive systems.
After our discussion of sharing we will show how a minimal kind
of sharing that involves everyone wanting to share some thing with
some people, can be used to argue for expansions of various sorts
so that individuals will be willing to share many goods with wide
circles of people.

The remaining sections argue that we need both good communal ties and sharing viewed in a certain way in order to formulate ethical criteria for distributive patterns. We will end up with a
conception of justice which should be whatever is the best way of
sharing within a community.

1. Fairness: to whom? On what basis?

It is commonly agreed that fairness in one way or another must
play a role in a description of a good system of justice. But this
leaves many questions unanswered. Is fairness a homogeneous
concept, or is it a combination of many aspects, functioning as dis-
juncts, with this or that component playing salient roles in this or
that context? Should fairness be linked conceptually to rationality and to equality?

One way of examining these issues is to list some of the intuitions that we have about fairness, and then see what kind of a
unity might emerge from this list. Herewith a sample.

1) This is unfair because it leaves us with inequalities.
2) This is unfair because we disregarded the respective merits
   of the participants.
3) This is unfair because we did not consider the different
   positions that participants play in this enterprise; hence
   bear different responsibilities.
4) This is unfair because my fundamental rights have been
   violated.

5) This is unfair because it takes no account of what society owes me.

6) This is unfair because it does not curb selfish tendencies in the participants.

Even this small sample supports the idea that fairness is not a homogenous notion. For example, 1) and 2) clash often since when we consider merit, we end up with a distribution that creates inequalities among the goods as distributed. Differences in responsibilities introduce further complications. Merit and responsibility often do not coincide, and the same goes for responsibility and equality. We must not forget that we are looking at these aspects of fairness within a communal setting, and within the history of the community in question. Thus 4) may clash with any of 1)–3), because of past developments that cannot be erased with "new start." E.g. Jones has a right to his property, but maybe his ancestors acquired that in fights of a variety of sorts, so that certain inequalities exist today as a result of past events. 5) too brings up historical questions, but this time within the life-span of one person. Furthermore, we can decide "what society owes" a certain person only in context; considering what are construed as good in that society, what are the existing rules of obligation, and other such matters.[2] 6) brings up psychological issues. To what extent should the practice of fairness bear the burden of moral education in the community? How much weight does this consideration have in comparison with the other ingredients?

Even when faced with these possible clashes, someone might try to bring in the notion of rationality, and claim that reliance on what is rational should resolve the conflicts that may surface. But a few examples can show that rationality by itself cannot bear the heavy conceptual burden that such a view would place on it.

Let us consider what on the surface seem like two rational distributive principles. One is: "justice in a community is whatever principle of distribution is willingly accepted by all those affected." One could support this by arguing that as long as the mode of distribution contemplated brings satisfaction to everyone affected, there is no reason to undertake upsetting this—maybe superficial—harmony. But one could argue also for the rationality of

2 Rawls, *op .cit.,* 284–292.

another principle. This says: "justice is the system of distribution for a community that enables it to achieve maximal gain." After all, communities want to be competitive, and remaining competitive might in some contexts require distributions of goods along the lines of this principle.

So both principles have some rationale underlying them. But both of these are likely to conflict with fairness.

The first one could create serious differences in the welfare of members of the community without sound ethical or economic justifications. The principles may be accepted by a community on the basis of ideological or religious pressures. The second principle too conflicts often with fairness, since one can increase overall economic gain in a community in some contexts by measures that create much injustice; i.e. increase hardships for some people without any consideration of their merits or what general respect we are bound by. The point here is not that either of these principles is beyond criticism. Both can be shown to be inadequate, but such demonstrations will not be able to rely on a sense of nationality that would show these proposals to be irrational without begging questions. Rawls has arguments against placing efficiency above justice,[3] but these assume giving among ethical goods fairness a special position. This, in turn, can be disputed by pointing out that in some contexts a desire for some version of fairness has no priority over such pressing matters as security or safety. This disagreement, in turn, leads us to larger considerations of what is human nature, and the nature of a community.

We encounter other difficulties with fairness when considering distributional problems over longer periods of time. For some of us justice as a sound distributional principle means to find the best arrangements of goods that enables us to distribute goods so as to make the development of individual and communal potentials, extended over all members, possible. But for many others it means that those previously oppressed should now have an equal chance to pay back their oppressors. We see arguments of this sort brought up, e.g. in debates between Israelis and Palestinians, or among some factions in South Africa. Fortunately, there are also different voices both in the Near East and in Africa. But one can-

3 Ibid. 78–80.

not simply rule out the "an eye for an eye" view. Furthermore, these arguments have to be brought into harmony with the ethical fact that in some contexts reparation for past damages is justified.

Next let us consider the relation between fairness and equality. Within some Kantian versions of justice questions of equality only arise in an ethically relevant way when the society operates under conditions of scarcity. E.g. Rawls dismisses cases in which people resent inequality even when everyone has enough, on the ground that this is a case of envy, and envy is not rational.[4] But one can argue that when inequalities are seen in a community as affecting self-esteem, this is not just envy, and problems about inequality do emerge as ethically relevant, even if there is no scarcity. In some societies, e.g. by and large in the USA, people are content to have some inequality in distribution as long as there is enough to go around, and some inequalities will be eliminated, even if the goods do not involve scarcity. The source of such a view need not be envy. Some people feel that the inequality takes away something valuable from communal life. This was, in fact, an argument used in the early development of the Kibbutz in Israel. Others claim that the inequalities, scarcity or not, robs them of self-esteem. One might argue that such people have an inadequate and shallow conception of self-esteem. But this takes us outside of discussions about fairness. This is precisely the kind of issue with which ideal ethics—as discussed in part I of this book—deals.

Does equality allow for exceptions? Every proposal allows for some exceptions. In Rawls' theory inequality is acceptable as long as it benefits the least advantaged section of society.[5] This raises the question of whether we can define the notion of being disadvantaged apart from contexts of communal values. E.g. it has been suggested that being in the relevant sense disadvantaged can involve economic conditions, or physical handicap, or having been previously oppressed.[6] There may be sound ethical criteria for sorting out these matters, but these are not grounded in fairness. This issue should bring out the need of shared values in a society,

4 Ibid. 530–541.
5 Ibid. 97–100.
6 Xiaorong, *Justice, Reason, and the Human Good.*

for without such agreements the status of being disadvantaged in that society will not be resolved.

Considerations of communal value, and possible transcultural ethical criteria for what should count as a communal value surface also when we consider the range of what should count as goods to be distributed. In addition to economical good, one needs to add, as Rawls stressed,[7] basic civic liberties. Amartya Sen has shown that one has to take an even broader view of the relevant qualities of life when dealing crossculturally with distributive problems.[8] Recent events across the globe suggest that a key communal good is security and safety. It might be thought that this is already included in Rawls' list of basic civic liberties under the heading of "right to life."[9] But right to life is not the same as a demand on the state that it should provide safety for a person, i.e. conditions minimizing the chances of burglary, theft, and other ways of depriving one of one's belongings, and for security, i.e. minimizing chances of being beaten up, raped, molested, prevented from reaching recreational facilities, etc. One can imagine a community within which murder is rare because of various deterrents, but millions live in fear and have to go through all sort of obstacles and install all kinds of safety devices so as to have a reasonable chance of arriving at home after work, with person, belongings, and car, still intact and in one's position. Unfortunately this description fits a considerable segment of the population of the USA, and the mere right to life will not solve the problem. This issue affects the matter of justice and fairness. For now security and safety become separate goods, vying for priority in various contexts with Rawlsian basic liberties as well as the goods provided by adequate communal ties. These priorities also affect such matters as what counts as a just system of taxation in a given community.

These considerations show that rationality cannot bear the burden it would have to carry if it were the foundation on which we can build fairness. Another line of thought would take equality as the cornerstone, and construe this as what explicates fairness in

---

7 Rawls, *op. cit.*, 61–62.
8 Sen, *Inequality Reexamined*.
9 I am indebted to conversation with Daniel Bell.

most important contexts. The following are considerations against taking this stance.

As we need to raise the questions "to whom?" and "on what basis?" in the case of fairness, so we need to consider the same issues in the case of equality. First, equality is a context-dependent concept. We may have a general understanding of the sorts of cases which we account for as cases of equality, but in specific contexts we need to ask: "what counts as equality in this set of circumstances?" Equality among teachers, equality among citizens, equality among wage-earners; these are all different types of applications of "equal" with different criteria. We can say in some cases, "they are equal, because each gets what he deserves." But when we consider minimal financial resources for paying basic medical bills, we consider equality in terms of same minimal earning power.

At times we consider equality in view of persons' contributions to a cooperative enterprise. In early stages of human culture, meat was distributed among the hunters. But one might insist that equal amount should be given to each, while others could argue that those with larger families should receive larger shares. Without considering communal values, outlooks on what should count as human goods, and similar issues, one cannot decide what the right distribution should be. Fairness has many sources, as our review of intuitions has shown. The same is true of equality. Neither of these can be brought in as a higher principle to settle problems that arise in connection with the application of the other. To insist that giving everyone a numerically and quantitatively equal share of what are agreed as goods seems both unethical and unrealistic. It is unrealistic because we cannot give that kind of quantitative analysis of all of our goods, and unethical because it would require us to ignore in all contexts merit and contribution. It is one thing to say that everyone should be treated as equal in court of law, and a very different thing to insist that in various contexts those who work harder should not be able to possess more than others with more lax working habits. This is a constant problem in many work places. We want equal distribution in some cases among all who work. In other cases, among all of those who deserve it. Still in other cases equal distribution is demanded in a group when receiving certain goods affects what others can receive. Some people will then add that when the reception of a certain good does not affect receptions by others, in other words we are not dealing with scarce goods, then "let everyone obtain as much as possible, regardless of need, equality." There are, however problems with such a view as well. Perhaps less significantly, some may object because their self-esteem will be hurt. But more significantly, obtaining even non-scarce goods can give some people a lot of power over others. Is it fair, then, to the community that it should allow such distorted power relations? At times researchers want to add the proviso that even though we cannot guarantee equal distribution of non-scarce goods, we should insist on equal opportunities for all members of the community to attain these sought after items. But this is unrealistic. People come to the distribution schemes with different histories, different abilities, and character. We cannot equalize all of this. And to say that at least everyone should have the same right to certain goods will not help much. How much does it help to say that everyone has the right to vote, if the community cannot guarantee to a large percent of the population that they will have the actual means to exercise their voting privileges? How much does it help to say that everyone has the right to run for a certain public office, if it turns out to be the case that unless an individual can collect 5 million dollars, he has—empirically speaking—no chance to run for the office?[10]

If we limit how much of a good that does not come under scarcity can be accumulated by a member of the community, the arguments will have to be not in terms of fairness and equality, but in terms of communal values and ties. How do enormous differences in the cases just mentioned affect communal ties and interpersonal relations? Furthermore, how much should these considerations about communal relation's weigh when formulating laws about what a person can or cannot gather in a given community? For example, is it good if some people in a community get much more attention than others, even if attention is not a good under scarcity?

These issues and question suggest that we seem to demand—even if not consciously—answers to the question, in various context: "when is equality and fairness deserved?" It makes good

---

10 Williams, "Equality."

sense to say in various contexts that members of this or that group "earned" fairness, or deserve equality. Justification has a variety of sources. At times it is a mode of cooperation among members, at other times it is the way each carries out responsibilities. The source can also be evidence about certain shared attitudes in a community.

Equality can also have as its source agnosticism. Underlying this agnosticism is the contention that we can never know with reasonable degree of confidence, who deserves what with regards to access to basic goods, and thus the safest way to distribute is to invoke equality. Our response to this is that such agnosticism too is context-dependent. In some cases it is more justifiable than in others. In some social contexts we know that a certain segment of the society handles responsibility better than members of another segment. In such cases awarding more responsibility and often more goods, is justifiable.

These considerations suggest that equality is not a foundational concept for justice. It has a variety of other notions governing its applications and interpretations. But having looked at both rationality and equality and construing these now as multifaceted, we can draw the same conclusions about fairness. Fairness is a "many-splendored thing." In some context this, and in others another element strikes reasonable people as salient. Hence at times equality, of certain kinds, is invoked to defend a proposed distribution as fair, and at other times merit, and amount of contributions from individuals to cooperative tasks.[11]

Yet it seems that in all of these contexts and distributions of goods, there is a common strand. For in all of the above we are dealing with varieties of SHARING. Individuals are moved to share goods, or to support certain ways in which the community will distribute goods. Having merely good will, or a sense of fairness and duty are not sufficient to sustain a system of justice. In order to be effective in matters of justice, these elements have to be incorporated in practices of sharing. Thus in the next section we shall explore this concept and show how it can be a part of the foundation of an adequate system of justice.

---

11 Baier, "Trust and Anti-trust."

2. Sharing

Sharing is an activity. We share some goods, we share the same fate with others, we can share fellowship. Given this variety of opportunities it is no wonder that adequate lexical definitions are hard to find, and translations into other languages, e.g. German, are difficult. It has been said that there is no word for "sharing" in Chinese. But the reason for this does not seem to be egoism, but the superfluousness of the word in a culture in which in a family objects are seen as common.

We share things for different reasons and with different motives. At times we share because that is what we want to do, at other times we are obliged to share, or do it under duress, and in still other contexts we share out of generosity, because we feel sorry for some people. These examples show that sharing has different aspects. There is the object to be shared, the recipients, the nature of our underlying attitudes, and hypotheses concerning the link between sharing and human nature.

Some of the objects we share, such as food, money, etc. have a determinate quantity so that if I share mine with someone else, my share decreases. The object need not be material. It can be shelter, or security, or affection. At times the means leading to what we want to share are of a determined quantity. E.g. we need money to buy what we want to share.

There are, however, other items that do not diminish when we share these. Furthermore, we cannot give them in literal sense to others. Some items do not increase or diminish as we share them. This class includes cultural goods such as songs, dances, carvings, etc. It makes no sense to talk of amounts of songs or dances; new ones can be created in a culture at any time. Furthermore, sharing these does not take anything away from them.

Likewise, we cannot talk about quantities of emotions to be shared. Sympathy, compassion, etc. do not lend themselves to quantitative analysis. To be sure, we describe humans at times as emotionally exhausted, but this refers to general psychic energy, not quantities of specific emotions or attitudes.

There are also goods that we do not share in any literal sense, but wish everyone had them, and we are willing to devote some energy to work towards this goal. Such goods include some aspects of character and cognitive ingredients. For example, in general we wish that wisdom could be incorporated into everyone's life, but this is not simply a matter of sharing one's own wisdom with others.

Under the genus "sharing" we distinguish two species; one of these is sharing in its normal sense, and the other of wishing certain goods would be possessed by everyone, or as many humans as possible. The first is to be divided into: sharing what is mine with others, sharing and thus distributing what is a common good, possessed by the community.

Health, for example is a good that ideally we wish everyone to have, and we are willing to work for this, e.g. build hospitals, train doctors, etc. As we shall see, this picture is complicated by the means to securing or maintaining health being affected by scarcity of resources.

At times we do not literally give people goods, but merely create opportunities for these goods to be obtainable. For example, Israel at one point built houses for Bedouins and invited them to occupy these. It did not force them to live in the houses. (Some who moved into the new houses kept the old tents "just in case.")

All of these goods need be defined by articulating a conceptual core and then adding contextual modifications, thus escaping relativism without adopting an overly rigid conceptual framework.[12]

In some cases what we share, and want to share cannot be described as a "good." E.g. in the opera AIDA the heroine wants to share the same fate as Rhadames. This need not be irrational. One might think that though the fate be bad, the two shared so much and had been through so much together that prolonged life separately does not seem worthwhile. In other cases we share indirectly by refusing to have more of something even though it will not immediately lead to improvement for others, simply because we do not feel good about having something that others do not have. I refused to eat in good expensive restaurants on my visits to Moscow, even when assured that the money assigned to this cannot be used for other more useful purposes. I simply could not have enjoyed a good meal, knowing how many people nearby lived in abject poverty.

---

12 Moravcsik, *Thought and Language,* chapter VI.

Some of the goods we might share are competitive, others are not, and can be even cooperative. Sharing communal activities is cooperative. Sharing a chance to go to the moon may or may not be competitive, depending on context. Sharing things under scarcity is to share competitive goods.

We turn now to accompanying attitudes. One of these is spontaneity. In some cases we encounter certain goods, and have a spontaneous urge to share it with others. We hear a beautiful symphony and wish immediately that everyone could hear it. We witness a truly courageous act, and wish that everyone could duplicate this. We wish that courage could be shared widely, not because it is either in our interest or because it is our duty, but because we think that the world would be better that way. We observe this spontaneity in children.[13] Children are often anxious to share with close family members something that they discovered or came into their possession. It can be a nice flower, a new toy, one of their early accomplishments. There are no arguments underlying these acts of sharing. The sharing is neither egoistic nor altruistic. The child sees something beautiful and wants to share.

Some of this kind of spontaneity is preserved also for adulthood. It can be seen especially in connection with non-competitive goods that are not subject to scarcity. Thus we are happy to share experiences of encounter with great art or great music. Some of this could be altruistic, but often lacks any such background. What is behind it is more like an exclamation: "look people, how beautiful."

This kind of genuine sharing that centers on seeing value in the object, ignoring its beneficial or harmful effects on the humans who are to be exposed to it, can also be detected within contexts in which the spontaneous desire to share is preceded by thinking about what the value of the thing to be shared is. A clear such example is health. It takes some reflection to understanding what the value of health is, and that it is not merely instrumental.[14]

We shall now turn to an aspect of these kinds of sharing, be they experiences of childhood or mature reflection. This special kind of sharing is not underlying all kinds of sharing. Some are

---

13 Damon, *The Moral Child.*
14 Moravcsik, *Health, Healing, and their Values.*

purely altruistic (trivially, birthday presents), and some purely egoistic, in that we share because we expect to be rewarded for that. But after we have explained the peculiar sharing under discussion, it will be shown that this special kind of sharing underlies the sharing required for a sound system of justice.

We shall label this "Platonic sharing" for reasons that will emerge later. Let us start with distinguishing two types of cases. In one of these our judgment is that something is "good for me." This is called egoistic judgment. In other cases we say that something good is primarily good for others. This represents altruism. But now we need to consider how one can justify such judgments. On one level one can simply insist that, e.g. this is good for me because I like it or enjoy it. Or alternately this is good for others, and this can be seen by the fact that they are happy with it.

But in serious contexts when much is at stake, we do not want merely to please, either ourselves or others, but share something that we judge to be genuinely, or objectively, good. Initially we might try to specify what this kind of goodness is by reference to what we take the manifestation of human nature is at its best. This is easier in the case of health than in the case of psychological attributes involving agency, but as we saw earlier, we can do our best to choose justifiable ideals well. This kind of objective good is what Plato seems to have in mind within his Theory of Forms. He would insist that it is not enough to limit ourselves to human good. Humans live within the larger context of nature and reality, and our conception of goodness and harmony should go beyond the human. We should at least attempt to specify goodness for as large a segment of reality as we can understand.

So far, then, we have described one part of Platonic sharing, namely the objectivity of the nature of what is to be shared. The other half is the nature of the attitude of sharing that goes with this. This sharing seems to have much in common with what we described earlier as spontaneous sharing. It is the attitude of wanting to multiply and disperse as much as possible certain goods that we judge to be objectively good. This kind of sharing in some cases is like creating something, e.g. good character, or insightful self-examination, in others. In most cases this sort of sharing has this creative aspect, because what we share is not—somehow—a "part of what I have." When I share wisdom, I awaken something in another person, and I am not sharing mine with it the way in which I can share bread with someone by giving him some of what was mine.

We discussed earlier the importance of being a good agent. Brief reflection should convince us that helping others to become good agents involves this kind of sharing. Hence the importance of this kind of sharing in our ethical lives. One can appreciate this point even without subscribing to Platonic ontology. Finally, we should see that within this theory the sharing itself is a case of extension of harmony, and thus in itself a good.

There are, then two ways in which Platonic sharing underlies the sharings involved in an adequate system of justice. Underlying various ego or other-relative sharing, if we carry out justification fully, we will discover the objective good and thus also the good-oriented attitude of sharing on the basis we also want to share things with others for their sake. In this way we can start with a kind of sharing, show it on the basis of empirical evidence to be a fundamental human trait manifested from childhood onwards, and show it to underlie distribution and sharing of goods within a system of justice.

To posit this attitude and objects is, however, only the first step in establishing it as a key element in justice. For even if all that has been argued for is granted, we have so far only Platonic sharing with a few people, and involving a few—non-scarce—objects. Shortly we will argue for the extension of sharing goods both in terms of the kinds of goods to be shared, and in terms of the circle of humans with whom we share.

But first, a few remarks on this sharing. Those who share some goods in this way need not have in their minds anything like the theory of Platonic sharing we sketched. Children learn mathematics and perform mathematical operations without realizing what the ontology is that underlies their activities. The same holds for language learning and use. But issues of foundations emerge at times when we try to push justification to the limit. This is the relation that our theory perceives between how people share when at their best, and our theoretical account.

The introduction of sharing into schemes of justice has important psychological consequences. The alternative accounts rely on rules and thus on obedience to rules as the main psychological vehicle for abiding by the edicts of justice. But our proposal sees justice and its implementation as resting on a positive universal human attitude, and sees the task of ethics as showing ways in which the attitude can be expanded. We shall see in the next few pages how we can deal with some salient phenomena that tend to block sharing. These examples should serve as illustrations for how one can foster readiness to share and agree to distribution schemes, without relying exclusively on taboos, or vague and very general inclinations such as benevolence.

Some might say that the matter of how people become just or what prevents them is an empirical issue and not within the range of appropriate concerns of the philosopher. The philosopher should articulate what justice, fairness, basic rights, etc. are. He should leave to others how these items are to be embodied and implemented.

This essay rejects any such dichotomy. Apart from the question of whether the analytic–empirical distinction can be drawn adequately, such division of labor makes no sense, even if in a wide sense not all of these endeavors are empirical. We can see this best by drawing an analogy with the philosophy of language. Let us suppose that a philosopher has a theoretically interesting characterization of the semantics of natural languages. Should this be of serious interest to us if it can be shown that the characterization represents language as in principle unlearnable by humans or humanlike devices? Learnability must be a key requirement to any successful characterization of human languages. Likewise issues of implementation and embodiment must be essential parts of an adequate ethical theory. Kantian theories of right and duty should be in this respect compared to the moral psychology of our theory and empirical evidence concerning what humans can learn to embody and express is relevant to an overall assessment and comparison of these views.

Envy is the attitude of not wanting someone else to have more than we have, regardless of this affecting or not affecting communal and individual welfare.[15] This attitude works against sharing for it makes people fearful of their sharing creating inequalities that places one in positions of inferiority in a variety of ways, for example, loss of prestige. This attitude can be countered by get-

---

15 Schoeck, *Envy: A Theory of Social Behaviour.*

ting people to abandon the very narrow conception of self worth and basis for finding meaning in their lives that they entertain. If humans gain a degree of self-sufficiency in their conception of individual ideals, and rely more on having embodied values that do not rely mainly on competitive goods, then envy can be minimized.

Similar considerations apply to insecurity. The insecure person does not trust others and fears that sharing might enable others to get ahead or do other kinds of harm to the sharing individual. Such insecurity can be alleviated by the maintenance of what we described as appropriate communal ties. Helping humans to form adequate individual ideals that enable them to live well even under circumstances in which distributional conditions are inferior can also combat it.

Sharing can also be thwarted by a one-sided sense of injustice within which the basis of sharing is seen solely in terms of merit and accomplishment. "Why should I share this? I worked for it all my life!" is the motto of such people. The underlying conviction is that one's effort and earning achievement should be the only criterion for the distribution of goods that one's work has affected. In responses to such a stance it should be pointed out that the welfare of others affects communal life and its qualities of trust, respect, and other positive attitudes. Consequently effort and achievement by one person should not be the sole criterion for settling on distribution schemes. Furthermore, what one sees on the surface as one person's achievement often turns out on closer inspection to be the product of several humans. The conviction that one can draw a sharp line between one's own achievements and those of others turns out in most contexts to be illusory.

Indifference can also contribute to hindering impulses and orientation towards sharing. "Why should I bother wasting energy on sharing? Let others worry about themselves." This attitude emerges usually from a narrow conception of the self according to which we should draw the line between the self and extrinsic qualities at bodily separateness, and see the self as the seat of pleasures arising from activities within which we need to rely on others only minimally.[16] In response one can point to many other conceptions

---

16 Moravcsik "The Perils of Friendship and Conceptions of the Self."

of the self that comprise much more than the narrow one mentioned. Some of our relations with others can also be seen as parts of the self. If so, then the development and maintenance of these relationships is as much a part of one's self improvement as securing food and other material goods. In terms of impact on ourselves the wider conceptions of the self seem more realistic. Ups and downs in one's economic state are unlikely to have as much effect on a human as the drastic changes in relations with others. Our character is shaped by these relations more than by the increase or decrease of pleasures derived from material goods.

These are only very brief sketches how one can attack in a thriving community the sources of what blocks sharing, and offer such a campaign as an alternative to the dubious task of developing a conception of rationality that could serve as an anchor to fairness, seen as a psychological component drastically different from our human inclinations.

The most difficult case for our approach is that of the resentful individual. We should take up the gravest situation, that of the justifiably resentful individual.[17] One of the best treatments of such a case is the drama *Philoctetes* by Sophocles. The hero, Philoctetes, has been wronged by the Greek army, and is suffering solitude and harsh conditions without having done anything on his own to deserve this. The Greek army discovers that they need his help. Should he overcome his justified resentment and rejoin his former comrades? There are two philosophical arguments pointing in the affirmative direction. One of these rests on the importance of self-sufficiency in developing and maintaining an adequate life ideal. It starts with assuming that a human is to have goals in life that he or she judges to be good, and towards which he or she works. If such goal-orientedness is to be successful, it should bring with it a degree of self-sufficiency. That is to say, the pursuit and attainment of the goals should not depend on what others think and do except in special circumstances, and then only to a small extent. But not overcoming resentment clashes with this. For it urges us to depart from doing what we take to be good only because of bad and insensitive things that others have done in relation to us. Why should we have an impoverished life because of the flaws in oth-

17 Scheler, *Ressentiment*; Strawson, "Freedom and Resentment."

ers? Can the pleasure of stubbornness really outweigh the losses we suffer in trying to achieve worthwhile aims? The negative answer to this question leads to the conclusion that resentment, even when justified, should be overcome in order to enable the agent to pursue his own higher good.

These are, then, some of the ways in which psychological blocks to genuine sharing can be removed. The argument for sharing of the kind described takes the following shape:

(i)   I wish to share good G. with others.
      Comments: the range is left unspecified. This does not mean that the intended range is humanity, but that at no definite exclusory clauses are intended. Secondly, we need to have agreement between the person who shares and the recipient that the item in this transaction is really a good.

(ii) First level of justification.
      I wish to share G with others because it is an objective good and not under scarcity. Goods should be multiplied in the world; within this kind of sharing my goods will not diminish.

(iii) Second level. In fact, my interest in sharing of this sort is itself a good thing. It is a part of good character and having a good Ethical Ideal to be that kind of a person.

(iv) I can defend construing G as a good by listing its good-making characteristics.

(v)   Since I see sharing G with others as itself a good, I can recommend this to the community.

(vi) If other cooperate and agree, sharing G can become a part of communal justice.

Justification is based on G being an objective good. Our motivation, though it may involve wanting others as well as myself to benefit from the distribution, is based on our attitude to share and distribution being one of a basic aspiration to distribute good things, without this being based on some egoistic or altruistic motive.

In this way, the good-oriented, the selfish and the altruistic can mingle in our attitude triggering the sharing, with the first item having priority both in terms of motivation and in terms of justification.

As was said at the beginning, there are also many other types of sharing, both in terms of kinds of goods and in terms of underlying attitude. Many of these are in various contexts fully justifiable; but cannot be the foundation for a just system of distribution in a community.

3. Expanding Sharing

We have sketched the anatomy of sharing, and singled out a kind of "Platonic sharing" that we witness already—in inarticulate form—in children. We then showed that sharing oriented towards objective goods and whose underlying attitude is neither egoistic nor altruistic, but fuels the spreading of the objectively good things, could serve as one of the foundational elements of justice. It can mingle with the altruistic and is also not incompatible with self-care, but is needed as a special element. We are left so far, however, with sharing that need not be, but can be, limited to the sharing of a few goods with a few people. In order for this kind of sharing to be at the foundation of justice, we need to show how it can be expanded in both directions. On reflection reasonable humans will expand it both in terms of the variety of goods shared, and in terms of considering large groups of humans as potential objects of sharing.

There is altruistic sharing without the "Platonic" element, but such inclinations by themselves cannot be at the foundation of justice for the following reasons. Altruism need not imply respect for the other person. One can do things for others in a condescending way. But a just system of distribution does imply some degree of respect, even if this admits of degrees on account of differences in merit. Also, altruism need not imply concern for what is objectively good. But merely wanting to please others may clash with the demands of the objectively good. Merely being altruistic will not enable one to decide between pleasing others and the objectively good.

Egotistic sharing, that is sharing with the aim that this will repay the agent of sharing, will not lead to an adequate distributional system, since it cannot be expected that the sharing that benefits the agent will also be a reasonable way of distributing goods.

With these considerations in mind, and the acceptance of sharing as dealing partly with objective goods and having as its aim partly the multiplication of goods, let us address the question of why we should expand the range of those with whom we want to share. First let us consider the sharing of goods that are not under scarcity. Should we place sharing with others ahead of keeping these goods to ourselves? If a part of our aim is to have as many instances of nonscarce goods as possible, then placing the other-oriented increase ahead of the self-oriented effort is obviously the way to go. The issue is not how much of a good we can produce by sharing. Since there is no scarcity, quantitative comparisons are not important. But even in these cases the effort that goes into sharing is not unlimited. Let us consider wisdom as the good in question. This does not admit a quantitatively determinate way of comparisons as weight, height etc. allow. There is no "WISER," the name of what would be the quantitative equivalent of inches or pounds. Sharing wisdom means in many cases helping to create another wise person. The basic units of wisdom are agents, not quantities of "wisdom-glue." Furthermore, the sharing of wisdom is in itself a good, in particular, a wise thing to do.

In the typical cases, sharing with as many humans as possible will result in more of the nonscarce good being around than just trying to make one human extremely wise. Under the assumptions made here, we regard humans we meet as potential objects of sharing, and proceed with that until empirical evidence shows this not feasible. Goods not under scarcity are also non-competitive goods. If we assume adequate communal ties for the community in which sharing takes place, then "hoarding goods" of this type will run counter to the adequate communal ties. Given lack of scarcity, we should make efforts both for maintaining the ties and acquire other non-competitive goods, but in key cases the ties should have priority.

As we move to expanding the range of humans with whom we want to share, we also need to consider the maintenance of those who now instantiate the goods in question. But in the case of humans, this will mean making provisions for their physical well-being and survival. Thus moving from the non-scarce to the scarce goods is required by our concern with those who represent good elements. We respond to those who potentially represent goods by attending to their needs, and these will necessarily include goods under scarcity.

So far, however, we have arrived at a conception of why we should share even scarce goods that is purely instrumental. We need to consider argument showing that sharing scarce goods with others has also intrinsic value, and should outweigh in many contexts the drive to secure these goods for oneself.

Our task presupposes some view about the relation between the non-scarce intellectual or psychological goods and the scarce physical goods. We shall treat the latter summarily under the rubric of health. According to one extreme view health and its constituents have only instrumental value. They serve as the means to the intellectual and other psychological goods. The view advocated in this book is that health also has non-instrumental value.[18] Health is constitutive of the good human agent. We judge what is instrumentally good by comparing it to what we take to be the standard of the healthy person, and we take the latter to be having non-instrumental goodness. Viewed that way we can see sharing health-preserving goods is to share elements of what is the good person who, in turn, is exemplifying one of the final goods.

Why should we share health-producing goods rather than working on accumulating all of these for ourselves? Here we need to refer to the social aspects of the human self. On reflection we see more order and harmony in the world if there are many healthy people with fine minds, than when we have only a few very healthy speciments. We regard the healthy society as non-instrumental goods, among other things.

The above does not say that we should always pay more attention to the health-producing elements in other people than in ourselves. In many cases this brings more harmony into the world, but not always. Respecting others comes also with self-respect. Self-respect involves taking care of our own health. At times we see the need to sacrifice some of our health for others, and at other times we think that it is appropriate for us to demand that society share a considerable amount of some goods to improve or maintain our health. Philosophy cannot provide ironclad rules to decide each such question in the abstract. We assess cases in terms of

---

18 Moravcsik, *Health, Healing and Their Values.*

merit, and equality. The history of the goods in question varies much from one cultural context to another. The theory of this book prepares only guidelines. The task of these guidelines includes pointing to the non-irrational nature of sharing that is objective good-oriented and need not center on the agent at the expense of the larger community. It also construes the task of acting justly as taking place within a value-based community—or approximate of such—and links the challenge of sharing to the acceptance of adequate communal ties and their being among the top non-instrumental values.

The argument for the desirability of extending the sharing potentials can also be formulated in the following way.

We are inclined to share non-scarce goods that have non-instrumental value. These may be cultural goods, intellectual goods, or objects of aesthetic value. We share discoveries of neglected classical musical pieces, or poems we find in all local volumes of poetry. We like to share sunsets or bird migrations with others. In all of these sharings we need to assume that the partner with whom we share appreciates the goods in question, and also their non-instrumental aspect. Would I really share spontaneously a violin sonata that I never heard before if I thought that my partner would use the music only as a substitute for his non-functioning alarm clock?

To regard someone else as an agent who can appreciate these cultural goods in the appropriate ways involves having some respect and concern for them. An agent that can appreciate a cultural good as having value of its own is to that extent an autonomous agent, and thus an appropriate object of value and concern. Concern is the key notion here, for it is my concern for my music or philosophy loving friends or those potentially such, that also leads me to want to share scarce goods with them. Their survival and good health is of importance to me, not only my own. But there is no general abstract rule telling me to what extent and when shall I place the value of sharing scarce goods with others over accumulating goods that will constitute my health and survival. In this section we merely build the foundation of the possibility of such sharing having in many cases top priority. The task of fashioning from this material the philosophical component of theories of justice is left to the next section.

We can now compare this kind of sharing with previous ideals surveyed in this book. First we saw criteria for the good individual ideal. We then saw criteria for good social interactions that centered on good communal ties and their importance. Thus we can now see sharing as the adequate and good way of dealing with goods. Good individual agency and good communal ties by themselves do not indicate how we should deal with goods to be shared and distributed. But there is an analogy between individual ideals, social ideals, and the ideal of dealing soundly with the acquisition and distribution of goods. Humans are not only aim-setting people, and socially interacting people. Humans have needs; require goods to be used for meeting these. The appropriate way to deal with goods is to draw on deep and universal psychological properties such as the drive to share, and use this to show what can lead the good agent in a good community to viewing goods as to be shared in ways that require in various contexts different specifications. In the next section we turn to sketching components of good systems of justice on this basis. We assume that humans want to share. The system of justice should show then what are better and worse ways of sharing and distributing.

4. Justice Based on Appropriate Sharing and Sound Communal Ties

This section will argue for the thesis that the justice and the associated system of administering justice, especially a distribution should be whatever is the best way of sharing in a community.

First, let us contrast sharing among persons and communal sharing. As we have seen, sharing is based on a deep human yearning. As this aspiration becomes intertwined with more complex thinking, we can distinguish egotistic, altruistic, and "Platonic" sharing. A key feature of personal sharing is that it is a relation between specific persons. I share goods with certain other human beings, and my motivation may be selfish, altruistic, or objective good-oriented. The agents involved are individuals. In the case of communal sharing, we surrender some of our autonomy and let the community through its institutions and officials determine the details of what goods will be shared in which ways. Thus communal sharing at its best presupposes: a) a desire on the part of the members to share, and b) Trust on the part of the members in the institutions and officials that the sharing will take place in accordance with what a critical mass of members would approve, and that it takes place within the bounds of adequate communal ties. In a typical modern philosophic theory of justice distribution is explained in semi-formal terms as the "right" or "equitable" system of justice. In our theory we place the whole issue of justice within the community. Justice is realized, implemented within communities, and not within abstract systems. In real life any distribution of justice takes place in a functioning community, and hence it requires trust on the part of those who give, or distribute, and also trust on the side of those who receive. Needless to say, the two classes can overlap.

The picture sketched so far is overly simplistic. It seems to assume that in each case there is a "ready-made" community into which we need to inject justice. But this is even as an idealization, misleading. Sharing itself creates a kind of community, in the sense in which this notion was introduced in this book. Successful sharing involves agreement on what are goods to be distributed, and thus a partial agreement on what are goods. It also involves agreement on delegation of responsibilities and conditions placed on this. Still, even if sharing in some cultural contexts starts with personal sharing, and this then develops into communal sharing, in a full-blown sense the kind of sharing that is involved in justice does require some form of institutionalization. Institutionalized sharing brings with it an aspect of the impersonal. Charity can be purely personal, but just distribution requires delegating power and hence the impersonal. At the same time, successful sharing in a community requires also a—at least tacit—agreement on who is worthy of receiving shares, and on what ground. Once this issue is settled in the community, the notion of people having claims on certain goods arises. This is not meant to lead to complete relativism. There are better and worse decisions on who is entitled to share, who is worthy of receiving and distributing shares. What we said earlier about adequate communal ties, and our characterization of what work should be in a community provide some guidelines for such construals.

As we shall see, communal ties are only guidelines for determining the participants and nature of a distribution process.

Regarding someone as having a claim on certain goods in a community and thus being worthy of our sharing goods with that person is a unique assignment of value to a person. It is not a mere equivalent to having respect and concern for that person.

The position that is marked out here is between Rawls' stand that is less contextual than ours,[19] and Walzer's that is more relativistic than the theory of this book.[20]

First, let us consider in more detail why one could not generate a theory of justice based solely on the theory of adequate communal ties. Basically, this amounts to the question of whether one could derive a good way of sharing from the tie constituted by respect, concern, and trust as well as care.

Clearly, respect is not enough. One can respect someone else without wanting to share goods with the person. I can respect a great pianist without wanting to share goods, especially of the ones under scarcity. Furthermore, there can be two quite different and incompatible systems of distribution, both of which acknowledge the need to respect the participants. For example both communists and capitalists claim that in their systems there is room for respect for all humans.

The same can be said about concern. One can be concerned about poor people in a community without being willing to share scarce goods with them. People sign petitions, vote for those who claim that they will better the lot of the disadvantaged. This can be regarded as a kind of concern, but hardly counts as the basis for distribution. Nor is it the question of HOW MUCH concern one has for others. Magnitude of concern can be measured in terms of intensity of feeling, or even of vigor in action, but the concern that underlies distribution must be coupled with the willingness and interest in sharing scarce goods. The commitment to sharing is a unique state of mind. It involves appreciating what it is to be a member of a community in which goods are shared, and the willingness to delegate what would be matters of individual rights to institutions. At best, these institutions must be in some ways accountable to the members, but the fact of power delegation remains a key requirement.

---

19 Rawls, *op. cit.*
20 Walzer, *Spheres of Justice.*

So far we have looked at the two ingredients that contain quality-dependent attitudes. Even if we conjoin the two, we cannot derive right patterns of distribution. Respect and concern can still be practiced without concern for sharing goods. The only goods that the adequate tie construes as shared in the community are the non-scarce, non-competitive spiritual or psychological goods. But sharing those will not yield distribution patterns for physical goods. For example Christian communities have come up with quite diverse systems of distribution, while claiming to subscribe to the same ethical goods.

We need not look at the direct attitudes of trust and care, because by their very nature these are not suited to be the foundation of systems such as distribution that rests on assumptions of what kind of a person deserves having a claim and sharing, and on the basis of what kind of warranting qualities.

Thus we see that while adequate ties can function as guidelines towards better distribution they do not have direct relations to acknowledging claims and extending the sharing to scarce material goods under the framework of delegated authority. Concern for the welfare of others can be paternalistic and thus not the basis of acknowledging claims. Respect can become a form of admiration and thus again not the foundation of a reasonable distribution system. For example, if everyone admires the head of state, the ensuing distribution scheme might lead to a tyrannical or at least oligarchic structure.

These remarks show also that one cannot look at the right kind of sharing as the mere application of the adequate tie to matters of goods distribution. Different factors, such as work done, achievement, the history of the goods, the nature of exchange of goods in that society, come into consideration. This goes beyond the mere applicability of respect, concern, and the other ingredients.

So we see that sharing is one of the pillars of good distribution. On the other hand, we can see that adequate ties are needed for good distribution schemes. Respecting participants and having genuine concern for their welfare within a scheme of respect are factors that should lead distributions away from exploitation, arbitrariness, and similar abuses.

There is an analogy between adequate ties and good sharing. Adequate ties specify what one might call the CHARACTER OF THE

COMMUNITY. We look at the ties and can read off communal character. Likewise the system of sharing and distribution used in a good exchanging and ascribing community represents the CHARACTER OF THE DISTRIBUTION SYSTEM. To be a just system is to have a good handling framework with GOOD CHARACTER. In the case of the ties we do not say merely that good ties will make people happy, but also that having those ties and those ways of making happy makes this a better world in a sense of "better" that is objective, and cannot be exhausted by relativizations. The analogous truth holds for justice.

These reflections bring into focus a key question one might raise about the theory proposed. What does sharing contribute to justice? To say that it is a necessary component does not yet say what its function is. To be analogous to character is a promising metaphor but not yet a full answer.

In response, we should first reformulate the question. What is at issue is not what sharing in general contributes to justice. As an answer to THAT question our theory merely points out that some sort of sharing seems to be a deep-seated human inclination, and thus in developing justice one should take account of this.

The key question for our purposes is: what does communal sharing contribute to justice? First, as was mentioned in the previous arguments, the communal aspect of the sharing proposed involves making sharing a partly impersonal element, and it involves delegation of certain powers and actions that in other contexts we regard as our own. These matters regard motivations from the participants that are quite different from mere altruism. Altruism is typically involved already in purely informal and personal transactions such as those taking place in a family. But sharing in justice goes way beyond that. In that context the issues of "what is mine?" "what claims do others have on what I helped to bring about?" become elements over which I have no full control, though in a truly democratic context I have some indirect say about these.

There is something analogous to this in our personal relations. For this surrender is also an aspect of friendship; at least the kind of friendship that is based on shared values, and not on merely utilitarian or hedonistic basis. But the analogy should not be pushed too far. Elements like personal contact and direct emotions are mostly parts of friendship, while this is neither a typical ingredient nor even a desirable one in communal sharing. To accept and not just tolerate, or conform to grudgingly, like a purely moral taboo, communal sharing is not based on the recognition of interdependence, though such recognition might in practice facilitate the development of the right attitudes. Interdependence is still an interest-related concept. Realizing its presence can be the ground of enlightened egoism. The claim of our theory is that acceptance of communal sharing goes beyond this, and construes this aspect of our lives as an enabling condition. It enables us to transcend narrow conceptions of the self, and to see in such relations a key mitigation of the I vs. of others dichotomy. In construing this sharing and resulting justice as also having non-consequential value it acknowledges the importance of the well functioning community as a distinct ontological entity, on par in fundamentality with that of the individual.

It has been said by cynics that the envisaged sharing occurs, if at all, in wealthy communities in which many people have much that they can give up for others without leaving themselves in life with hardships. Powerful evidence has been presented against this hypothesis by the description of a part of Calcutta in which misery is worse than what characterized the district in which Mother Theresa was active.[21] A fine book describing an amazing community that was formed even under unbelievably poor conditions shows how joy in the kind of sharing we feature in our theory can flourish among people for whom every bit of material good is a vital condition of their survival. Books like this one are very useful, since one cannot PROVE in some mathematical or logical sense that necessity of this kind of love and sharing. As Wittgenstein often remarked, something cannot be proved, but can only be shown.[22] Our conception of justice is one of these elements. One has to envisage how it works and then "see" its superiority to alternatives proposed in the past or present.

So far we treated the underlying moral psychology of justice. This is in harmony with the other chapters in which we argued for individual and social ethics being intertwined, and the fundamen-

---

21 LaPierre, *The City of Joy.*
22 Wittgenstein, "A Lecture on Ethics."

tality of the communal dynamics, which we can also call underlying psychology for functioning units with laws and institutions and a responsive community moral. Still, we need to say a few things about how our kind of system of justice would function. Let us suppose that a community has the appropriate underlying dynamics. How then does distribution take place?

In answer, we shall draw on some of the material presented earlier in this chapter in our discussion of fairness. We pointed out that fairness has a pluralistic, rather than a monolithic, basis. It is not based on one thing, like equality, but on a plurality of elements, like merit, work, contribution, equality, non-arbitrariness, the history of the good in question in that particular community, and a few other items. It is important to leave the list open-ended, because we cannot survey all possible present and future cultural contexts and decide what is or will be relevant to fairness. At the same time, not anything goes. There must be continuity between how we introduced past candidates as what determines fairness and present ones. The situation is analogous to lists of virtues. Though there have been attempts in the past to give a closed list of virtues, these attempts either result in failure or in items specified so vaguely as to be of limited practical use. We now apply the same considerations to what factors are to be balanced when determining what should affect distribution. Furthermore, both the salience of the various factors and relative priority are contextual matters. No one ironclad rule can be invoked to settle all of the complex problems the solution of which constitutes the final distribution pattern in a given community in a given context. We want each participant to have what is needed to be a well functioning individual. This is, however, a normative notion. Thus the theory of Ethical Ideals becomes relevant from part I of this book. The same holds for the theory of adequate communal ties. But invoking these, and agreeing on the list of goods provide only partial guidance. The remaining matters depend on what are perceived as needs, and to some extent also the subjective preferences of the participants. But this last factor—in contrast with most contemporary benefit–cost analyses—cannot be the dominant factor in our theory, for reasons made clear throughout the book.

For some this will seem a lame conclusion. But the conclusion in its partial recommendation mirrors what we have said elsewhere about items like work, and responsibility. Philosophy in matters of justice, work, and responsibility should stick to its limitations. It can provide the analysis of basic constituents and structures including partial conditional priorities but given the nature of human experience it cannot and should not try to provide universal decision procedures.

In conclusion, we should show how this account of justice from a philosophical point of view relates to a philosophical analysis of an empirically very relevant factor, namely power.

Power has, as we know from the Platonic dialogues, two different senses. We shall ignore the fact that Plato wants to reduce what we shall regard as sense (1) to sense (2), because that point, correct or not, is not relevant to our purposes.

Power in sense one means "having control over animate or inanimate elements; being able to collect and keep for oneself various goods." "Power" in sense two means: "having the ability and opportunity to change things in the world in ways that achieve the spread of objectively good elements."

We need to distinguish power from selfishness. One may be selfish and not want power at all. Again, one might try to fight selfishness but still cling to power. For power as defined above can have as its roots insecurity and feelings of inferiority. As shown so well in Eisenstein's film, *Ivan the Terrible,* power can have at its roots fear and distrust. Thus one way to eliminate the drive for power in sense (1) is to eliminate the fear and distrust. Thus one way to eliminate the drive for power in sense (1) is to eliminate the fear and related insecurity. Being a member of what in our theory is a value-based community with adequate communal ties would be one way of accomplishing this.

It must be admitted, however, that for some people the drive for power in sense (a) is fuelled by the expectation of the sheer pleasure of pushing others around, suppressing them, and so on. This drive is diametrically opposed to what we call justice, sharing, and wanting to live in an adequate community as well as developing an adequate individual ideal. There may be various ways of transforming such drives into something more useful, such as reorienting the agent to power in sense two, namely "the ability and opportunity to accomplish good things, both for self and others"—in this formula "good" is used in a non-relative and objective sense. Plato seems to have thought that humans being rational creatures such a reorientation could be effected. But empirical evidence for these hypotheses is far from convincing. Perhaps in some people this destructive drive can never be extinguished, even if one gives all of the arguments of this book for adequate ethical ideal communal tie, and good sharing system: or arguments from other ethical traditions.

But there should be constraints even on wanting and exercising power in sense (2). Respect for others, recognizing some of their claims for sharing, even without perfect aims, are dictated by our theory, else the desire to do good can degenerate into paternalism. In our theory power in sense (2) can be part of a well functioning society if it is in the context of trust and responsibility.

Appendix to Chapter VI.
Communities and Outsiders

When a theory is presented in which so many of our basic moral notions, individual and political, are discussed within contexts of communities, it is natural for the reader to ask how the theory affects relationships with those outside the community. Are they mere outcasts? What if someone, through no fault of his own, failed to "get a ticket" into the community?

These questions mostly affect those theories that deal with communities defined by laws and institutions. In those cases the "in or out" question receives clear-cut answers, and claims, rights, and duties are defined for those meeting membership criteria.

In our theory membership is defined for a value-based community and as we saw, for these membership admits of degrees and other qualifications. The extreme outcast would be someone who neither actually nor potentially shares any values at all with members of the value-based community that happens to be under discussion. To be sure, in the cases in which the value-based and the institutional–legal coincide, there will be claims and responsibilities that apply only to those meeting the institutional criterion. But this is on the basis of the peculiar kinds of interactions that such communities partly demand, partly make possible.

Given this outlook, those subscribing to the theory presented or to some reasonable facsimile will interpret the notion of the outsider contextually and rarely if ever in terms of complete exclusion. This outlook, however, entails that not everyone will be regarded within a value-based community as meriting equal treatment. Thinkers in liberal traditions will immediately raise the question: are there not some basic rights that everyone has, regardless of how much or little they are outside a given community? As we have already seen, this theory remains agnostic on this issue. All rights and privileges are conditional. There are no unconditional ethical principles in this moral philosophy. But it may be the case that the person who has nothing in common, potentially or actually, in terms of values with the adequate value-based community is a piece of fiction.

The idea that one owes more to those with whom we share values and interact in communal activities is hardly news. It is a part of basic common sense for many societies. Even if we meet persons with whom we seem not to share sufficiently rich clusters of values, while we might not feel obligated to include them in various schemes of sharing as part of our system of justice, we might still treat them with some kindness as a matter of philanthropy, or help those disadvantaged, even if not on merit.

There are two ways, then, in which a value-based and institutionally defined community can provide goods for those regarded as outsiders by legal criteria. One of these is to recognize the good qualities we share, and see these as a basis for extending the sharing of goods outside political boundaries. The other is to treat some extensions of providing goods as charity or philanthropy. Some modern philosophers might miss in this theory a treatment of the claim "why should not all humans receive equally the best of what human life can offer?" But, as we have seen, we must distinguish two questions: "Would it not be good if everyone could possess certain goods that would enable her to live a good life?" and "Do I have an obligation to do everything in my power to help to realize the above articulated state of affairs?" Our theory denies that, while the answer to the first question is affirmative, this would impose on everyone a duty to realize the state described in the second question. In everyday life we think that we owe more to family members than to others, and more to colleagues than to randomly selected workers, and so on. This theory provides a rational basis for such a stance without ruling out the possibility that one day we might be able to raise the global level of well-being in dramatic ways. And those value-based communities would include working for this as a part of their communal aims.

The word "theory" has been used a fair amount throughout this chapter. This use requires qualifications. What is presented here is not a theory of justice in the usual sense. Rather it is a proposal for what the adequate moral psychology is that should underlie communal activities involving the distribution of goods, and reflection on ways in which this distribution should take place. The material of this chapter presents a view on the psychological background that facilitates successful communal discussion of more specific matters. Given the outlook of our conception, the philosophical theory need not, and perhaps should not be too specific, since our views on communities and sharing allow for considerable pluralism for what adequate distribution systems in a given community could be. Fairness, need, merit, welfare, and other such ingredients should play roles in distribution systems, but the mixture of the ingredients can vary considerably from context to context.

The pragmatic effect of our Theory should be that humans do not only worry about specific distributional schemes, but work hard in communities to have the psychological outlook prescribed by our theory firmly implanted. As we have seen, this does not involve "new men," but merely to take something that is already a part of human nature, and give it priority.

Our theory is pluralistic with regard to political and economic systems. Thus is should not be surprising if it is also pluralistic with regards to systems of justice. A theory that construes certain attitudes as more fundamental than the rule systems associated with these is likely to have a pluralistic flavor.

EPILOGUE

Recently, one of the best known global investors said that capitalism has shown how we can serve efficiently individual needs, but have yet to come to grips with the challenge of how to develop out of these individual satisfactions a concern for and viable economic foundation of the common good. Around the same time, a retired professor of psychiatry said that psychiatry helped us to lead people to feel good about themselves, but that out of this collection of individual well-beings one cannot build a community.

Thus we see here coming from two very different sources the same concern with the problem on how to construct an ethics that takes care of individual well-being and also provides a foundation both for how individuals should see their role in community building and for how we should conceive of the common good.

This book centers around this challenge. There are two main directions in which solution for this problem can be searched. One is the tradition of seeing individual and communal goods as two separate realms, and then introducing an autonomous moral dimension. Within this rules and duties—either in utilitarian or in Kantian terms—will be formulated that restrain concern with the individual good, and also lay down laws for the individual to contribute to the common good.

The other approach is advocated, among others, by this book. Within this approach we reconsider what individual good really is, and also take a sharp look at what should tie a thriving community together. It can be shown that a well functioning community has other than mere economic aims, and that the ties that bind it together center on humane values rather than on mere economic success. The book shows also that the individual good need be defined not in terms of the kind of self-interest that assumes a narrowly egotistic individual self, but the human self in classical and pragmatic senses in which social interaction, concern with others and respectful mutual interactions are parts of the individual human essence.

Thus within our approach the conceptual framework construes individual and communal values as intertwined, without the sharp separation of the alternative mode. Furthermore, it does not need the importation of an independent moral component at the fundamental level, since what the separate moral component within the alternate approach prescribes for individuals has its analogues in our system in those values that are seen as both individual and communal. This does not mean that in appropriate interpersonal contexts we do not posit obligations and duties. But these have the individual and communal ideals as their background, and thus do not have foundational roles. For example, we can agree on ideal friendship along roughly Aristotelian lines, and agree also that some components of that enter into communal values as well. Within that context we can go on to discuss what obligations friends, in typical cases, have to each other.

When Love Grows Cold

The communal ties sketched in this book, and key parts of adequate individual ideals can be subsumed under the more traditional conceptions of love, in which love is not restricted to sensual aspects of life but includes what is called in more modern times charity, kindness, and in general the kind of love that friends whose tie is based on shared non-utilitarian values and family members whose mutual affection does not change in time, experience. This kind of "love" need be nourished and real efforts need be made toward its maintenance. This book centers on guidelines towards how to build up this kind of love, and how one can work towards its persistence.

The ills of human life can be summed up both on the individual and social level as different aspects of "love growing cold." (This conception of individual and communal thriving must not be confused with naïve cries that "everything is all right as long as we love each other" and other simplistic superficial slogans.) The various chapters have shown how much intellectual and individual effort must go in to the building and maintaining of the deep traditional sense of love and charity.

There are many ways in which love can grow cold in a community. When a community is ruled tyrannically, not much love—in our sense of this notion—is left. Love is replaced by fear and trust. At the other extreme there are societies bordering on anarchy. Love is scarce in these units as well. Distrust permeates these units, and this makes typically both sharing and receptivity more difficult. Hence anarchistic tendencies work against the social glue that the previous chapters articulate.

The most typical, and not easily recognizable, manifestation of the cooling of love is, however, indifference. This is the indifference that people have towards the communal good, communal ties, aims, activities, sharing, and receptivity towards the outsider. As we have seen, an adequate value-based community is not a static state. It cannot be secured by laws. It requires the constant dynamic of activity, and the expression of the attitudes already listed. Indifference saps energy, and takes away attention and concentration. Hence the cooling of love caused by indifference deadens the communal tie and the underlying attitudes. We become indifferent towards respect, care, trust, concern, and the other needed communal ingredient. Such indifference typically does not manifest itself in open disavowals of these values. But the acceptance of these values becomes gradually more just a matter of what we say and what routines we follow. More narrowly self-centered thinking and activities replace the difficult cognitive and emotional burden required of us by an adequate community. A typical excuse for the indifference—and the favoring of more immediately lucrative self-centered activities—is the claim of lack of time. This is well exemplified by contrasts we can see in the poet Donald Hall's description of fathers playing catch (baseball) with their sons. Unfortunately in many families the father does not have "time any more for such activities." The result is a familiar cop-out. The child is given money to buy something he wants, in place of the joint play. Such routines create in the child a conception of familiar ties based on consumerism, and love begins to grow cold, ending up with friendship based on mere utility. (This danger was pointed out to me by a social worker in Singapore.)

Another symptom surfaces when helping neighbors and others in need who are in our vicinity becomes not a spontaneous volunteer activity but a job entrusted to people who earn their living this way. In the fall of 1994 a congressional committee visited Singapore. A congresswoman was heard exclaiming how amazing it was for her that so much work for which you have to pay people in the USA was done here by volunteers.

Indifference is a general condition of not being concerned with certain matters. A particular type of indifference emerges from loss of interest. When what is supposed to be a matter of activity and underlying attitudes becomes mere routine, people tend to become bored with it. We see this phenomenon in countries that are described as "becoming bored with democracy." The remedy is not "hype" for communal values, but quiet painstaking grassroot activities that involve everyone on the ground level (communal outings, free readings of stories to children in public libraries, much dialogue between political leaders and dwellers of city blocks, etc.). Maintaining interest in the community cannot be accomplished by decrees "from above." Loss of interest in communal matters is camouflaged at times by the slogan "people should just do what they feel like doing as long as they do not harm others and obey the law." The "should" in this proclamation can be interpreted as a harmless legal permission. Indeed, it is permitted for people to take this point of view; attitudes cannot be forced on humans. But if taken as ethical advice, then it conflicts with the ideals of chapter one. To be sure, maybe what someone wants is participation in the community. But people with the slogan cited typically have a narrow conception of self and self-interest in mind, and thus interpret the slogan as a call to withdrawal from the public arena. As such, this stance is subject to all of the criticisms developed in part I as well as the social ethics of part II.

So far we have dealt with internal, psychological obstacles to the development of an adequate normative community. There are, however, external conditions that can also have a negative effect on such developments. For example, extreme poverty and the lack of hope that improvements might come can make the maintaining of good ties very difficult. Still, as the report in *The City of Joy* shows, humans can rise even under incredibly bad conditions to high levels of individual and communal excellence.

Another external factor preventing the maintenance of good communal ties is at times extreme lack of stability. Lack of stability can make planning very difficult and this leaves us with scant possibilities for exercising responsibility, concern, and thus sharing over the long haul. This is why in this essay stability was proposed as a criterion of adequacy for communal planning. Modern industrial societies have failed to find a golden mean between stagnation on the one hand, and obsession with novelty and change on the other. Yet discovery of such patterns will be crucial if adequate schemes for individual and communal living are to be found.

Thus we see that love growing cold can take a variety of shapes. It is not tied to the traditional political villains of tyranny and anarchy. The indifference of individuals who live in structurally sound societies can also lead to the kind of indifference that is devastating for a community. The communal tie ingredients disappear, to be followed by relationships based mostly on expected mutual utility or gratification. The weaknesses and fragility of such relationships has been explored already. The indifference towards deep communal values tends also to erase awareness of differences in levels of depth between lifestyles, cultural variety on the one hand and the aims, values, and character traits that transcend such variety, and define the adequate normative community on the other. Hence strife in the community, and thus also level of violence, grows with leaps and bounds. The less we are aware of the deep values that tie us together, the better the chance that sound cooperative values will be replaced by competitive ones.

A brief glance across borders indicates mixed signals. There are indeed some bad signs, including skepticism towards objective values. Such skepticism tends to spread mistrust. Hence some industrial societies turn into litigatious communities, in which everyone is suing everyone else, since it is imagined that a lack of objective values leads to lack of possibility for peaceful compromises. Another bad sign is a widespread tendency to place economic values above all others. A sad manifestation of this surfaced in European debates in the spring of 1994 about whether to join the European Union. Those insisting that the issue must be judged on other than mere economic considerations were denounced by the opponents as "being merely emotional!"

There is also widespread acceptance of what we called earlier economic determinism, and with this the prevalence of consumer attitudes dominating people's lives. All of this in spite of the fact that there is no evidence supporting this stance. There is also a lack of interest in developing theories of emotions and attitudes except in manipulative contexts, though recent strains of feminist ethics have tried to remedy the situation. Finally, genuine interest in friendship, loyalty, and respect disappears underneath an avalanche of books written about our human capacities and emotional lives in the pattern of the "how to do it" books giving us advice about our mechanical devices.

There are, however, also encouraging signs. In various countries, including the USA and South Africa, attention to that part of medical ethics that deals with humane qualities in the physician and in the doctor–patient relationship, as well as its economic and structural consequences, is making headway, spelling out implications for medical education, institutional structure, and economic sponsoring agencies. In South Africa we see also a renewed interest in tribal traditions centering on deep friendship and family loyalty. Similar themes can be detected also in public discussions in Israel, though there the problem of how to extend such communal values to larger units, including ones that transcend ethnic and religious differences still seem enormous.

In Austria some university students refuse to acquire driver's licenses as a protest against urban conditions that make it prohibitive for them to rely on public transportation. In Switzerland some young people take on jobs at less than 100% time so that they can devote the time and energy this freed to social work or artistic activities. There are also encouraging signs in Singapore. For though some of the implementations of law and order and accountability of the leadership do not coincide with Western conceptions, there is a great deal of public discussion, in house blocks as well as in newspapers and television programs, of the problems facing the small nation of reconciling the maintenance of economic progress with the upkeep and expansion of the spread of humane values and character traits in the society.

Various parts of this book provide material for how to combat communal indifference. The fact that the community is based on attitudes and not merely on laws gives us a start. Laws do not have built in dynamic; attitudes do. Maintaining attitudes is a matter of sound interpersonal relations that we want in one or the other of our interaction with others.

Secondly, we saw the arguments earlier for what we called the wide in contrast with the narrow conception of the self. Once we adopt the wide conception of the self we face the unavoidable question of what are better and worse ways for such a self to function. The adoption of the key attitudes underling an adequate normative communitarian structure serve as a good way to construct adequate models of functioning.

The ingredients of the adequate communal tie and the other underlying attitudes of taking on responsibility well, inclination to share, and receptivity, jointly work against the cooling of love and growth of indifference. The ingredients introduced in Chapter 1 and the other key elements surfacing in chapters 3,4, and 5, mutually support each other. It is this dynamic interaction between the attitudinal ingredients that keeps our cognitive and affective structures and processes vital. In this way it acts against indifference.

Finally, unlike a merely rule-oriented system, our conception of the anatomy of a value-based community prescribes constant activity and in this way also a constantly active state. It is a theory built for providing guidelines in periods of change as well as stability. The changes may be within the framework of adequate tie ingredients, since—as we have said—these are subject to change in degree and kind. Alternatively, the changes may be within a society that is attempting to develop better communal ties, aims, and sharing.

Here are some of the contemporary problems to which the theory of this work provides at least sketches of solutions.

(i) There are pressures for larger economic and political units in the world today. (E.g. the European Community, alliances in North America, and South-East Asia).

(ii) There is a global trend towards nationalism and emotional identifications with ethnic groups.

(iii) We are witnessing the rise of large-scale bureaucratic administrative structures across the world.

(iv) There is—across nationalities—a demand or yearning for more personal human interactions, and being viewed primarily as both thinking and feeling human beings.

(v)   In some parts of the world there is widespread skepticism about objective values.

(vi)   In various parts of the world there is hostility towards those with different customs. This involves often a minority, or outsiders, and brings with it the likelihood of violence.

(vii) In many parts of the world violence is on the rise.

(viii) We witness in many countries widespread corruption, and lack of trust in legal authority.

The fruitfulness of our approach can be shown by reflecting on how much, if any, help it gives towards adequate dealings with the eight statements listed above.

The first statement deals with the pressures towards larger economical and political units. This essay distinguishes between large economic–political units that are purely legal and not value-based, and then communities of communities, arranged in a hierarchical way, with local and more specific values at the bases of the smallest communities, and more general values within the larger communities. Within the latter the original small organizations remain, and the values for the higher level communities emerge from the ground up. Our theory supports this kind of enlargement, while it opposes the first type mentioned. The first type may lead to mere efficiency and productivity, but leads also in most cases to corruption and the erosion of local cultures that are tied, psychologically if not conceptually to values that need be preserved in these communities.

Our reply to the second statement about trends towards identification with national and ethnic groups is to show how such identification arises often from feelings of alienation and not finding values to tie together larger units. We go on then to show that these identifications by themselves are superficial, and should be combined with the kinds of values that our ethical ideals and communal ties contain.

Thirdly, within a community with adequate ties and members aspiring towards adequate ideals, bureaucratic structures will be accepted or not, depending on how well these are explained, and how well their aims coincide with communal aims that can be defended on ethical grounds.

Our comments on the first three points contain already the

answer to the question that the fourth point raises. For both in our account of individual ethics and in the social ethics intertwined with the individual one, personal relations organized around joint and cooperative values that have also affective elements constitute essential ingredients for individual and communal well-being.

Our theory attempts to combat the widespread skepticism towards objective values by presenting an anatomy of key normative concepts within which we distinguish a conceptual core and a wide variety of different contextual implementations. Surface variety is acknowledged but held together by the underlying core that does not consist of rules but of guidelines.

The sixth point too receives in our theory a treatment that relies on distinguishing surface variety and underlying unification. Clinging to custom and showing hostility towards those with different customs reveals the shortsightedness of those who cannot look beneath the surface and see—as finally Achilles comes to see in the *Iliad*—that we are "all in the same boat" and that good ways of handling our conditions will cut across ethnic and national boarders, without destroying these.

In the light of the events of September 11, a careful consideration of violence is especially timely. To respond to violence simply with increased force will not solve the problem. For a fanatic, the death of a comrade is typically merely a call to recruit more in his place. To be sure people bent on murder need be segregated one way or another from the rest of the population. But we need also to get at the psychological roots of the violence in order to work out ways of healing.

It does not help to denounce those adopting violence as irrational. Such denunciations may say the truth, but how will that cure the problem? Besides, as is stressed in this book all along, ethics cannot be merely a matter of reason. Emotions too play important roles, especially as ingredients in attitudes. Thus trying to overcome the temptations of violence must contain emotional elements as well.

Some of the sources may not be respectable from a Western intellectual point of view. Much of it is envy and misguided egalitarianism. We cannot meet this by changing fundamental ideas of what a good person should be or a healthy community, just to please wild irrationality. But we can offer people vistas of good lives and qualities of interpersonal relations that will seem more inviting than a life of holding grudges and dreaming of revenge.

As we said before, communal dynamic, especially ties, play a more crucial role in improving our lives than mere laws, even if these are democratic laws. Within the right communal dynamic it is crucial to make the communal life something interesting and full of vitality. It must not degenerate into mass indifference. For indifference leads to boredom, and in that state even small flaws of the political system can seem large. This, in turn, invites the demagogue and potential tyrant to try to take over.

We may be able to "stamp out violence" temporarily, but we cannot stamp out frustration. It is not the kind of phenomenon that lends itself to that kind of treatment. But the functioning of what we described as the right communal dynamic and ties yield more hope towards making frustration at least non-violent. As long as there is a lot of frustration among the citizenry, there will always be the threat of the rise of terrorism. Mere rules and law cannot lessen the danger.

Apart from making the well functioning community an exciting place to live in, we also must not let scores of citizens feel that the system has it "in for them," no matter what they do. This applies not only to poor districts, but also to ethic groups. Ethnic groups must feel assured that responsibility is a matter of individual action or action by a well-defined organization. To punish an ethnic group because some of its members might have acted in ways not approved by the government is the worst way to try to build a community. Furthermore, according to the ethics sketched in this book, removing or in other ways harming whole ethnic groups because of what some members might have done is a paradigm of what is immoral, both for individuals and communities. Killing or deporting a whole ethnic group on the alleged ground that some members violated rules is barbaric, and will only lead to more frustration and the start of new cycles of revenge.

Finally, the lack of trust and spreading corruption is addressed head on in our theory. Mere rules will not provide a cure. We need to build up trust to back our system of communal ties, and this will bring with it many of the other ingredients of our individual and communal aspirations. After the initial stages the many other ingredients will also help to form trust. Our approach is a bootstrap maneuver.

It would be absurd to suggest that these features of our theory provide a panacea or "snake-oil medicine" to the woes of the world. But hopefully the features do provide the foundations for guidelines that can spawn a variety of implementations that do indeed tackle normative problems on the concrete level.

We bridge the gap between aspects of human psychology and features of communal life that have been shown desirable by such earlier writers as David Riesmann and Robert Bellah, though theirs is a more individualistic moral psychology, with a revised moral and social psychology that shows the individual and the communal goods have common ingredients, and need not be viewed as strictly separate. Within that conception there is no need for an autonomous moral element, since the self- and other-oriented are interdependent already within the value theory.

The outlook of this essay and its program should be seen as more plausible now that the pioneering work of Amartya Sen has shown the need to include cooperative humane attributes in what economists call quality of life, and examples like the *City of Joy* referred to already earlier show that economics by itself does not determine the possibility of building a thriving community.

Some will object that the positive proposals of this work, since these are based on psychological factors that cannot be created instantly by laws and economic inducements, require too much time and test the patience of today's fast moving world too much. But we plead guilty to the charge that the proposal of this plan requires for its implementation much patience. The world needs to become accustomed to the idea that there are no quick fixes to today's problems, and that we cannot solve social problems and crisis in achieving individual happiness by just throwing a lot of money at these. There are signs that in some parts of the world people are beginning to understand the need for patience and endurance. In a conversation with a black woman in South Africa a few years ago, she said to me: "I cannot hope for much political and economic improvement within the remaining years of my life. But I have hope and trust in what we are doing. I am confident that even if I do not live to see the coming of major improvements, my children will. And that is what keeps me going." The faith and patience of this woman could, and should, be an inspiration for us all.

This book shows that the patience required examine and absorb new procedures, customs and rules is easier if there is an adequate communal dynamic underlying these efforts. This dynamic is analyzed in this book as adequate communal ties, and modes of work, responsibility and sharing. The resulting scheme is pluralistic and context-sensitive without lapsing into relativism. It does not pretend to present the end of the story of valuations, but it offers, a way to construe the beginning of that story.

Let us return to the two quotes listed in the beginning of this section. From two diverse points of view we hear the same complaint, and hence the push to try to heal the gap between the individual and the communal. Our theory does construe the problem not as one of merely constructing many rules that chain the two components together, but more as healing, i.e. helping to tie together two elements that in an adequate conception of human nature and interactions should be seen as a whole. Modern liberal idealogy centers on the problems of how to create a democratic society among people with differing values, and how to solve the problem of individuals having to sacrifice a part of themselves for communal goods. These are undoubtedly important problems. But above we have sketched roughly how the conceptual framework of this essay can ameliorate, if not cure, these vexing conflicts. One of the key conceptual tools emerging from our conception is that of "layered thinking" about the self. We are engineers, Spaniards, opera lovers, etc. But on a deeper level we have fundamental common elements. These are our capacities to develop what are called in this essay adequate communal ties, and develop our capacities to share, and search for adequate values in a cooperative manner. As an overview let us contrast fashionable slogans with the message of this book. One such slogan is: "give it enough money and everything will be all right!" This has been applied especially to projects in developing countries. The deficiencies of this approach have been well summed up by Elinor Ostrom. After listing the "minuses," e.g. too many politicians made rich, only crumbling remains of roads, irrigation systems, etc. her conclusion: "There is a serious need to rethink the overemphasis on physical capital alone." (Social Capital, a Multifaceted Perspective, ed. by Partha

Dasgupta and Ismail Serageldin, The World Bank, 2000, pp. 172–214.) Presumably agreeing with this, here is a quote from a Swiss banker: "we have learned that you cannot solve most problems by just throwing money at these."

This book is meant to be a modest attempt to fill in some of the gaps. In our view much of what is described here as communal dynamics and ties could be used to substitute for some of the monetary items. Ostrom seems to agree with this. She lists many items that we would accept as "social goods." One big difference between her list and ours is that ours includes emotion-involving and not just reason-involving items. Thus she urges more local autonomy over what to sow and how among farmers. In this book, as we have seen, items such as emotional spontaneity and cooperative attitudes that also contain emotional elements, are listed. Money may be used cooperatively, but often is not. Even when it is, the result might not be what one wants. For example, some plans involve giving money to this or that country, but only on condition that this unit will install democratic reforms. Is this: "democracy for money" plan likely to work? If the required communal dynamic is missing, the following scenario might become reality. A country is paid, and introduces some democratic reforms. Then another wealthy country enters the picture, and pays even more money if the one in need dissolves the democratic reforms and introduces new anti-democratic ones. If the nature of the political structure in a given country depends solely on who paid them how much money, the result will be lack of stability and thus certainly no democracy.

Opposition to what this book contains is expressed at times in the following terms. "Are you really against giving people some incentive to do the right things? Even in religious texts some successful incentive givings are described." In reply we need to point to the vagueness of the term "incentive." We usually associate the term with material goods and for power. One could also construe the term in a very wide sense, covering any conceivable kind of reward or encouragement for what someone has done. When this book criticizes the model of incentive-caused progress, we have mostly material incentives in mind. Whether we should use the term in a wider sense is problematic. We should not use it so widely that we blur the distinction between doing it for some reward and doing it because we believe that is the right thing to do, regardless of rewards. The crucial issue in this context is, that our book envisions in the case of the genuine social change a reorientation of values in most cases, and not just doing the right thing not for its own value, but for something exterraneous that is pushed at us at the same time.

Some newly developed notions seem to point in the right direction. There are groups of artificial intelligence researchers for social responsibility, and similar organizations for physicians. Some universities offer courses on social responsibility for transmitting new technologies to developing countries. As of now, however, such efforts are still on the parameter of our social–political life, and their significance has not been noted by mainstream philosophical ethics. We have attained a level of political discourse at which looking at the consequences of the relevant plans for the environment is mandatory. It would be a great step forward if such a "check" would be seen by society at large and philosophers in particular as equally needed in matters of "social responsibility." The latter phrase is merely a cover-term for a variety of ethical concerns. Our theory is meant to supply a conceptual unifying framework for these concerns, and to show a picture of our lives that suggests making such a "check" more than that; we should make such concerns the primary reflection on any technological, economical, or political proposal. We do not owe this to any one person or persons. We owe it to our humanity.

BIBLIOGRAPHY

Aiken, S., D. Mechanic, and J. Moravcsik. "Organizational Aspects of Caring." *The Milbank Quarterly* 79 (1995): 77–95.

Annas, J. *An Introduction to Plato's Republic.* Oxford: Oxford University Press, 1981.

Anscombe, G. E. M. "Pretending." In *Proceedings of the Aristotelian Society.* Suppl. Vol. 32 (1958): 279–294.

Aristotle, *Nichomachean Ethics.* Oxford: Clarendon Press, 1894.

Arpaly, N. *In Defense of Deep Virtue Ethics.* Stanford University Ph.D. dissertation, 1998.

Austin, J. *Philosophical Papers.* Oxford: Clarendon Press, 1961.

Axelrod, R. and W. Hamilton. "The Evolution of Cooperation." *Science* 211 (1981): 1390–1396.

Baier, A. "Trust and Anti-trust." *Ethics* 96 (1986): 213–260.

Baier, K. "Types of Responsibility." In *Individual and Collective Responsibility,* ed. French, P. New York: St. Martin's Press, 1991, 117–122.

Bell, D. *Communitarianism and Its Critics.* Oxford: Clarendon Press, 1993.

Bellah, R., R. Madsen, W. Sullivan, A. Swidler, and S. Tipton. *Habits of the Heart.* Berkeley: University of California Press, 1985.

Bellah, R. et al. *The Good Society.* New York: Alfred Knopf, 1991.

Ben-Zeev, A. "Envy and Equality." *Journal of Philosophy* 89 (1992): 551–581.

Berlin, I. "Two Concepts of Liberty." in *Four Essays on Liberty,* Vol. I. Oxford: Oxford University Press, 1969: 118–172.

Berovsky, B. ed. *Free Will and Determinism*. New York: Harper & Row, 1966.

Biko, S. "Black Consciousness, and the Quest for a True Humanity." In *Black Theology: The South African Voice*, ed. Moore, B. London: C. Hurst Co., 1973, 41–43.

Blum, L. *Friendship, Morality, and Altruism*. London: Routledge Kegan Paul, 1980.

Blum, L. "Vocation, Friendship, and Community: Limitations on the Personal–Impersonal Framework." In *Identity, Character, and Morality*, eds. Flanagan, O. and A. Rorty. Cambridge: MIT Press, 1990, 173–197.

Bok, H. *Freedom and Responsibility*. Princeton: Princeton University Press, 1998.

Bok, S. *Lying*. New York: Vintage Books, 1978.

Bok, S. *Alva Myrdal*. New York: Addison–Wellesley, 1991.

Bosanquet, B. *A Companion to Plato's REPUBLIC*. London: Rivington, Percival and Co., 1895.

Brandt, R. *A Theory of the Good and the Right*. Oxford: Clarendon Press, 1979.

Bratman, M. *Intentions, Plans and Practical Reasons*. Cambridge, Mass.: Harvard University Press, 1980.

Bratman, M. "Shared Cooperative Activities." *Philosophical Review* vol. 103 (1992): 327–341.

Bratman, M. "Shared Intention." *Ethics* 104 (1993): 97–113.

Brink, D. "Rational Egoism, Self, and Others." In *Identity, Character, and Morality*, eds. Flanagan, O. and Rorty A. Cambridge: MIT Press, 1990, 339–378.

Buber, M. *Paths in Utopia*. London: Routledge & Kegan Paul, 1949.

Camus, A. *The Plague*. New York: Knopf, 1948.

Chomsky, N. *Aspects of the Theory of Syntax*. Cambridge: MIT Press, 1965.

Chomsky, N. *Cartesian linguistics*. New York: Harper & Row, 1966.

Chomsky, N. *Language and Responsibility*. New York: Pantheon Books, 1977.

Clowney, D. "Virtues, Roles, and the Foundation of Ethics." *Philosophia* 70 (1990): 49–68.

Code, A. and M. Moravcsik. "Explaining Various Forms of Living." In *Essays on Aristotle's De Anima*, eds. Nussbaum, N. and A. Rorty. Oxford: Clarendon Press, 1992, 129–145.

Collins, J. and J. Porras. *Built to Last*. New York: Harper, 1994.

Copp, D. "What Collectives Are: Agency, Individualism and Legal Theory." *Dialogue* 23 (1984): 249–269.

Copp, D. "The Concept of a Society." *Dialogue* 31 (1992): 183–212.

Damon, W. *The Moral Child*. New York: Norton, 1983.

Dancy, J., Moravcsik, J. and C. Taylor, eds. *Human Agency*. Stanford: Stanford University Press, 1988.

Darwall, S. "Two Kinds of Respect." *Ethics* 88 (1977): 36–49.

Dasgupta, P. "Well-being and the Extent of its Realization in Poor Countries." *Economic Journal* 100 (1990): 1–32.

Davidson, D. "Actions, Reasons, and Causes." In *Essays on Actions and Events*, Oxford: Oxford University Press, 1980, 3–20.

Dewey, J. *The School and Society*. New York: Arcturus, 1980.

Dunn, J. "Review of *Moral Prejudices: Essays on Ethics by Baier, A.*" *Journal of Philosophy* 92 (1995): 44–47.

Durkheim, E. *The Rules of Sociological Method*. New York: Free Press, 1938.

Dworkin, R. *A Matter of Principle*. Oxford: Oxford University Press, 1985.

Dworkin, R. "Obligations of community." In *Authority*, ed. Raz, J. Oxford: Blackwell, 1990, 218–239.

Etzione, A. *Rights and the Common Good*. New York: St. Martin, 1994.

Feinberg, J. "The Moral and Legal Responsibility of the Bad Samaritan." *Criminal Justice Ethics* 3 (1984): 56–66.

Fisher, C. *America Calling: A Social History of the Telephone till 1940*. Berkeley: University of California Press, 1992.

Flanagan, O. and A. Rorty, eds. *Identity, Character, and Morality*. Cambridge: MIT Press, 1990.

Fogel, R. *Without Consent or Contract: The Rise and Fall of American Slavery*. New York: Norton, 1989.

Foot, Ph. *Virtues and Vices and other Essays in Moral Philosophy*. Berkeley: University of California Press, 1978.

Frankena, W. *Ethics*. Englewood: Prentice-Hall, 1963.

Frankena, W. *Three Historical Philosophies of Education*. Chicago: Scott, Foreman and Co., 1965.

Frankena, W. "The Ethics of Respect for Persons." *Philosophical Topics* 14 (1986): 149–67.

Frankfurt, H. "Alternate Responsibilities and Responsibility." *Journal of Philosophy* 66 (1969): 828–839.

French, P. ed. *The Spectrum of Responsibility*. New York: St. Martin's Press, 1991.

French, P. "The Corporation as a Moral Person." In *The Spectrum of Responsibility*, ed. French P. New York: St. Martin's Press, 1991, 290–304.

Gewirth, A. *Reason and Morality*. Chicago: The University of Chicago Press, 1978.

Gewirth, A. "Are There Any Absolute Rights?" In *Theories of Rights*, ed. Waldron, J. Oxford: Oxford University Press, 1984, 91–109.

Giligan, C. *In a Different Voice*. Cambridge, Mass.: Harvard University Press, 1982.

Green, L. "Commitment and Community." In *Authority*, ed. Raz, J. Oxford: Blackwell, 1990, 240–266.

Greenspan, P. "Guilt and Virtue." *Journal of Philosophy* 91 (1994) 57–70.

Gutmann, A. *Liberal Equality*. Cambridge: Cambridge University Press, 1980.

Gutmann, A. "Communitarian Critics of Liberalism." *Philosophy and Public Affairs* 14 (1985) 308–322.

Gutmann, A. *Democratic Education*. Princeton: Princeton University Press, 1987.

Hampshire, S. *Innocence and Experience*. Cambridge, Mass.: Harvard University Press, 1989.

Heller, A. *Beyond Justice*. Oxford: Blackwell, 1987.

Herman, B. "Obligation and Performance; a Kantian Account of Moral Conflict." In *Identity, Character, and Morality*, eds. Flanagan, O. and A. Rorty. Cambridge: MIT Press, 1990, 311–337.

Homiak, M. "Politics as Soul-making: Aristotle on Becoming Good." *Philosophia* 70 (1990): 167–193.

Hursthouse, R. *On Virtue Ethics*. Oxford: Oxford University Press, 1999.

James, W. *Varieties of Religious Experience*. New York: Longman and Green, 1903.

James, W. *Pragmatism and Other Essays*. New York: Washington Press, 1963.

Kingwell, M. "The Polite Citizen; Or, Justice as Civil Discourse." *The Philosophical Forum* 25 (1994): 241–266.

Kittay, E. "In Whose Different Voice?" *Journal of Philosophy* 88 (1991): 645–646.

Konner, M. *Becoming a Doctor*. New York: Viking Press, 1987.

Korsgaard, K. *Creating the Kingdom of Ends*. Cambridge: Cambridge University Press, 1996.

Kothian, J. *Tribes*. New York: Random House, 1992.

Kymlicka, W. *Liberalism, Community, and Culture*. Oxford: Oxford University Press, 1989.

Lapierre, D. *The City of Joy*. Garden City, N.Y.: Doubleday, 1985.

Larmore, Ch. *Patterns of Moral Complexity*. Cambridge: Cambridge University Press, 1987.

Larmore, Ch. "The Right and the Good." *Philosophia* 70 (1990): 15–32.

Lewis, D. *Convention*. Cambridge, Mass.: Harvard University Press, 1969.

Locke, J. *Second Treatise of Government*. Oxford: Blackwell, 1976.

Loetter, H. *Justice for an Unjust Society*. Amsterdam: Rodopi, 1993.

Lott, T., ed. *Subjugation and Bondage*. Lanham: Rowman & Littlefield, 1998.

Lukas, S. "Perspectives on Authority." In *Authority*, ed. Raz, J. Oxford: Blackwell, 1990, 203–217.

Macedo, S. *Liberal Virtues: Citizenship, Virtue, and Community in Liberal Constitutionalism*. Oxford: Clarendon Press, 1990.

MacIntyre, A. *After Virtue*. London: Duckworth, 1981.

Macleod, A. "Distributive Justice, Contract, and Equality." *Journal of Philosophy* 81 (1984): 709–718.

Martineau, J. *Types of Ethical Theory*. Oxford: Oxford University Press, 1888.

Massie, R. K. "Understanding Corruption." *Die Suid Afrikaan* 45 (1993): 38–41.

McGary, H. and B. Lawson. *Between Slavery and Freedom*. Bloomington: Indiana University Press, 1993.

Meinberg, E. *Die Moral im Sport*. Düsseldorf: Meyer & Meyer Verlag, 1991.

Miller, F. *Nature, Justice, and Rights, in Aristotle's Politics*. Oxford: Clarendon Press, 1995.

Minow, M. "Equalities." *Journal of Philosophy* 88 (1991): 663–644.

Moravcsik, J. "Ancient and Modern Conceptions of Health and Medicine." *The Journal of Medicine and Philosophy* 1 (1976): 337–348.

Moravcsik, J. "On What We Aim at and How We Live." In *The Greeks and the Good Life*, ed. Depew, D. Indianapolis: Hackett, 1980, 198–235.

Moravcsik J. "Understanding and the Emotions." *Dialectica* 36 (1982): 207–224.

Moravcsik, J. "Plato and Pericles on Freedom and Politics." *Canadian Journal of Philosophy*, Suppl. Vol. 9 (1983): 1–17.

Moravcsik, J. "The Philosophical Foundations of Religious Tolerance." *Immanuel* (1984): 77–87.

Moravcsik, J. "Communal Ties." *American Philosophical Society: Proceedings and Addresses* 62 (1988): 221–25.

Moravcsik, J. "The Perils of Friendship and Conceptions of the Self." In *Human Agency*, eds. Dancy, J., Moravcsik, J. and C. Taylor. Stanford: Stanford University Press, 1988, 133–151.

Moravcsik, J. "The Role of Virtues in Alternatives to Kantian and Utilitarian ethics." *Philosophia* 20 (1990): 33–48.

Moravcsik, J. *Thought and Language*. London: Routledge, 1990.

Moravcsik, J. *Plato and Platonism*. Oxford: Blackwell, 1992.

Moravcsik, J. "Why Philosophy of art in Cross-Cultural Perspectives?" *The Journal of Aesthetics and Art Criticism* 51 (1993): 425–435.

Moravcsik, J. "Generiticity and Linguistic Competence." In *Theorie des Lexikons*. Wuppertal, 1994.

Moravcsik, J. "The Development of Friendship and Values in the *Philoctetes*." In *Proceedings of the Boston Area Colloquium in Ancient Philosophy*, ed. Cleary J., m: Brill Academic Publisher, 1998, 253–281.

Moravcsik, J. "Two Types of Ethical Attitudes." *Christian Theism and Moral Philosophy*, eds. Beaty, M., Fisher C. and M. Nelsen, Macon: Mercer University Press, 1998, 163–180.

Moravcsik, J. *Meaning Creativity, and the Partial Inscrutability of the Human Mind*. Stanford: CSLI Publications, 1998.

Moravcsik, J. *Health, Healing and Their Values*. Cambridge: Harvard Center for Population and Development Studies, 1999.

Mulhall, S. and A. Swift eds. *Liberals and Communitarians*. Oxford: Blackwell, 1992.

Noddings, N. *Caring*. Berkeley: University of California Press, 1984.

Nozick, R. *Anarchy, State, and Utopia*. New York: Basic Books, 1974.

Oruka, O. *The Philosophy of Liberty*. Nairobi: Standard Textbooks Graphics, 1991.

Pakaluk, M. ed. *Other Selves: Philosophers on Friendship*. Indianapolis: Hackett Publishing Co., 1991.

Pettit, Ph. *The Common Mind*. Oxford: Oxford University Press, 1993.

Pettit, Ph. "Review of *Political Liberalism* by Rawls, J." *Journal of Philosophy* 91 (1994) 215–220.

Pitkin, H. *Wittgenstein and Justice*. Berkeley: University of California Press, 1972.

Plato, *Republic*. Oxford: Clarendon Press, 1902.

Putman, R. "The Moral Life of a Pragmatist." In *Identity, Character, and Morality*, eds. Flanagan, O. and A. Rorty. Cambridge: MIT Press, 1990, 67–89.

Railton, P. "Moral Realism." *Philosophical Review* 95 (1986) 163–20.

Ramsey, F. "Universals." In *Foundations of Mathematics*, London: Routledge, Kegan & Paul, 1931, 112–137.

Rawls, J. *A Theory of Justice*. Cambridge, Mass.: Harvard University Press, 1971.

Rawls, J. *Political Liberalism*, New York: Columbia University Press, 1993.

Raz, J. *The Morality of Freedom*. Oxford: Oxford University Press, 1986.

Raz, J. ed. *Authority*, Oxford: Blackwell, 1990.

Rorty, A. ed. *Identities of Persons*. Berkeley: University of California Press, 1976.

Rousseau, J. J. *Du Contrat Social*. In *Oeuvres Completes,* vol. 3. Paris: Gallimard, 1964.

Royce, J. *The Philosophy of Loyalty*. New York: MacMillan, 1906.

Royce, J. *The Hope of the Great Community*. New York: MacMillan, 1916.

Sacks, O. *A Man Who Mistook his Wife for a Hat*. New York: Harper & Row, 1987.

Sandel, M. *Liberalism and the Limits of Justice*. Cambridge: Cambridge University Press, 1982.

Satz, D. "Markets in Women's Reproductive Labor." *Philosophy and Public Affairs* 21 (1992): 107–131.

Satz, D. and J. Ferejohn. "Rational Choice and Social Theory." *Journal of Philosophy* 91 (1994): 71–87.

Scheler, M. *Ressentiment*. Glencoe: Free Press, 1961.

Schoeck, H. *Envy: A Theory of Social Behavior*. London: Martin Secker and Warburg, 1969.

Schwarzenbach, S. "On Civic Friendship." *Ethics* 107 (1996): 97–128.

Sen, A. "On Optimizing the Rate of Saving." *Economic Journal* 71 (1961): 479–496.

Sen, A. *Choice, Welfare, and Measurement*. Cambridge: MIT Press, 1982.

Sen, A. "Well-being, Agency, and Freedom: the Dewey Lectures." *Journal of Philosophy* 82 (1985): 169–220.

Sen, A. *Inequality Reexamined*. Cambridge: Harvard University Press, 1992.

Shorey, P. *Platonism, Ancient and Modern*. Berkeley: University of California Press, 1938.

Simpson, E. and M. Williams. "The Ideal of Social Disillusionment." *The Philosophical Forum* 26 (1994): 63–77.

Slote, M. *Beyond Optimizing*. Cambridge, Mass.: Harvard University Press, 1989.

Solomon, R. and M. Murphy. *What is Justice?* Oxford: Oxford University Press, 2000.

Stevenson, C. *Ethics and Language*. New Haven: Yale University Press, 1944.

Strawson, P. ed. "Freedom and Resentment." In *Studies in the Philosophy of Thought and Action*, ed. P. Strawson Oxford: Oxford University Press, 1968, 71–96.

Taylor, Ch. "Responsibility for Self." In *Identities of Persons*, ed. Rorty, A. Berkeley: University of California Press, 1976, 281–299.

Taylor, Ch. "Atomism." In *Philosophical Papers*, vol. II, Cambridge: Cambridge University Press, 1985, 187–209.

Taylor, Ch. *Philosophical Papers*, vol II, Cambridge: Cambridge University Press, 1985.

Thorpe, C. *Non-contingent Reasons*. Stanford University Ph.D. thesis, 1999.

Tomasi, J. "Individual Rights and Communal Virtues." *Ethics,* vol. 202. (1991): 521–536.

Trianosky, G. "National Affection and Responsibility for Character." In *Identity, Character, and Morality*, eds. Flanagan, O. and A. Rorty, Cambridge: MIT Press, 1990, 93–109.

Tugendhat, E. *Philosophische Aufsätze*. Berlin: Surkamp, 1992.

Tugendhat, E. *Vorlesungen in der Ethik*. Berlin: Surkamp, 1993.

Tyler, T. *Why Do people Obey the Law*. New Haven: Yale University Press, 1992.

Urmson, J. *Aristotle's Ethics*. Oxford: Blackwell, 1988.

Waldron, J. ed. *Theories of Rights*. Oxford: Oxford University Press, 1984.

Walker, A. *The Color Purple*. New York: Harcourt and Brace, 1982.

Walzer, M. *Spheres of Justice*, New York: Basic Books, 1983.

Watson, G. "On the Primacy of Character." In *Identity, Character, and Morality*, eds. Flanagan, O. and A. Rorty. Cambridge: MIT Press, 1990, 449–469.

White, N. "Review of Williams, G., *Shame and Necessity.*" *Journal of Philosophy* 91 (1994): 619–622.

Williams, B. "Equality." In *Problems of the Self*. Cambridge, Cambridge University Press, 1976), 230–249.

Williams, B. *Moral Luck*. Cambridge: Cambridge University Press, 1981.

Wittgenstein, L. "A Lecture on Ethics." *Philosophical Review* 74 (1965): 3–12.

Wolf, S. "Self-interest and Interest in Selves." *Ethics* 96 (1986): 704–720.

Wolgast, E. *Ethics of an Artificial person*. Stanford: Stanford University Press, 1992.

Young, Ch. "Virtue and Flourishing in Aristotle's Ethics" in *The Greeks and the Good Life*, ed. Depew, D., Indianapolis: Hackett, 1980, 138–156.

Xiaorong, Li. *Justice, Reason, and the Human Good*. Stanford Ph.D. dissertation, 1993

Zelger, J. "GABEK—A new Method for Qualitative Evaluation of Interviews and Model Construction with PC-Support." In *Enhancing Human Capacity to Solve Ecological and Socioeconomic Problems*, eds. Stuhler, E. and M. O. Suilleabhain, Muenchen-Mering: Rainer Hamp, 1993, 128–172.

Zemach, E. *Types: Essays in Metaphysics*. Leiden-Dordrecht: Brill and Reidel, 1992.

INDEX